EUROPE BETWEEN DEMOCRACY
AND ANARCHY

EUROPE BETWEEN DEMOCRACY AND ANARCHY

by

FERDINAND A. HERMENS

Professor of Political Science
University of Notre Dame

"A majority . . . is the only true sovereign of a free people. Whoever rejects it does, of necessity, fly into anarchy or despotism. Unanimity is impossible; the rule of the minority, as a permanent arrangement, is wholly inadmissible; so that, rejecting the majority principle, anarchy or despotism in some form is all that is left."—ABRAHAM LINCOLN

*A Publication of
The Committee on International Relations
University of Notre Dame*

UNIVERSITY OF NOTRE DAME
Notre Dame, Indiana
1951

Copyright, 1951 by
University of Notre Dame Press

Printed at Ave Maria Press

PREFACE

This book is the first part of a more general investigation of the relationship between peace and democracy. It is to be followed by a study on "Peace, Democracy, and World Government," and, subsequently, by more general studies on the constitutional, as well as the economic and social, conditions which determine the success or failure of democratic government. These studies will be concentrated on what might be called the danger zone of democracy: Continental Europe, and those countries in the Near and Far East which have entered, or are preparing to enter, the path of constitutional government.

The material contained in this book was given priority because it seemed more urgent, in particular after a four months' stay in Europe during the summer of 1948. The people of Continental Europe, in particular the young people, are repelled by what is offered to them in the name of democracy. Unless a way to something radically different is pointed out to them they will, at best, continue to drag their feet in the defense of democracy; at worst, their freedom may have been lost to internal enemies before they become the victims of external attack.

Concentration upon systems of voting as the key to the necessary reforms is, as will be shown below, readily understood by a growing number of observers in Europe, especially in France and Germany. The reasons are less obvious in the Anglo-Saxon countries, where the plurality system is so firmly entrenched that it is taken for granted, and its essential relation to the democratic process does not become readily apparent. The author is aware that this fact can, on his part, lead to over-emphasis on systems of voting; the impression may arise that this little volume is based upon a monistic interpretation where, in reality, a plurality of factors is involved. In the long run, the only defense against possible misunderstandings along these lines will be a balanced treatment of all the basic conditions affecting democracy in its danger zone. Work on such a project has proceeded simultaneously with the preparation of this book.

A great many people have been generous with their assistance in the preparation of this volume, and those at least should be mentioned without whom essential information could not have been obtained.

Dr. Jacques Cadart, Senator Michel Debré, Dr. Raoul Husson and Dr. Auguste Soulier have gone to a great deal of trouble in order to provide material on France. Professors Giuseppe Ferri of the University of Rome and Mario Einaudi of Cornell University have done the same for Italy. For Germany it was always possible to rely on the advice of Professors Ernst W. Meyer of the University of Frankfurt and Ottmar Buehler of the University of Cologne, as well as upon Mr. Georg Joestingmeier, a member of the Diet of North Rhine-Westphalia. In addition, the officers of the *Deutsche Waehlergesellschaft* have been helpful, in particular its executive secretary, Mr. Baer, and Dr. Ursula Wetzel, whose translation of my earlier volume, *Democracy or Anarchy?* will be published by the Wolfgang Metzner Verlag in Frankfurt simultaneously with this book, a fact which may be of interest to those who find the condensed treatment of pre-war developments in this study insufficient and may not have access to a copy of *Democracy or Anarchy?* which has been out of print for several years. For Belgium, information was provided by Professors Frans Brusselmans of the University of Louvain and Felix Oppenheim of the University of Delaware. The material on England was checked by Professor John Hooker and the Introduction was read by Professor Francis O'Malley of the University of Notre Dame. Professor James Hogan of the University College of Cork has furnished essential materials on Ireland. Various State and War Department officials in Washington have provided material on Germany, Austria and Japan; the Embassy of Israel and the Israeli Ministry of Justice, as well as Dr. Abraham Weinshall, have done the same for Israel. For information on Switzerland I have, for years, relied upon Professor W. A. Joehr of the Institute of Commerce in St. Gallen; Mr. George Bacopoulos, a member of the Greek Diet, made available to me a memorandum (since published) on the Greek constitutional system in general, and Greek P.R. in particular.

This list does not include those who, during the summer and fall of 1950, discussed with the author various aspects of the issues treated in this study, in Paris, Rome, Innsbruck, Munich, Bonn, Duesseldorf, The Hague, Brussels, and London. Since the text of the book was being set up at the time, most of the material which they made available will have to be used on subsequent occasions, although an attempt has been made to incorporate as much of it as possible in the footnotes. Several persons were good enough to read chapters of the manuscript; for this courtesy the author is particularly indebted to members of the United States Embassies in Paris and Rome whose names it would not be proper to mention, and to Mr. Arnaldo Cortesi of the Rome office of *The New York Times*. It should be added forthwith that they are in no way responsible for the contents of this book; that responsibility devolves upon the author alone.

It is also a pleasure to thank the officials of the University of Notre Dame, in particular the President, the Rev. John Cavanaugh, c.s.c., and the successive Vice-Presidents in Charge of Academic Affairs, Rev. Howard S. Kenna, c.s.c. and Rev. James Norton, c.s.c., for their help and encouragement, as well as the author's colleagues of the University of Notre Dame Committee on International Relations, in particular its chairman, Professor Waldemar Gurian. Both before and since the establishment of the Committee, the Rev. Philip S. Moore, c.s.c., Dean of the Graduate School, greatly facilitated the author's work. Dr. Bruno Schlesinger, Mr. Paul Chang, and Mr. Joseph Reninger rendered research assistance; Mr. Reninger made the Index. The task of both editing and typing the successive drafts of the manuscript has, as on previous occasions, evolved upon Mrs. Hermens, without whose assistance this study could not have been completed.—F.A.H.

South Bend, Indiana
January, 1951

TABLE OF CONTENTS

	PAGE
INTRODUCTION . . .	
Positive or Negative Democracy	xi

SECTION I. THE FORMATION AND DEFORMATION OF POLITICAL WILL: THE MAJORITY SYSTEM AND PROPORTIONAL REPRESENTATION 1

CHAPTER 1. POSITIVE DEMOCRACY IN ENGLAND 1
English and Continental Institutions 1
Voting Systems and English Democracy 3
Pluralities and Governments 5
P.R. and Splintering 6
Problems of Principle 11
Types of Majority Voting 14
The Elections of February 1950 17

CHAPTER 2. POSITIVE AND NEGATIVE DEMOCRACY IN THE FRANCE OF THE THIRD REPUBLIC (1870-1940) 29
Party Patterns and Government Weakness 29
Institutional Weaknesses 31
Successful Defense of the Republic 38

CHAPTER 3. NEGATIVE DEMOCRACY AND DICTATORSHIP IN ITALY.. 45
Pre-Fascist Italy 45
P.R. in Operation 47
Objections 58
One or Many Causes 58
Form and Matter in Politics 58
The King and the Intriguers 61
Matter versus Form 61

CHAPTER 4. P.R. AND THE TRIUMPH OF HITLER 63
The Period of Pluralistic Stagnation 66
Totalitarian Revolution 72
Objections 75
The World Economic Crisis 76

Intrigues and the President	76
Politics and the Class Structure	79

CHAPTER 5. NEGATIVE DEMOCRACY IN SMALLER COUNTRIES ... 83
The Austrian Tragedy	83
Poland	86
Czechoslovakia	88
Greece	94

CHAPTER 6. POSITIVE AND NEGATIVE DEMOCRACY IN
SMALLER COUNTRIES	99
Belgium	99
Ireland	106
The Scandinavian Countries	113
The Netherlands	115
Switzerland	116
Finland	121
Additional Countries	123

SECTION II. POSITIVE AND NEGATIVE DEMOCRACY AFTER
WORLD WAR II	125

CHAPTER 7. FRANCE 125
Resistance and Reconstruction	125
Two Majority Elections	130
P.R. Enters the Picture	132
Formation of Governments	140
Experiments With Majority Voting	144
The Opposition to P.R.	149

CHAPTER 8. P.R. IN POST-WAR ITALY 160
P.R. Discussions	160
The First Elections	164
Formation of Governments	166
Polarization	167
Panic and Victory	171
Prospects of "Normalcy"	173
The Republic and the Future	179

CHAPTER 9. GERMANY 182
The Chance for a Two-Party System	182

Turning Away From the Two-Party System 192
P.R. and the Federal Constitution 199
The First Bundestag 202
The Election and the Prospects for a Two-Party System........207
Bonn and Weimar 209
P.R. and Future Allied Policy 216

CHAPTER 10. RECENT DEVELOPMENTS IN AUSTRIA, ISRAEL,
JAPAN, INDIA AND TURKEY 220
Austria 220
Israel 227
Japan 235
India and Turkey 244

SUMMARY AND CONCLUSION 247
THE NEED FOR A POLITICAL MARSHALL PLAN 247
APPENDIX 257
REFERENCES 261
INDEX 287

INTRODUCTION

POSITIVE OR NEGATIVE DEMOCRACY

Modern democracy was born out of a spirit of negation. Its tragedy lies in the failure to outgrow this spirit. The opposition to absolutism which was inherent in the early struggles for modern democracy made negation inevitable. It was indeed necessary to eliminate the old state with its suppression of the individual. The negation of a particular historical form of the state led, however, on the part of many intellectual and political leaders of the democratic movement, to a negation of the state as such. All authority, not only the exaggerated authority of absolutism, was rejected.

The hostility to authority is clearly indicated by Rousseau. For him even the election of representatives was undemocratic:

"Sovereignty cannot be represented for the same reason that it cannot be alienated; it consists essentially in the general will and the will cannot be represented; it is the same or it is different; there is no medium. . . . The English nation thinks that it is free but is greatly mistaken for it is so only during the election of members of Parliament; as soon as they are elected, it is enslaved and counts for nothing." [1]

At best, there might be commissaries who might conduct the people's business on its orders and according to its instructions. Rousseau himself, however, presented us with the *reductio ad absurdum* of his theory when he wrote that democracy — his democracy — was not possible among men, and required a society of gods. Politics, however, deals with men — with men as they are. A political science not given to empty speculation is not interested in what has been termed "impossible forms of government."

Negation is also too evident in the famous slogan of the French Revolution: Freedom, Equality, Fraternity.[2] The call for Fraternity seems closest to being of a positive nature. Basically, however, it is related to the anarchist dream of a "society of the free and equal." In the world in which we live people do not regard each other as brothers, at any rate not as long as they are sober.

The negative character of the demand for Freedom as formulated at that time is obvious. This does not indicate that it must remain negative. Freedom has, in the well-known formulation of Max Weber, a positive function if it is freedom within the state and not freedom from the state.[3] It must be the freedom of the *citizen,* who regards himself as part of the whole and as obligated to the whole, and not freedom of the individual who does not want any social obligations. Thus understood the demand for freedom includes respect of authority. Indeed, as Professor Yves Simon[4] has shown, liberty and authority belong together. Power without freedom is a mere physical fact devoid of moral sanction, and degenerates into arbitrary rule. Freedom without authority is license and provides anyone with the possibility of interfering with the sphere of others and thus limiting their freedom. Genuine freedom presupposes a political structure within which it is protected by authority. Where the edifice of government, and in particular the edifice of democratic government, collapses it buries freedom under its debris. The doctrinaires of democracy overlook that when they demand freedom without providing for authority, they destroy all possibility for freedom to exist.

The demand for Equality in its turn remains within the field of negation, if it is interpreted generally and mechanically. Only two specific forms of equality — equality before the law and equality of opportunity — are included in the essence of democracy. Equality before the law — which Herodotus[5] more than two thousand years ago mentioned as an advantage of democracy — is common to all forms of the state which guarantee law and order. Law and justice must indeed be the same, regardless of the person involved, or else they would not be law and justice.

The practical application of this principle is, to be sure, rendered difficult by many obstacles. The legislator must watch lest his intentions be frustrated by social facts, such as overpowering economic might. Practical problems of this kind, however, do not invalidate the principle; they are solved as well as conditions permit. What happened under the dictatorships established in the wake of the First World War has again demonstrated how great the difference is between a state which, in spite of all imperfections, attempts to secure equality before the law, and arbitrary rule, which is guided by the interests of the ruling party.

INTRODUCTION

Similar considerations apply to equality of opportunity. It is perhaps even more controversial than equality before the law; it seems to a particularly high degree to be subjected to the influences resulting from the unequal distribution of property. Again, we must guard against perfectionism. If we look at democratic reality, we shall see that the effects of the unequal distribution of property are limited, and that wealth can actually become a *privilegium odiosum,* a hindrance rather than a help to political influence. In the United States, for example, the power of hereditary aristocracy, never fully developed, has been narrowly limited since the time of Andrew Jackson, and in particular since the time of the Civil War.

The influence of industrial wealth on American politics has been more extensive, but confined to rather restricted limits, at least since the period of the New Deal. For over a century a political leader who was able to refer to his birth in a log cabin has done so with pride, and in the expectation of political success. Even in England, where political leadership was so long dominated by the aristocracy, the victory of the Labour Party in 1945 has all but completed a change which has long since been in preparation. Suffice it to mention the names of former trade union leaders who became cabinet members, such as Ernest Bevin and Herbert Morrison. These men are aware of what they owe to the principle of equality of opportunity.

With the equality before the law and the equality of opportunity the realm of meaningful equality is exhausted. A democratic theory which assumes that all men are equal in their political ability puts itself in contrast to reality, and gives to anti-democratic criticism a strength to which it is not entitled. When Mosca,[6] Michels[7] and Pareto[8] proved with a large array of factual material that the active direction of politics, even in a democracy, was in the hands of a minority, many were led to the assumption that the foundation of democracy had been shaken. Actually, what had been shaken was an ideology unrelated to the true meaning of democracy. There is a difference between equality of opportunity and equality of gifts and talents. Equality of opportunity merely creates a common background against which genuine inequality is made more visible.

The men engaged in the practice of democratic politics have long since been aware of this fact and expressed it well. There is, for example, an interesting remark by Pericles in his famous oration on which Hegel enlarged in his *Philosophy of History,* when he said:

"In the democratic constitution the widest scope is given to the development of great political characters; for it above all not only admits the individuals, but it asks them to make use of their talents . . .

"In Athens, there was a lively freedom and a lively equality of manners and of intellectual education, and if inequality of property could not fail to be present, it did not go to extremes. Beside this equality and within this liberty the inequality of character and of talent, all differences among individuals could assert themselves most freely, and find in their environment the richest stimulation to development." [9]

This problem is treated even more thoroughly in a letter by Thomas Jefferson to John Adams. In Jefferson's words:

"For I agree with you that there is a natural aristocracy among men. The grounds of this are virtue and talents. Formerly, bodily powers gave place among the aristoi. But since the invention of gunpowder has armed the weak as well as the strong with missile death, bodily strength, like beauty, good humor, politeness and other accomplishments, has become but an auxiliary ground of distinction. There is also an artificial aristocracy, founded on wealth and birth, without either virtue or talents; for with these it would belong to the first class. The natural aristocracy I consider as the most precious gift of nature, for the instruction, the trusts, and government of society." [10]

More recently Gladstone said: "I am a firm believer of the aristocratic principle, the rule of the best. I am out and out inegalitarian. . . . How are you to get the rule of the best? Freedom is the answer." [11]

Political leadership constitutes in fact the essence of democracy. It must, of course, be a genuine leadership and therefore spontaneous. If it is mechanized it is destroyed. The "leadership principle" of German national socialism represents such a mechanization. Leaders were appointed by the thousand whose position did not rest upon the voluntary recognition of their worth by those whom they were supposed to "lead," but on orders given from above. Their position was not maintained by the active consent of their followers, but by coercion, if necessary backed by the might of the Gestapo and the terror of the concentration camp. It is characteristic that the anti-democratic practice of today appeals to democratic termin-

INTRODUCTION

of a democracy functioning for more than five generations is in itself so impressive that it contains the living answer to the question whether modern democracy can exist and whether freedom and authority can be effectively combined.

The English example is in some respects even more significant than the American. First, because the English type of democracy, characterized by the parliamentary system, comes closer to European experience than the American type with the separation of powers. Second, because the experience with the English type is not limited to England. The same type of constitution governs the political experience of countries which are as different as Canada, Australia, New Zealand and South Africa. Yet in all of them this constitutional pattern shows the characteristics of political success.

Section I

THE FORMATION AND THE DEFORMATION OF POLITICAL WILL: THE MAJORITY SYSTEM AND PROPORTIONAL REPRESENTATION*

Chapter 1. Positive Democracy in England

The successful combination of authority and freedom in the Anglo-Saxon democracies is generally admitted. The question is raised, however, whether Anglo-Saxon experience is relevant to the problems of Continental Europe and other areas. Reference is made to the differences of a material nature which, according to widespread opinion, exclude the possibility of applying successfully the same kind of constitutional form.

English and Continental Institutions

The presence of such material differences is obvious. Some of them will have to be dealt with later. That the constitutional pattern of countries like France, Italy and Germany has never been identical with that of the Anglo-Saxon nations must, however, also be taken into consideration. This applies in particular to the system of voting, which Montesquieu said was the basic problem of democracy, comparable in its importance to the law governing the succession to the throne in a monarchy.[1] Proportional representation (or

---

* The basic purpose of proportional representation is to give each party a percentage of seats which is as close as possible to its percentage of the votes. For this purpose, it is necessary to establish large constituencies which elect a number of members. Let us, for the sake of simplicity, assume that the state of New York elected its congressmen by proportional representation, and that the state is subdivided into districts electing ten representatives each. The distribution of votes might, in a district forming part of New York City, be as follows: Democrats 300,000, Republicans 200,000, Liberal party 200,000, American Labor Party 200,000, Communists 100,000. In this simplified case, a party would elect a congressman for each 100,000 votes. The Democrats would have three, the Republicans two, the Liberal party two, the American Labor party two, the Communists one. Under the plurality system as now used each district elects one congressman; under proportional representation the cake would be enlarged and slices presented to each party in proportion to its numerical strength.

P.R., as it is commonly designated) is in use nearly everywhere on the continent of Europe, whereas in the Anglo-Saxon countries it has never been applied on a substantial scale.

Even during the time, however, when the countries of Continental Europe used the majority system of voting, they did so in a form different from the English type. England as well as the United States uses the so-called plurality system, under which the candidate with the highest number of votes is declared elected. No country on the continent of Europe has applied this system, and, as will be discussed below, this entails important differences.

In comparing constitutional developments on the continent of Europe and in the Anglo-Saxon countries, it must further be emphasized that a two-party system does not presuppose as large a measure of social homogeneity as is often assumed. So far as the United States is concerned, Professor Jerome Kerwin recently commented on this as follows:

"American political parties are not homogeneous groups. In this country a multi-party system exists within the confines of two parties. These two parties constitute the chief agencies in the country of political unification. Each one is compounded of forces left of center, center, and right, forces of labor and capital, forces of agriculture and of urban areas, forces of professional groups and of artisans, forces of plutocracy and of the proletariat, forces of divergent geographical areas. The Republican party, indeed, may represent more definitely conservative interests, but it is by no means a unit, for agricultural interests and urban workers still work within its ranks. For the sake of the smooth-functioning of governmental machinery, it is far better that the process of unification and compromise take place for the most part outside the sphere of government." [2]

What Professor Kerwin says with regard to the United States, applies with certain modifications to England. In both cases there hides behind the simplicity of the two-party system a multiplicity of tendencies. In the Anglo-Saxon countries this multiplicity is controlled by the effects of the plurality system. In Continental Europe this control was first weakened by less effective varieties of the majority system. Subsequently, P.R. was introduced. Its ultimate implication is to eliminate political control entirely and to give free rein to all the divergent forces which exist in a nation. It is the most radical institutional embodiment of negative democracy.

POSITIVE DEMOCRACY IN ENGLAND

Voting Systems and English Democracy

Englishmen are little inclined to make general assertions in regard to political problems. It is interesting to note that systems of voting led to an exception from this rule. While in other countries P.R. was adopted without systematic investigation, the English appointed a parliamentary commission which examined the problem with a completeness unprecedented up to that time. When, in 1910, this commission, after carefully weighing the arguments advanced by both sides, submitted its report, it contained the following sentences:

"This statement of the aims of Proportional Representation (i.e., to represent the parties in proportion to their strength at the polls) is in reality very incomplete; for the title conceals a root-and-branch attack on the single member majority system and all its works — its effects upon the elector, upon the candidate, upon the member of the House of Commons and upon politics, no less than upon the justice of representation."

These remarks mean that the introduction of P.R. would bring about a radical change in British constitutional life. A brief analysis of the actual content of this constitutional life will make such a conclusion understandable. English constitutional practice is characterized by one-party majority government. No matter how many parties may exist at a given time one of them has, as a rule, an over-all majority. Therefore, it forms, except in times of war or crisis, a government of its own, and the authority of this government is promoted by its political homogeneity.

It is no less important that this government is based upon a direct decision by the people. Theoretically, English government is parliamentary; the supremacy of parliament is the highest political maxim. Practically, however, parliament has been subjected to a process of mediatization. Significantly, this happened as a result of the second electoral reform in 1867 when a large number of people were, for the first time, given the vote. The political parties found it necessary to organize these voters systematically. They were, at first, afraid of the new element being introduced into British politics, and Robert Lowe said: "Now we shall have to educate our masters." Practically, however, the would-be educators were educated by those whom they expected to be their pupils. When the popular party organization was established throughout the country its membership demanded simple decisions. As it was put: "We now think in battalions."

These new political battalions wanted to fight for or against a particular leader who then, in case of victory, became the prime minister. They also wanted the issues of the campaign to be presented to them as simply and clearly as possible. The result was a clear popular decision on men as well as on measures.

These changes at the same time eliminated the need for the bargaining among parliamentary groups characteristic of coalition governments. England has now a government which is democratic rather than parliamentary. The people themselves, with the help of the two-party system, form and overthrow governments; the task is no longer handled by parliamentary leaders, and there can be no English equivalent of the "smoke-filled room" in which, if an American convention is deadlocked, a few men may make a "dark horse" the presidential nominee of a major party.

The British government is able to govern. What it means to govern was recently expressed by Professor Mirkine-Guetzévitch, against the background of the weak governments of the Third French Republic, in these words: "To govern does not simply mean to execute laws and apply them: To govern means to give its impulse to public life, to take the initiative, to propose laws, to appoint officials, to recall them, to punish, to act. Always to act!" [3]

The British cabinet can govern in the fullest sense of this definition. It knows that in all likelihood it will be in office for the full length of the parliamentary term. It can, therefore, plan a coherent program of action without having to confront the voters before the fruits of its policy have had a chance to mature. Legislation is a part of this program. Much of the work to be done by the government requires new legislation, apart from the fact that the budget which deals with all forms of government activity, is voted as a law.

Laws have long since become a practical domain of the British cabinet. It is an exception if a law introduced by a private member is seriously discussed, let alone passed. The power of the government goes far, and in the case of an emergency it can deviate from a law and request an act of indemnity with the certainty of obtaining it. The government alone has the power to initiate expenditures, a fact which not only leaves the control of financial policy in its hands, but also strengthens its control over policy as a whole, since in Parliament no motion is admissible which would require an increase of expenditures.

If the basis for the extraordinary power of the British cabinet is to be found in the democratic character of British government, this at the same time establishes the necessary limitations. Even the appearance of an abuse of power is unpopular, in particular with the independent voters. It is their task to place a ceiling on partisanship. They can solve it because a majority would like to remain a majority. The views of the independent voter are subject to constant study — in particular by the members of the House who were elected by small pluralities, and who, if possible, spend every weekend in their constituencies, where they will notice any opposition. The government is not inclined to act contrary to the advice of this group of members upon whom its majority usually depends. As a result, though the individual member of Parliament is now no longer as influential as he was before the rise of cabinet supremacy, he retains the task of control. Ivor Jennings, in his book, *Parliament*, has demonstrated that this control can even now find ways and means to assert itself.[4]

Pluralities and Governments

The combination of authority and liberty which the English government professes is typically the result of the majority system. P.R. would destroy it from one election to the next. The report of the Royal Commission of 1910 contains a compilation of the shift in party strength which would take place if, under P.R., the distribution of the popular vote were to remain the same, the number of seats being adjusted to the percentage of the popular vote obtained by the parties. In all elections which were examined (those from 1885 to 1910) it results that the party on which the burden of government eventually came to rest would suffer a considerable loss of seats under P.R. In the elections of 1895 and 1900, the majority would have declined to two seats, in 1886 to eighteen and in 1892 to forty. The commission did not hesitate to regard this weakening of the majority as a serious interference with the work of the government, which would have been too dependent upon the accident of the presence or absence of a few individual members. The results of the elections of February, 1950, were to bear them out. It must be borne in mind that wherever a two-party system exists both parties include very different tendencies. These tendencies cannot be handled by the rigid system of parliamentary discipline which exists in certain countries where the authority of the party bureaucracy has been strengthened by P.R. In England it is possible as long as a "safe" majority exists for a particular group of majority members to vote against the government without doing serious harm. This safety valve is necessary and, of course, unobjectionable as long as the government majority remains sufficient. If, however, majorities should regularly — rather than exceptionally — fall below a certain level this type of government could not be continued.

If the Royal Commission drew such conclusions from the material available in 1910, its conclusions are greatly strengthened by the experience of the subsequent decades. In the elections held since the end of the First World War we find, if we disregard the coalitions of 1918 and of 1931, that there was not a single case in which one party secured a majority of the popular vote. Instead, a plurality of the popular vote obtained by the leading party led to an absolute majority of the seats. The exceptions are the two elections of 1923 and 1929, when Labour was not strong enough to secure a majority of the seats, but benefited sufficiently by the plurality system to underline its claim to leadership. P.R. would, therefore, have created a multiple-party system in England a generation ago; no party would since that time have possessed an over-all majority in the House of Commons.

This is the decisive point. Proponents of P.R. often emphasize that there exists in England a considerable number of parties even now. The number of parties is irrelevant, however, as long as one party normally has a majority, and the British type of one-party majority government can continue. Coalitions of a continental type would have been the only alternative. British politics would, therefore, under P.R. have lost the essential characteristics which distinguish them from the political pattern of Continental Europe.

P.R. and Splintering

The consequences of P.R. would not have been limited to a mere change in the number of seats in the House of Commons. The distribution of the popular vote would have been altered, the small parties being strengthened at the expense of the large ones. This applies, first, to the Liberals who, until 1922, had been one of the pillars of the two-party system, and who then lost ground to Labour. In the majority of the constituencies Liberal candidates have had, after 1924, no chance to be elected. Therefore, either no candidates were presented or they received a comparatively small number of votes, since the voter did not want "to throw his vote away." Under existing conditions the absorption of the remnants of the Liberal votes through the two large parties is only a matter of time, even though the length of time required has been greater than expected. P.R. would change this fundamentally and at once; all of the votes cast for the Liberal party could be utilized and it would, therefore, receive many more votes than at present. The Liberal leaders are aware of this fact and consequently they now demand P.R., without taking into consideration the results which such a step would have for British constitutional life. This attitude was bound to evoke criticism. Sir Austen Chamberlain wrote:

". . . the Liberal party in the long heyday of its power persistently opposed, with a few exceptions, this innovation (i.e., P.R.). It is only since it ceased to be a great party that the rump has professed to find salvation in it. Its adoption is more likely to destroy the constitution than to strengthen parliament." [5]

On another occasion Sir Austen said:

"Mr. Gladstone bitterly opposed this change on a similar occasion. Mr. Bright, with the strong, bold, common sense which clung to him always, repeatedly and consistently condemned all freakish schemes of this kind throughout his long career. Now the party which claims them as two of its most illustrious leaders is, I am told, invited by its present leader to go into the Lobby in support of this amendment. If so, a profound change has been worked on their party. This scheme used to be the monopoly of a few cranks, very distinguished men in some cases, but always unable to work in harness with other men, unable to make the concessions which are necessary, I do not care whether in politics, in business or in life, if men are to get on together and help one another. I protest against facilitating the entry into this House of that class of person. I protest against embarking on a scheme which sets sectional interests and little cliques above the broad genuine opinion of the nation . . ." [6]

What Sir Austen objected to in the case of the British Liberals is a general phenomenon which we shall encounter again repeatedly. Parties regard their self-preservation as their highest goal; whatever serves or seems to serve this aim is promoted, no matter how much damage may be inflicted upon the general welfare. To such opportunism P.R. owes a large part of its success.

In this connection it is characteristic that parties are blind in regard to the permanent effects of P.R. They forget, in particular, that what benefits them also promotes the success of other groups which might nullify all they could possibly accomplish. In England, for example, the Liberals assume that the results of P.R. would be limited to returning them to a position of political power. They forget how much the worst enemies of liberalism, the Fascists and the Communists, would in their turn gain from P.R.

Let us now consider in detail the effects which P.R. would produce in the case of minor groups. Certain assumptions must be made concerning the concrete form of P.R. applied. Before the First World War 300 different brands of P.R. were already counted, some of them differing considerably in their political results. The principal source of such differences lies where it is seldom suspected, namely, in the size of the constituencies and in the provisions governing the utilization of surpluses, if any. In a parliament of 400 members the logic of P.R. would require that a party receives a seat for each one-fourth of one per cent of the total valid vote cast. There is no technical difficulty in securing this result: unlimited utilization of surpluses would accomplish it. If one asks where such thoroughness would lead it is only necessary to quote what Thomas Hare, one of the inventors of the single-transferable vote, the only form of P.R. now advocated by the English and American proponents of P.R., predicted in case of the application of his system:

"Many more candidates will be everywhere put in nomination . . . minorities . . . (will, under the single-transferable vote) far exceed the entire number of any minorities now existing, by the operation of numberless affinities and compulsions, which, in a state of liberalism, *will dissolve the present majorities.*" (Italics mine) [7]

The present supporters of Thomas Hare would no longer agree with such a radical application of P.R. On account of technical difficulties which stand in the way of the application of the single-transferable vote in large constituencies, they demand small constituencies. They usually place the limit at five members, and they exclude all utilization of surpluses. This means, of course, that the principle of proportionality is strongly weakened; the result would contain some of the effects of the majority system.

In Ireland, for example, there are a number of constituencies which elect only three members to the Dáil. It follows that a candidate is certain of being elected only if he receives one-third of the popular vote, whereas with the majority system only one vote more than the majority would be required. Small parties rarely succeed in securing one-third of the votes. What they lose in unutilized votes accrues to their larger rivals. Thus, in a three-member constituency a party which secures more than fifty per cent of the votes automatically obtains two of the three seats. P.R. is, therefore, comparable to an accordion which one may open and compress arbitrarily.

The following comparisons are based on the conditions prevailing under the German law of 1920. At that time the utilization of surpluses was limited only by the provision that no more seats could be obtained from the national lists than had been obtained in the comparatively large provincial constituencies, and in the unions of several provincial constituencies (*Wahlkreisverbände*). In general about three per cent of the votes cast in a constituency were needed to secure a seat. This limitation was comparatively insignificant, and it was the result of a threat made by a delegation of midwives. This delegation appeared before the then Minister of the Interior, Koch-Weser — who later, shortly before his death, was to make a thoroughgoing attack on the entire principle of P.R. — and told him that in case certain of their demands were rejected a midwives party would be founded and elect several members of the Reichstag. Koch-Weser forestalled this possibility by limiting the number of seats which a party could secure from the national list to the total of those secured in the provincial constituencies and the *"Wahlkreisverbände."* In these units very small parties secured no seats, even if in the whole country they polled several times the quota of 60,000.

This process of limiting proportionality may be carried on indefinitely. Parties can be eliminated which are not even "splinter parties" in the proper sense of the term. It will be seen later, however, when we discuss the experiences made in France in recent years, that provision against small parties may confer benefits on large parties even if they are radical. The French Communists are a case in point; and of course when the small parties are placed under a handicap for the benefit of large radical parties the resultant reduction in the number of parties only renders the functioning of democracy more difficult. When, on the other hand, the majority system reduces the number of parties, it favors the moderate groups; the dependence of the candidates upon the marginal voter in the center erects a dam in front of the radicals, which they can rarely breach.

Space does not permit the presentation of statistics showing that in England Communists as well as Fascists might, under the assumed type of P.R., each receive something like one or two dozen parliamentary seats. This calculation[8] is based on the percentages of the popular vote, which the Communist and Fascist candidates actually secured in English elections and which make it probable that both would receive enough seats in the provincial constituencies to enable them to utilize their surpluses from all over the country.

One to two dozen Communists and Fascists can, in spite of their small number, already influence majority conditions substantially, at any rate in a parliament elected under P.R. in which majorities often consist of a very few seats. Thus, in the vote of July 18, 1930, when Dr. Brüning's emergency decree was rejected by the German Reichstag, entailing the dissolution of that body, the vote was 236 to 221. A shift of eight votes would have reversed the result. In view of the fact that the twelve National Socialists, who were in the Reichstag at that time, had received their seats with such small percentages of the total vote that under a majority system one would hardly have paid attention to them, it is obvious that the defeat of the government is due to P.R. The vote in question led to the elections of September 14, 1930, in which democratic parties suffered a defeat from which there was to be no recovery.

The fact that even small groups of Fascists and Communists could, under P.R., render the formation of majorities difficult constitutes only a part of the political effects of P.R. The Labour party, for example, would be confronted in every constituency with serious Communist competition. That would make it difficult for its leaders to pursue a moderate attitude, in particular in the field of foreign affairs. Similarly, the Conservatives would have to suffer from the competition of the Fascists, who resumed their activities after the Second World War. In both cases centrifugal forces would be strengthened and centripetal forces weakened.

Problems of Principle

This entire process has its consequences also in regard to the will of the people which P.R. is supposed to express with clarity and precision. If there is to be a will of the people, it must be one. Therefore, there must be clear political fronts during the campaign, and on this basis a clear decision. In England, the plurality system leads to such clear fronts and clear decisions. P.R. would promote the splitting up of parties, would destroy present majorities, and no popular will would be discernible any longer. There would remain only the will of a number of parties — a babel of voices each bent on drowning out the other.

It must further be borne in mind that the claim of P.R. to represent the will of the people assumes the act of voting to be a kind of census or, as the English say, a counting of noses. Actually, there is, in the political field no objective and quantitative fact which could simply be measured. Political attitudes are the result of a thousand shifting impressions and considerations. The direction of the shift is to a considerable extent governed by the system of voting. The two major systems confront the voter with entirely different questions. As a well-known Italian scholar at one time put it in conversation with this writer: "The majority system asks the voter to do something, which he can do, namely, to give an answer to the concrete question concerning political leaders and the measures which they propose. P.R. demands something from him which he cannot do: he is asked to exercise an option between different political world outlooks which he is not able to understand."

The implication is that the majority system invites the voter to participate in a process which promotes agreement and integration, whereas P.R. causes him to participate in a process of disagreement and disintegration; it divides a people against itself. The difference in the reply is caused by the difference in the question. Neither system of voting is a "mirror" which reflects what exists. Elections are a dynamic political process, in the direction of which the system of voting plays an active part. Our choice is limited to deciding whether we want to guide this process into channels which lead to a working democracy or into those which lead to a weakened democracy, which in a time of crisis might yield to a dictatorship.

The opinion is often expressed that English political attitudes are the product of a tradition built up in generations. We shall return to this point shortly, but we might emphasize without delay that, as traditions have their beginning they may also come to an end. When Walter Bagehot in his book, *The English Constitution,* discussed P.R. in the form proposed by Thomas Hare a few years earlier, he reached this conclusion:

". . . the mass of a Parliament ought to be men of moderate sentiments, or they will elect an immoderate ministry, and enact violent laws. But upon the plan suggested, the House would be made up of party politicians selected by a party committee, chained to that committee and pledged to party violence, and of characteristic, and therefore immoderate representatives, for every 'ism' in all England. Instead of a deliberate assembly of moderate and judicious men, we should have a various compound of all sorts of violence." [9]

What Bagehot said could be taken as a faithful description of conditions as they had developed in Germany immediately before Hitler came to power. Bagehot's comments were, however, made in a book which was the first modern analysis of the British constitution, an analysis which, until this day, has not been exceeded in clarity. Bagehot's views could be reworded as follows: take British politics as they are after having been shaped for generations through a number of factors, including tradition. Vary the one factor of the voting system, and a radical change will occur, rendering the continuation of the present system of government impossible.

A few additional remarks on the nature of the majority system will serve to make Bagehot's argument more readily understandable. Reference has already been made to the fact that elections under the majority system necessitate a process of integration. Candidates must find a common political denominator for voters belonging to a multiplicity of groups. In the United States, for example, there are Protestants, Catholics and Jews; whites, blacks and people of mixed color; industrial workers, white collar workers, middle-class people and business men; voters of English, Irish, Scandinavian, German, Slav and Latin descent. Certain candidates run in constituencies where they can win without the help of some of these groups. Large political parties can never do so. They need voters from all groups, because each one of them may be able to make them lose enough doubtful constituencies to turn the scales against them. Party leaders, therefore, systematically aim at winning as many voters as possible from all groups. They know that a majority is possible only as a combination of minorities. This is the reason why Thomas Woodlock was able to say: "Democracy is the protection of minorities by the rule of the majority." As long as a majority is unable to maintain itself without minority groups it must do justice to them.

The establishment of a common denominator for the members of the majority may be termed intra-party integration. This has already, to a large extent, the function of blunting the edges of conflict, of playing down what divides, and of emphasizing, thereby strengthening, what is common. Common convictions develop; their social function cannot easily be overestimated. By way of example we may mention that, in the state of New York, there usually are, among the candidates for the offices of governor, lieutenant-governor, and attorney-general, a Protestant, a Catholic and a Jew. The fact that leading members of these three denominations stand shoulder to shoulder in the campaign after speaking from the same platform, and that they must win the support of millions, means a mitigation of religious conflicts, which is much more effective than all calls for tolerance, no matter how sincere they may be. If, in the United States, we have not yet overcome religious and racial intolerance we have at least largely succeeded in keeping its political manifestations under control. This is vital, because it means that instrumentalities of the state cannot be used to foster intolerance; they may instead be mobilized, as is now being done, to curtail the social manifestations of intolerance in such fields as employment in private as well as in public business.

Intra-party integration is supplemented by inter-party integration. Both large parties depend upon the same group of independent votes needed for victory, and as a result they will be inclined to compete for for it with the same promises. This process leads to a mutual assimilation which has often been subjected to ridicule, as where people speak of American parties being like "tweedledum" and "tweedledee," but which nevertheless constitutes a social necessity. Reference is often made to what Lord Balfour said in his introduction to Walter Bagehot's *The English Constitution*:

"Our alternating Cabinets, though belonging to different Parties, have never differed about the foundations of society. And it is evident that our whole political machinery pre-supposes a people so fundamentally at one that they can safely afford to bicker; and so sure of their own moderation that they are not dangerously disturbed by the never-ending din of political confflict. May it always be so." [10]

Thus Balfour regarded agreement on fundamentals as a condition for the successful working of the party system. Actually it is, to a large extent, a result of this system, brought about by the dependence of both major parties upon the marginal voter.

Inter-party integration is most effective under a two-party system; in that case the moderating and unifying influence of the independent vote reaches from the center into every significant political area, be it to the right or to the left. The question arises as to what causes a two-party system. It should be evident that, while marriages may be made in heaven, the same can hardly be said about party systems. Considerations of a very earthly nature are involved. One of them is the simple fact that a hundred divided into fifty is two: the task of securing more than fifty per cent of the votes can obviously be tackled with a real chance of success only by two parties. Smaller parties are "interlopers" who risk bringing about the defeat of what they stand for.

Types of Majority Voting

The details differ according to the particular types of majority voting applied. Let us, following common usage, employ the general term "majority system" to designate any kind of voting in which the aim is to bring about the election of candidates by a majority, even if this aim is not reached.

The simplest type of majority voting is the plurality system. Suppose the political preferences of those who intend to vote in a given English constituency are: Conservatives 25,000, Labour 20,000, Independent Labour (as represented by the Zilliacus group in the 1950 elections) 10,000. England uses the plurality system, which means that the candidate with the highest vote is elected. In this case the

Conservative candidate will benefit, provided that the votes are cast in accordance with the assumed political preferences. The result would hardly be popular with the Zilliacus supporters. They would not only feel that they "wasted their votes," but also that they brought about the election of the candidate whom they liked least. Foreseeing this result, most of those who sympathize with Independent Labour will be inclined to vote for the regular Labour candidate. Experience shows that such voters are often fully reassimilated by their old party after only a brief interval.

The second and third forms of majority voting have the purpose of making certain that the candidate elected is supported by an overall majority. One way to accomplish this is the system of "run-off" elections, which permits only the two leading candidates of the first ballot to compete in the second. On the other hand, the law may permit all candidates to run in the second election. It is assumed that a political consolidation will take place between the two ballots which will give the winner an absolute majority, but if this is not the case, a plurality will suffice. This system was used for most of the elections held during the Third Republic in France, where it was even possible for new candidates to present themselves for the second ballot.

In England the proposals to make sure of an absolute majority for the winning candidate usually take the form of the alternative vote, which completes the process in one election. Voters are given the right to express one alternative choice. If no candidate has obtained a majority of the first choices the candidate with the smallest first choice vote is eliminated. His ballots are recounted, and those which contain an alternative choice are transferred to the candidate for whom they are marked. If necessary, this process is repeated until only two candidates remain, one of whom will have an absolute majority. If we return to the above-mentioned example, let us assume that the 10,000 votes cast for the Independent Labour candidate are all marked for the regular Labour party candidate as the alternative choice. The latter would then have 30,000 votes as against 25,000 for his Conservative rival.

Paradoxically, the safest way to provide for absolute majorities in the long run is the plurality system. It contains the strongest incentive for the voters to group themselves in two large political parties. Each of the three systems aiming at an absolute majority facilitates the splitting up of parties. The founders of new parties are not faced with the simple alternative of either producing a winner immediately, or else being irrevocably defeated. They can present a candidate of their own in the knowledge that, if he is not elected in the first ballot, he will at least not have brought about the defeat of the candidate whom his supporters like next best. The voters will be aware of this fact and, therefore, willing to support a new party even if they would not have done so under a plurality system.

American experience provides the best illustrations for the political effects of the plurality system as compared with any of the systems intended to secure an over-all majority. In presidential elections the plurality system is used on the largest possible scale. The results show clearly how it penalizes political divisions and rewards party unity, while remaining compatible with the requirements of democracy. In 1912 the split among the Republicans made it possible for the Democratic candidate, Woodrow Wilson, to be elected with 41.8 per cent of the total popular vote, his Republican rivals polling between them 50.6 per cent.

Any doubts that the resultant administration might be undemocratic were soon dispelled. If ever a President made an intelligent and successful attempt to govern with the consent of the governed, Woodrow Wilson did so during his first term. He was aware that he could not expect the Republican split to continue, and that he was unlikely to be reelected unless his administration appealed to millions of voters who were previously either Republicans or Independents. He obtained almost three million votes more — an increase of close to fifty per cent — in 1916, when his record was submitted to the test of popular approval, than he had obtained in 1912; he had managed to lead his party out of the political wilderness of Bryanism and to make it a serious, and for the time being successful, contender for political power.

The Republicans, on the other hand, realized that they had fought each other so bitterly only to present the Democrats with a victory. The split was healed in time for the election of 1916, when the Republican candidate, supported by both factions, came so close to a majority in the Electoral College that on the evening of the vote he retired in the belief that he was the next President of the United States, although Wilson had a clear lead in the popular vote.

POSITIVE DEMOCRACY IN ENGLAND

It is difficult to imagine a similar result if a second ballot is required. In that case two factions of the Republican party could, in 1912, have united on the candidate of one of them — or, as in the case of the French system, on a neutral candidate — and elected him. There would not have been the pitiless punishment for division which the plurality system exacted. Nor would it have been necessary to heal the split so rapidly. The two wings of the party might well have become two political parties.

This is the reason why the British Liberal party, after Ramsay MacDonald, in 1929, had declined to accept P.R. as the price for their support, agreed to the alternative vote. The Liberals knew that under such a system they would receive more votes and more seats than under the plurality system. The accident that the House of Lords failed to approve of this law, and that the House of Commons was dissolved before the two years required for the final adoption of the bill had passed, prevented a far-reaching change in the pattern of British politics.

Fullfledged P.R. would, of course, have modified British constitutional life much more thoroughly than the alternative vote. The Royal Commission on Systems of Election rightly concluded in 1910: "What arrangements might ultimately have to be made to induce any party to undertake the administration of the country in such circumstances (i.e., the destruction of majorities by P.R.) . . . it is impossible to forecast; it is only clear that parliamentary government as now understood in England would become impossible." Forty years later we must add that in addition to a revolution in British constitutional life, P.R. would also bring about a revolution in political thinking, producing a House of Commons containing, as Walter Bagehot predicted, representatives "for every 'ism' in all England." [11] In other words, the major features of what we now consider typically English would be destroyed, and a pattern not unlike that of Continental Europe would develop.

The Elections of February 1950

The general election of February 23, 1950, led to a result which, in the opinion of some observers, invalidates, or at least weakens, the conclusions drawn above. The standings of the parties in the House of Commons, after an election postponed on account of the death of a candidate had taken place, was as follows:

PARTIES	SEATS
Labour	315
Conservatives	297
Liberals	9
Irish Nationalists	2
Independent	1
Speaker	1
Total	625

Thus, Labour had an over-all majority of six, excluding the Speaker. This majority rises to eight, when we consider that the two Irish Nationalists have not taken their seats. In a typical P.R. country such as France, even so slender a majority for a moderate party would have appeared miraculous. Great Britain, voting under the plurality system, and accustomed to substantial majorities, has different standards. Measured by these the outcome of the elections had glaring defects.

The safety valve of dissent was closed; in every seriously contested vote Labour had to muster its entire strength. The accidents of ill-health became of vital importance, in particular since the age of the Labour members was higher than that of the Conservatives. The latter had benefited from the rejuvenation process characteristic of the majority system. The Conservatives had lost a large number of seats in 1945; the arduous task of recapturing them was entrusted, so far as possible, to young and vigorous candidates, more than a hundred of whom were successful. In addition, Labour suffered from the handicap that those of its members of Parliament who were also ministers had to choose between work in their offices and attendance in the House of Commons. Inevitably, the opposition held the initiative. It could afford to lose without ill effect, but it could also, at a time of its own choosing, marshall its full strength in an attempt to defeat the government, for which every lost vote was a serious setback even though it lay within its power to disregard any defeat save one on a vote of confidence.

POSITIVE DEMOCRACY IN ENGLAND

Before we go into details, it is well to recall the reason for the near stalemate. The distribution of the popular vote among the major parties was as follows: Labour 13,306,614, Conservatives 11,504,851, Liberals 2,637,089.[12] In such a case, the plurality system ordinarily gives the leading party an appreciably larger number of seats than Labour received. A special correspondent of *The Economist* had calculated that the law of statistical averages called for Labour to secure eighteen seats more, and the Conservatives eighteen seats less, than they actually obtained.[13]

The combined efforts of two changes prevented such an outcome. First, there had been a reapportionment of seats necessitated by the population increase in the Conservative suburbs. This factor was expected to increase Conservative strength by about thirty seats. While this redistribution was an overdue measure of fairness, the previous situation had served to compensate for a factor which operated to the disadvantage of Labour. The latter had been "carrying coals to Newcastle"; it enjoyed top-heavy majorities in a number of constituencies from which it benefited no more than in the United States the Democrats benefit from their top-heavy majorities in the solid South. The Conservative vote was more evenly, and much more advantageously, distributed. The correspondent of *The Economist* concluded: "It is probable that, for the time being, to get a clear majority of seats in a general election, Labour will have to get at least one per cent more of the popular vote than the Conservatives would need for the same result." [14]

Where such a condition prevails, and the division of the popular vote is fairly even, with the handicapped party enjoying a small lead, near-deadlocks may repeat themselves. Awareness of this fact could suggest the adoption of measures designed to mitigate the effects of this condition until such a time as a sufficient shift in the popular vote is expected to give a clear parliamentary majority to one side or the other. As mentioned above, in the literature on government, frequent reference is made to British political traditions. Their influence can be overestimated. Political traditions may be compared to the ivy entwining an ancient structure; it embellishes the structure but, while it is the first thing to strike the eye, it does not support the edifice. When, however, wind and rain loosen a part of the structure, the ivy may hold it in place until the necessary repairs can be made.

BETWEEN DEMOCRACY AND ANARCHY

One of the strongest British traditions is expressed in the saying, attributed to the Duke of Wellington: "The King's government must be carried on." An opposition which is not strong enough to replace the government, although it has sufficient strength either to overthrow it or to make its life difficult, is expected to restrain its attacks. There is an example which, while referring to a somewhat different situation, well illustrates the basic principles. After the election of 1923 the Conservatives had 258 seats, the Liberals 159, and Labour 191. In Continental Europe a coalition would have been regarded as the most natural solution for such a problem. In a memorable speech made in the House of Commons on January 17, 1924, the Liberal leader, Asquith, told his audience that he had been urged again and again that it was his duty to society to ally himself with the Conservatives and to block Labour's road to power. He concluded, however: "I think there is no ground for departing from the normal usage, and if the Labour party is willing, as I understand it is, to assume the burden of office . . . , it has the absolute undoubted right to claim it." [15]

What Asquith designated as "normal usage" is what we have termed "tradition." It called, in this case, for a one-party rather than a coalition government. The Liberals stepped aside, refused to exploit their bargaining position, and allowed Labour to proceed with a government of its own.

In 1950 a corresponding attitude on the part of the Conservatives, while reserving the right to press the government hard as soon as a defeat and a dissolution appeared desirable, would have required moderation until that point was reached. British newspapers were all but unanimous in recommending such a course and, "as a practical matter," *The Economist* suggested that the opposition provide "pairs for those ministers who are compelled to be absent from the House of Commons on public business." [16] "Pairs" for members too ill to attend were also recommended.

What actually happened was expressed by *The New York Times* in these words:

"It was taken for granted when the results of the Feb. 23 election were known that the Conservatives would give the country a breathing spell and not really try to overthrow the Government except on an issue of grave import like steel nationalization. Anthony Eden promised as much in a speech at the beginning of the new Parliament. Winston

Churchill evidently has other ideas. Here were the Tories yesterday, with the support of the small Liberal contingent, doing their best to defeat the Government and bring about a general election on a small gasoline tax and a purchase tax on trucks!" [17]

While the Duke of Wellington had insisted that, "The King's government must be carried on," another maxim proclaimed that, "The duty of the opposition is to oppose." It is perhaps no accident that this maxim is ascribed to Lord Randolph Churchill, the irrepressible father of an irrepressible son. There is little use to engage in hortatory arguments on such an occasion; the Conservatives had the power to act as they did under Churchill's leadership. The tactics which they pursued only go to show, once again, that traditions are a weak reed on which to lean; they consist in mental attitudes which can be discontinued at will and, in the long run, will be discontinued if the conditions which led to their rise come to an end.

Still, if ever there was a time to refer to these traditions, it was in the spring of 1950. The cause of both democracy and stability had been served well by the British plurality system; if, for the first and only time in modern parliamentary history, it had led to a result which was less than satisfactory, it was also clear that if enough patience could be mustered on the part of the opposition to postpone a general onslaught on the government until such time as the electorate could be expected to have shifted its support sufficiently in one direction or the other, a return to the old condition of safe majorities could be anticipated. Most surgeons do not recommend the amputation of the leg as a cure for a blister on the foot.

Doctors anxious to prescribe surgery did, however, crowd the British political scene as soon as the election results became known. What they advocated would at best perpetuate the evil of which they complained. Their method consisted in condemning the plurality system on the basis of its own high standards, while they were ready to evaluate the results of their respective alternatives on the basis of the lax and lenient standards which these imply.

It is well, however, before discussing the alternatives, to recall what the opponents of the plurality system fail to remember, namely, that the elections of February 1950, in addition to an undesirable division of major party strength, had also some rather positive results.

In the first place, a clean sweep was made of political splinters.

The Communists, who held two seats in the old House, presented 100 candidates and elected none. Only three managed to secure more than one-eighth of the votes cast in their respective constituencies and to save their deposits; even so their percentages were large enough to produce, under a P.R. system comparable to the one used in Germany after 1920, the original seats needed to make possible the utilization of additional votes from all over the country on a national list.

At the right, Sir Oswald Mosley's followers did not even try their luck. It must be borne in mind that fascism usually flourishes as the counterpart of communism, and that, in a democratic country, the defeat of the one is the defeat of the other.

What *The Times* termed "the execution" [18] of the minor parties, was accompanied by that moderation, and agreement upon essentials, which Lord Balfour mentioned, hopefully rather than confidently, as the prime requirement of a system of alternating cabinets. English observers took this development so much for granted that they barely referred to it. Still, it is not so many years ago that Harold Laski predicted civil war as a possible result of a Socialist victory. That victory occurred in 1945, and it did mean socialism, surprising though it was to see a party whose leaders had been brought up on the Fabian diet of gradualism and moderation turn to Marxian dogmatism. Major industries were nationalized, but the Tories who, according to Laski, should have been sharpening their swords, reacted by accelerating their development from "Tory democracy" to what some observers have called "Tory socialism." Perhaps Lord Beveridge's version of the welfare state more adequately expresses the essence of current Tory policies.

It must be added that, if the Conservatives proved unwilling to go beyond the welfare state, Labour showed signs of regret for having gone beyond it. During the campaign Labour's left-wingers, such as Aneurin Bevan, were kept as carefully under control as their Conservative counterparts. After the campaign, as prominent a supporter of the Labour party as Barbara Ward expressed misgivings that, "Nationalization remained as the distinctive Labour policy," and added that it was "difficult to win an election on a program half of which is identical with that of the opposition and the rest only half believed in by the party itself." [19] Her views seemed to be shared by the party leaders, in particular by Mr. Attlee and Mr. Morrison, and the report of *The New York Times* on the first meeting of the new parliamentary group of the Labour party is entitled: "British Labour Views Election as Mandate for Moderation." [20]

Moderation and agreement were complete in the field of foreign affairs. Instead of going into details, let us quote from what C. L. Sulzberger reported to *The New York Times*: "This fundamental bi-partisan attitude of the two major parties is not crystallized on any formal basis such as that attempted in Washington. Nevertheless, some people suspect that despite its tenuous and informal nature it is more successful." [21] Mr. Sulzberger proceeded to mention that Socialist policy in Britain had its repercussions upon international economic planning, which were different from those implied in Conservative proposals. Yet, agreement went deeper than disagreement, and the French daily, *Le Monde,* headlined an article by Anthony Eden, "England's Authority in International Affairs Is Not Diminished." [22] In this article Mr. Eden emphasized that the extreme Leftists, the only real critics of Mr. Bevin's foreign policy, had all been defeated, and added: "I personally believe that the present equilibrium among the parties will, in fact, permit us to attack with firmness and even with imagination the problems concerning the Commonwealth and the world." Certainly, this means unanimity to an extent which no coalition government could achieve even within its own ranks.

These considerations must be emphasized in regard to the argument of Professor Gilbert Murray, according to whom it was necessary to introduce P.R. in order to save the British Liberal party, because "The elimination of moderates is not good for any country, and is ruinous to international cooperation." [23] Under the existing system, moderation triumphs because it is characteristic of both major parties and, therefore, of British policy as a whole. P.R. would tend to make moderation a monopoly of a minority group in the center, which could become politically effective only by selling its parliamentary strength to one of the major parties, which then would be separated from the marginal voter, and inevitably become less moderate. Such bargaining would be certain to be less democratic, as it would replace British democracy, with its direct electoral decision on government, by an aristocracy of party leaders and party bureaucrats, inside and outside parliaments. How much moderation would stand at the end of the bargaining process is anybody's guess, and the time might come when the inevitable periods of paralysis would make the call for "the strong man" heard even in England.

A few words will suffice on the general position of the Liberals. They had entered 475 candidates in the election, and their leaders had been provident enough to insure them with Lloyd's against losing their deposits, which 315 of them did. The voters responded to the more than fifty per cent increase in the number of Liberal candidates by increasing the Liberal vote by one-tenth of one per cent, leaving it practically stable with 9.1 per cent of the total as compared with 9.0 per cent in 1945. With a repetition of the experiment — *The Economist* called it "a gamble" [24] — neither the British voter nor Lloyd's can be expected to be in sympathy.

Liberalism would not perish in England if the Liberal party should cease to be a major contender in the elections. Economic liberalism, to begin with, is no longer championed by the official Liberal party. A grandson of a former Liberal prime minister, Gladstone, wrote to *The Times*: "I am entirely unable to offer my support or my vote to the Liberal party. I do not believe it to be truly liberal. Liberalism is the antithesis of State-Socialism. But the Liberal party has been pandering to State Socialism since 1945. Frequently Liberal members of Parliament have either voted for or acquiesced in projects of nationalization. Monopoly is the bane of history and State monopoly is the worst form of all. And yet the Liberal party has tended to acquiesce in it." [25] *The Economist* discussed both sides of the picture in these words: "The general character of the Liberals returned to the House is radical, but they had stated in their eve of poll message that they will have no truck with further socialisation." [26] In other words, while Labour has come to accept, temporarily at least, Karl Marx as its patron saint, the Liberals prefer Lord Keynes. Tendency and temper propel both parties in the same direction, but as Labour shows certain dogmatic traits, the Liberals attempt to remain discriminatory in their approach to the same economic goal. That makes a difference, but it is basically also the attitude of the Conservatives. A *New York Times* report on party platforms was entitled: "Thin Line Is Drawn by British Parties; 'Socialism' in Conservatives' Program Is Dismaying to Some of Their Adherents." [27] To be more concrete, the "welfare state," so controversial in the United States, was accepted by all British parties.

So far as Liberal prospects are concerned, we can only agree with what *The Times* wrote, after first training its editorial artillery on the Liberals' "irresponsible splattering of the electoral map with hundreds of candidatures for which there never was the remotest chance of substantial support":

"Liberalism is immortal. Its victories from the great Reform Act to 1914 are the main thread of British political history. Its triumph has been so complete that Conservatives and Socialists alike must endeavour to embody Liberal principles in their policies, and those who deny Liberalism altogether may expect to be dismissed with the contempt that the electors have just shown for the Communists. But it has been shown that, in the great majority of constituencies, the Liberal Party can best serve Liberalism by leaving, or helping, its supporters to judge for themselves which of the two larger parties can do most to put the Liberal spirit into practice." [28]

It must be added that if anything is apt to translate the "Liberal spirit" into political reality, it is the present type of British democracy, with direct popular decision on the government. A large Liberal party which would be unable to hope for a majority would constitute the most direct threat to this political embodiment of Liberalism. Furthermore, by working from within the two major parties the Liberals could do a great deal more to make their ideals effective than they are now able to do. Liberal voters at present, for the most part, either waste their votes by supporting Liberal candidates, or they are confined to a choice between the candidates selected by the major party organizations, even though one of the criteria for the latter's selection is their ability to attract the Liberal vote. As members of Conservative or Labour associations the Liberals would have a direct rather than an indirect influence on the selection of candidates, and they would also have a voice in the selection of the local delegates to the national party congresses. The editors of *The Economist* may not have been averse to such a solution when they wrote:

"If the influence of Liberalism is to be felt in the country, the leaders of the Liberal party must begin to consider whether the time has not come to transform it from an organisation with purely electoral ambitions into an extra-parliamentary movement. Such a movement, working towards defined Liberal objectives and capable of undertaking the kind of research which is outside the range of the ordinary political parties, might come to have an influence far greater than the contemporary Liberal party could ever command in Parliament. The very dispersion of the Liberal millions across the country, which is the source of their weakness when they put up their own candidates, could be turned into a source of strength if the candidates of the larger parties were compelled to compete for their votes. Such a Liberal movement . . . might be capable of exercising a moderating and invigorating influence upon the two major parties without wasting money, energy or prestige in putting up Parliamentary candidates." [29]

The alternative to the Liberal party's acceptance of these facts is a change in the system of voting. The elections were followed by a lively debate on this subject, spurred to greater intensity than was otherwise to be expected by Mr. Churchill's House of Commons speech of March.[30] Mr. Churchill began by expressing agreement with an editorial in *The Times* which had termed the large number of Liberal candidatures "frivolous," and contrary to the rules intended by the legislator, who wanted not just to punish, but to eliminate candidates without a serious chance to win. He continued by saying: "The object of the Liberal leaders was nakedly stated by Lord Samuel in his broadcast of 7th February when he said: 'It may be that no party will have a working majority in the new House of Commons. In such an event the Liberals might be called upon to form a government.'" Mr. Churchill saw in this what a *New York Times* reporter termed the "'balance of power' complex," which, he added, "dominates Liberal thinking." [31] On this issue Mr. Churchill said: "I hope that the House of Commons is not going to allow itself to be dominated or let its fate and future to be decided by any small number of Hon. Members. We do not wish to emulate some foreign parliaments where small parliamentary parties are able, by putting themselves and their favors in the balance, to sway the course of considerable events. Indeed, it seems to me that this would be an undignified attitude for the Mother of Parliaments, especially in a time so serious as this."

After this introduction Mr. Churchill complained of "the constitutional injustices done to 2,600,000 voters who, voting upon a strong tradition, have been able to return only nine members to Parliament." The remedy was to lie in electoral reform, and Mr. Churchill suggested to the government that a Select Committee of the House of Commons be set up to report on available methods.

There can be little objection to an investigation of the problem, although the example of the Royal Commission, examining the matter from the point of view of intervening thought and experience, would be preferable. Still, one wonders why Mr. Churchill — always an "irregular" in politics, and in past years quoted by the British Proportional Representation Society as having endorsed P.R. for the major cities — objects to the plurality system as long as his views are as stated in his introductory remarks. If P.R. were adopted even for a substantial part of the country, it would be certain to perpetuate the very deadlock which Mr. Churchill regretted; it would necessitate the very bargaining which he excoriated. Professor Neville was right when he concluded a letter to *The Times* with these words: "The choice is not between two electoral systems; it is a choice between two systems of government." [32]

In Britain, the alternative vote would have a more serious chance than P.R. It was, as mentioned above, adopted by the House of Commons in 1931, and failed to become law on account of the opposition of the House of Lords. It was planned to form a Liberal-Labour campaign alliance on the basis of the changed election system (for which the Liberals were willing to pay the price by supporting the Labour government). Dr. Karl Braunias wrote that if the measure had gone into effect, "The reform itself would, in case of continued Liberal-Labour cooperation, have led, at the following elections, to great successes of the two parties and to a smashing of the Conservatives." [33]

How would the alternative vote work under present circumstances? As *The Economist* put it: "If to give one's first preference to the Liberal were not to waste the vote, many more votes might be so given, enough to bring the Liberal into second place in a number of seats and thus benefit (as the party of the middle would) from the second preferences of whichever party was at the bottom." [34] Again one of the major parties — in this case the Conservatives — might accept the alternative vote as the price for Liberal support. *The Economist* remarks that the Liberal party would, by the new system of voting, be guaranteed "both seats and independence."

That, of course, would mean the end of the two-party system. If the Liberals are guaranteed "seats and independence" there is a chance that the revival of their party would take on more extensive form than the Conservative partners to such a bargain would be prepared to welcome. Also, there is no way to limit the benefits of the scheme to the Liberals. The Communists, the left-wing Socialists, and the Fascists would be grateful to be reinsured against wasting their votes. No one can tell who would benefit and by how much.

A multiple-party system would, however, be certain to develop. It would, to be sure, be a multiple system of *related* parties, quite different from the multiple system of unrelated parties characteristic of P.R. No candidate standing at the right of the present Conservatives, or at the left of the present Labour party, could be elected except when moderate enough to be accepted by the marginal voter in the center. That, of course, is a very important safeguard, and for countries which at present use P.R. the alternative vote would constitute a great forward step. In Britain, however, where the inconvenience produced on February 23 is neither major nor permanent, one should think that few would want to trade the certainty of a very minor evil against the possibility of a grave danger.

Even the alternative vote would mean a journey to a "point of no return." A new party system would develop, containing so many vested interests connected with the new order that an abolition of the alternative vote would hardly be possible. There is a difference between a political experiment which one may try and stop, and a political plunge in which the law of gravitation pulls downward rather than up. It may be mentioned in passing that if Australia [35] has had preferential voting (which is similar to the alternative vote except that more than one alternative preference may be expressed) for its House of Representatives, it has now also adopted P.R. for its senatorial elections. Besides, as the centrifugal tendencies of British politics are stronger than those of Australia — this is nearly always the case when a large country is compared with a small one — deviations from the plurality system are likely to bring about greater effects in Britain than in the southernmost member of the Commonwealth.

The Economist, in commenting on the chances for electoral reform, calls P.R. "certainly unattainable" and the alternative vote "just faintly conceivable." A systematic analysis of the subject would lead to the conclusion that what British institutions owe to the plurality system pertains to the very core of British democracy. This realization would eliminate from further consideration even a reform apparently as moderate as the alternative vote.

Chapter 2. Positive and Negative Democracy in the France of the Third Republic (1870-1940)

The political patterns of Continental Europe, and of France in particular, differ from those of England in about as many characteristics as it can be possible for one country to differ from another. Some of these differences arose from the social material with which French politics had to deal, such as Latin individualism, and the heritage of the struggles between monarchists and republicans, clericals and anticlericals. Other differences belong to the field of political institutions and will be discussed in some detail later.

Party Patterns and Government Weakness

Whatever the causes for the basic features of French politics, their effects were plain for all to see. Political parties which are the pillars on which a stable parliamentary government must rest, existed before the Second World War only in their beginnings. There was, of course, a Communist party held together so tightly by the bonds of a Moscow ordained "unity" that in this case the victory of political "form" over the "matter" of Latin individualism was complete. The Socialists had established a "unified" party in 1905, but it was torn by the contest of tendencies. The Radicals (the old republican party which at that time represented the moderate Left) made efforts to establish a popular organization in the years immediately preceding the First World War, without, however, accomplishing much more than the establishment of party headquarters in the Place de Valois, which provided the party with the nickname of *les Valoisiens*. At the moderate Right there was the Popular Democratic group, a Christian Democratic party which was well enough organized but too weak to be a political power.

The majority of the deputies was, at any rate before 1936, elected more by their own efforts than by those of their party. They established a campaign committee in their constituency before the elections, which afterwards receded into oblivion with the possible exception of an annual banquet. As a rule, deputies belonged to a party in name and were independents in fact. In the Chamber (as well as in the Senate) they joined whichever parliamentary group they liked best, and changed their allegiance if that was opportune. Political discipline was, outside of the parties mentioned above, an ideal rather than a reality. Even the leader of a parliamentary group might, as Louis Marin did repeatedly, value his freedom so highly that he voted one way even if all of his "followers" voted the opposite way.

Thus a French cabinet could, as a rule, not rest on the foundation of a stable coalition. The prime minister had, instead, to appeal to the individual deputies — by means of eloquence, or by favors. These weapons might easily prove inadequate. In fact, there was a total of 106 cabinets during the period of the Third Republic, with an average duration of less than eight months.

Governments which do not last cannot govern. Before the First World War, the weakness of French governments became obvious first of all in the general field of legislation, where work needed for generations could not be accomplished. The legal codes were sadly out of date, going back to Napoleon I, and much of the administrative system dated either from Napoleon I or from King Louis XIV. The administration of justice was equally deficient and, together with a number of deputies and senators being amenable to corruption, this led to scandals of which the Panama scandal was the most notorious. These events did much to keep the opposition to the Republic alive.

After the First World War, matters went from bad to worse. Deputies and senators no longer left foreign affairs to the foreign minister and the president of the Republic, as they had done, in the main, before 1914; they were agitated about every detail and stood so much in the way of the various foreign ministers that no active and coherent policy could be pursued. Equally serious was the spreading of disruption from the political into the economic field, in particular to financial matters. The inflation accompanying and following the First World War in France should, in a country normally so rich in savings, have been terminated quickly. Political indecision allowed matters to drift and get worse; stabilization came only after a serious financial and political crisis in 1926.

POSITIVE AND NEGATIVE DEMOCRACY IN FRANCE (1870-1940)

Institutional Weaknesses

The France of the Third Republic had, then, its share of the effects of negative democracy. If we ask to what extent institutional shortcomings were at fault, let us first quote, at the price of repetition, what Woodrow Wilson had to say on the second ballot:

"The law governing the election of Deputies provides against choice by plurality on the first ballot; and the result is unfortunate. If there are more than two candidates in an electoral district (an *arrondissement*), an election on the first ballot is possible only if one of the candidates receives an absolute majority of all the votes cast not only, but also at least one-fourth as many votes as there are registered voters in the district. If no one receives such a majority, another vote must be taken two weeks later, and at this a plurality is sufficient to elect. The result is, that the multiplication of parties, or rather the multiplication of groups and factions within the larger party lines, from which France naturally suffers overmuch, is directly encouraged. Rival groups are tempted to show their strength on the first ballot in an election, for the purpose of winning a place or exchanging favor for favor in the second. They lose nothing by failing in the first; they may gain concessions or be more regarded another time by showing a little strength; and rivalry is encouraged, instead of consolidation. France cannot afford to foster factions." [1]

Wilson's views fall into the same general pattern which has been developed in the discussion of the second ballot in the preceding chapter. Our agreement with Wilson clearly extends into the field of methodology; for him as well as for us systems of voting do not simply "mirror" a static political fact, but have a share in molding the political forces of a country, the specific effect of the second ballot being to "foster factions."

The institutional framework of the Third Republic was, however, deficient for another reason; there was no workable right of parliamentary dissolution. English writers state unanimously that the possibility of dissolving the House of Commons is an essential part of their constitutional system; if the House can overthrow the cabinet, the latter must be able to overthrow the House. Theoretically, the right of dissolution is exercised by the king. The king's political acts require, however, the counter signature of a responsible minister, in this case the prime minister, who in reality decides whether there is to be a dissolution. The king's participation gives to this act a greater solemnity; also, it is not inconceivable that he might refuse his cooperation if a patent abuse were intended.

Parliamentary dissolution is a democratic measure, since new elections are held within a few weeks, and the voters finally decide the conflict between cabinet and parliament. If the cabinet wins, it continues in power with renewed popular sanction; if it loses, it will resign. In a case where there is no doubt as to the character of the new majority, and the person of its leader, resignation may take place immediately. Thus, on the evening of July 26, 1945, Winston Churchill resigned, and Mr. Attlee was appointed, even before the counting of the votes, begun on the morning of that day, was completed. As a result of such prompt compliance with the popular verdict, no one is afraid that the right of dissolution might be abused. Should a prime minister apply it injudiciously, as Ramsay MacDonald did in 1924, he and his party would be the first ones to suffer.

The framers of the French constitution intended to follow the British example and to confer an unrestricted right to dissolve the Chamber of Deputies upon the President of the Republic. Two historical accidents, however, deflected France from the path of positive to that of negative democracy. First, Marshal MacMahon, then President, expressed fear in assuming responsibility on his own accord for a dissolution; at his request, the head of the State was given this right subject to the approval of the Senate. This condition went far toward invalidating the right of dissolution. Its usefulness lies less in its practical application than in its constant availability. It should be obvious that if the government can be overthrown at any time, it must also be able to retort at any time with a decree of dissolution. Dependence upon the approval of another body, such as the French Senate, means at best delay and at worst uncertainty and a defeat for partisan reasons. A weapon which must be sharp if it is to be useful would be so blunted as to make it all but useless.

The second historical accident to render ineffective the right of dissolution was again due to Marshal MacMahon. The elections of 1876 had resulted in a republican majority, and a republican cabinet took office. The monarchist President soon disagreed with it fundamentally. He caused the prime minister to resign and appointed a monarchist in his stead. The new government did all it could to win the subsequent elections for the monarchists. MacMahon had stayed within the letter of the law, as the Senate, which then still had a monarchist majority, had approved the dissolution. From the point of view of the unwritten, but fundamental, rules of the parliamentary system, however, the French President had committed a grave abuse of his power. It is the purpose of a dissolution to submit, in case of a conflict between the government and the parliament, the issue to the people. In the France of 1877 there was no such conflict; the republican government enjoyed the confidence of the republican majority in the Chamber. Actually, MacMahon was challenging the people, who in 1876 had sided with the republicans rather than with the monarchists.

French republicans were right in denouncing the Marshal; they were wrong in holding the institution itself responsible for its abuses. In subsequent years, no prime minister dared propose a dissolution; to do so would have provoked the charge of preparing a *coup d'état* against the Republic. It was completely overlooked that the institution had proven itself on the very occasion when the attempt was made to pervert it. The republicans managed, in the elections of 1877, to return a majority to the Chamber. MacMahon had to accept this fact; first he agreed to appoint a republican cabinet and, when the latter's actions went too deeply against his convictions, he resigned, and was replaced by a republican. Ultimately the entire sequence of events meant that the republicans had completed their assumption of power several years sooner than would have been the case without MacMahon's actions. Appearance was, however, in this case as in others, allowed to "tyrannize over truth";[2] the contention that the right of dissolution was undemocratic became an accepted part of French republican dogma.

There are reasons for assuming that the right of parliamentary dissolution would have been particularly effective in France. The very fact that so many deputies did not owe their election to a political party, but to their own efforts, would have made them reflect long and carefully before casting a vote against the government, all the more so since such votes were often successful only because of collusion between the extreme Right and the extreme Left. The voters, and in particular the independent voters, seldom approved such a combination; in addition, many deputies had to budget their campaign expenditures carefully over several years, apart from the physical strain and uncertainty of a new election. No party could lighten these burdens appreciably for them; no party leader could have forced them into a vote against the government from which they recoiled.

The other factor which would have operated to make the right of parliamentary dissolution particularly effective in France was the clear-cut division of the French electorate into a Right and a Left. The voter might not know, or care, to which particular group of the Right or Left his candidate belonged. He did know, however, whether it was the Right or the Left, and he insisted that his candidate agree with his own preference. One of the most important aspects of French political life, noticed first by Charles Seignobos,[3] and then emphasized by others, was that almost all French deputies owed their election either to the entire Right or to the entire Left. The second ballot was, as a rule, characterized by the withdrawal of the weaker candidates of both sides and a united front of Right against Left.

This cooperation had important implications. The French multiple-party system was, due to the influence of the majority system, a multiple system of *related* parties, rather than a multiple system of *unrelated* parties, as is the case under P.R. Campaign alliances brought about rather close relationships between the Rightist and the Leftist group. Their alliances could be effective only if the candidate was personally acceptable to all the groups needed for his election, and also, if there was substantial agreement on the more important issues of the campaign. The process went so far that a common leadership of the entire Right and Left tended to develop. The leader of the strongest party within the winning combination was generally regarded as the leader of the entire combination, and if his side won he expected to form the new cabinet. Thus Herriot enjoyed the advantage of popular designation to the premiership in 1924, and Léon Blum in 1936. The agreement on men and measures did not, however, last. Within six months or so after an election the elements of the majority would be at loggerheads. That could hardly have been the case had the prime minister been able to renew the contact with the people to which he owed his original strength, or had he, in other words, like his English counterpart, been able to dissolve the Chamber.

POSITIVE AND NEGATIVE DEMOCRACY IN FRANCE (1870-1940)

Some French observers, such as René Capitant, have gone so far as to state that out of the system of "two blocs" there might eventually have developed a system of two parties. An effective right of dissolution would have established stronger bonds between the prime minister and all of the elements of his majority; their coalition might, as was often remarked, have led to a fusion. It might be added that so astute an observer as Walter Bagehot emphasized the importance of the right of dissolution for party cohesion:

" . . . though the leaders of party no longer have the vast patronage of the last century with which to bribe, they can coerce by a threat far more potent than any allurement — they can dissolve. This is the secret which keeps parties together." [4]

The basic facts were admitted even by some of those who were unwilling to draw the logical conclusions. In 1934 the cabinet of Gaston Doumergue attempted to reform the constitution by facilitating the dissolution of the Chamber. One of the reasons why Doumergue failed was a series of brilliant articles published by the Socialist leader, Léon Blum, in the daily of his party, *Le Populaire*.[5] Blum argued that if Doumergue's proposals were adopted, the French political system would be radically changed. There would be common leaders for the Right — in that case André Tardieu, who combined so much partisan bitterness with his brilliance that he was detested by his opponents — and for the Left, Herriot at that time, Léon Blum failing to anticipate the strengthening of his own party in 1936, which put him in the place of the Radical leader. Blum argued that the concentration of political leadership upon two men would terminate the existing condition under which the sovereignty of the people was embodied in parliament. Power would instead be shared by the electorate, and the two leaders of the Right and the Left.

Léon Blum did not realize that the system he defended was the one Rousseau attacked as undemocratic, and that the system he attacked was democratic in the true sense of the word. France had to choose between an aristocratic parliamentarism in which the deputies were supreme, and a democratic system, which divided the power between a government whose leader was designated directly by the people, and the people themselves. Blum was, of course, repelled by some of the supporters of Doumergue, such as Tardieu, and the semi-

Fascist, *Croix de Feu*. He overlooked that institutions have their own dynamics, which bear no relation to the motives of those who establish them. Thus the constitution of the Third Republic was drawn up by monarchists; the Senate was expected to be a pillar of monarchist power, and was attacked relentlessly by the republicans, only to become a stronghold of the Radicals, the principal republican party. Similarly, as mentioned before, the first one to benefit from a simpler method of dissolving the Chamber would have been the victor of the elections of 1936, Léon Blum, whose government began with a very active program but was, a year later, forced out of office, in this case by the Senate, without being able to appeal to the people.

There is, among writers on this subject, a considerable number who feel that a workable right of dissolution would have sufficed to correct the worst evils of parliamentary government in France. It might be recalled that the evils which flow from the lack of the right of dissolution could have been foreseen, and were in fact predicted in the early 1870's by Walter Bagehot, who wrote:

" . . . the present policy of France is not a copy of the whole effective part of the British Constitution, but only a part of it. By our Constitution nominally the Queen, but really the Prime Minister, has the power of dissolving the Assembly. But M. Thiers has no such power; and therefore, under ordinary circumstances, I believe, the policy would soon become unmanageable. The result would be, as I have tried to explain, that the Assembly would be always changing its Ministry, that having no reason to fear the penalty which that change so often brings in England, they would be ready to make it once a month. Caprice is the characteristic vice of miscellaneous Assemblies, and without some check their selection would be unceasingly mutable." [6]

What Bagehot says does not call for further comment, except that, with an observer as keen as he was, the omission of any reference to the second ballot is significant. Bagehot must have felt that even if the second ballot were maintained the introduction of the right of parliamentary dissolution would be sufficient to put French government on the right track.

A number of French writers have recently expressed views similar to those of Bagehot. They were particularly numerous in the early 1930's, when a vigorous call for the reform of the right of dissolution was made, with the result that in 1934, following the crisis of February of that year, the government of Doumergue was formed for the specific purpose of amending the constitution. At that time, André Maurois wrote a lucid article[7] in which he contended that if only the right of dissolution were adopted without too many restrictions French parliamentarism might become as stable — he might have added as democratic — as the parliamentarism of Great Britain. The Right or the Left would secure a majority in a given election. Its leader would be known after the election, and thanks to the right of dissolution he could expect to maintain his position as a rule for the full term of the particular parliament. Prof. Marcel Prélot said that the only reform of the constitution required would be the elimination of the five words which made the dissolution of the Chamber contingent upon the advice and consent of the Senate. In that case, "The obstruction would be removed and the mechanism would be free and ready to function." [8] More recently, Professor Lowenstein wrote: "The indissoluble parliament was the biggest nail in the coffin of the French Third Republic." [9]

It would seem, therefore, that the most urgent reform to be adopted in France was to introduce an untrammelled right of parliamentary dissolution. The system of the second ballot had grave defects. But, it did not prevent the crystallization of a clear majority of either the Right or the Left, nor the general agreement of Rightist and Leftist parties among themselves on major issues, nor the emergence after each election of one man whom common opinion designated as the leader of the majority. The adoption of the plurality system could have done much to accelerate the process of consolidation. When certain political evils have developed, however, it is often advisable to bring about the reform gradually. In France several minor parties would have been afraid of being wiped out entirely under a plurality system. This applies even to the Radical party which, for so many years, was the strongest party of the Third Republic but which was, at that time, losing ground for somewhat similar reasons for which the Liberals in Great Britain were losing ground. With a plurality system the Socialists would most likely have assumed undisputed leadership of the Left. They would, undoubtedly, have had to become more moderate before they could expect to win the allegiance of the marginal vote to a sufficient extent to come even close to being a majority, but the prospect would have been nonetheless alarming for the Radicals.

If, in the French case, a workable right of dissolution had been accepted first, time could have been allowed to intervene and to clarify to what extent the second ballot created problems of its own. Even the steps from a negative toward a positive democracy may have to be taken one after the other.

Successful Defense of the Republic

The Third Republic, with all of its shortcomings, did, however, have its strong points. As the saying went: "The Third Republic governs badly but it defends itself well." [10] It is not difficult to see that this effective defense of the Third Republic was an effect of the majority system, weakened as it was by the substitution of the second ballot for the plurality system. The defense of the Republic by the majority system was made possible by the severe handicap under which the majority system places extremist groups. They have, to be sure, the same right as everybody to participate in elections. They will soon notice, however, that they are in a bad strategic position. Standing at the extreme Right and at the extreme Left they are farthest removed from the independent vote, without which nobody is elected. A moderate Rightist party, for example, has an opportunity to attract the independent vote, and for that reason voters who might otherwise be inclined to support the extreme Right will prefer to vote for the moderates because they have a better chance. The French voter is as reluctant as his British or American counterpart to "throw his vote away."

One is inclined to say that all the majority system does in regard to the radicals' vote is to give them enough rope to hang themselves. The result of such a situation usually is that such a party is not even founded. If it is founded and is defeated in elections, the result invariably is that the majority of its supporters turn away from it. They return to the moderate parties which they used to support, and are reintegrated into a party system in which the moderates dominate. If the followers of a radical party are assimilated, the same may happen to the leaders.

In France it was a constant experience to see a young politician start at the extreme Left and move gradually toward the Center, if not to the Right. Suffice it to mention the names of Clemenceau,

Millerand, and Laval. If, on the other hand, political leaders refuse to be drawn into this process of assimilation, they are neutralized. Like Maurras and the other leaders of the Rightist *Action Française*, they will in the end become a nuisance rather than a danger. As Waldemar Gurian has emphasized, they criticize the existing political system without realizing that they live on it, as it provides them with their reason for existence.[11]

French political life is full of illustration for the effects of the majority system on extremists. Let us begin with the Communists. An analysis of their position is rendered easy by the fact that George Lachapelle who, for a generation, was the leader of the French P.R. movement, has provided us with a set of figures which prove the point.[12] The following table summarizes the results:

ELECTIONS	1924	1928	1932	1936
Number of seats actually obtained by the Communists	26	14	10	72
Number of seats which Communists would have obtained in the case of full proportionality between the votes cast and seats received	56	68	50	93

The table indicates that in every one of the four elections covered the Communists would have secured more seats under P.R. than they received under the majority system. We assume, of course, that the number of votes received by the respective parties would be the same regardless of the system of voting. Actually, it is likely that under P.R. the number of Communist votes would have decreased because, under the majority system, the Communists had no chance in most of the constituencies.

A few remarks must be added for the elections of 1919 and 1924, and those of 1936. The first two elections after the First World War were held under a hybrid system. From the practical point of view it meant P.R. in the large cities and an aggravated form of majority voting in the rest of the country, because a list which secured an overall majority of the total popular vote obtained all the seats. In anticipation of this fact alliances were formed in most parts of the country by the combined Right and Left. As a result, outside the large cities, one or the other of the two combinations secured all of the seats, with nothing going to the minority. The reason the elections of 1928 were once again held under the customary majority system, with the second ballot, is that the Communists had done so well in the areas where no list secured a majority and P.R. was actually applied. As was expected, the readoption of the majority system made serious inroads into Communist strength.

The elections of 1936 are remarkable on account of the large number of Communists elected under the French type of majority system. Numerous were those who said: "You told us that under P.R. the Communists would obtain fifty seats. Now, under the majority system, they secured seventy-two." The answer is, of course, that if the Communists secured many seats under the majority system they would have secured even more under P.R., and it will be seen that the difference was vital.

In the second place, we must not forget that, properly speaking, the Communist candidates elected in 1936 were as much members of the Popular Front as of the Communist party. In view of the threat the Rightist, often Fascist, leagues presented to the Republic at that time all Republican groups, including the Communists, who had received orders from Moscow to "defend the remnants of bourgeois democracy," formed a pact. In the first ballot, each party was free to present its own candidate, but in the second it bound itself to support the Republican candidate who had the highest vote in the first. The Communists benefited from this tremendously, as this policy excluded the alliances against them with Leftist support.

Lastly, the Communist candidates who had been elected under the majority system were not the free agents of communism which P.R. would have allowed them to be. They owed their seats in most constituencies to the support of the moderate Left, which included the small Christian Democratic Group of the Young Republic. Therefore, fighting under their own banner alone, they would have been defeated in most of the constituencies. This means that the Communists had to act or at any rate to pretend to act as defenders of the Republic rather than as the advocates of a "Soviet France."

It was not long before the Communists received an illustration of what the majority system might do to them, in spite of their gains.

POSITIVE AND NEGATIVE DEMOCRACY IN FRANCE (1870-1940)

In the provincial elections of 1937 they obtained, according to the statistics of the Ministry of the Interior, fourteen per cent of the popular vote, but according to the calculations of the newspaper, *Le Temps,* only 3.1 per cent of the total number of seats. These figures are not quite typical, but most observers agreed that the Communists had suffered a defeat under the majority system which would have been impossible under P.R. They had lost some of the popularity acquired in 1936, and even a small reduction in popular votes was sufficient to deprive them of the plurality over the Republican parties which they held in the Chamber elections of 1936.

It is equally significant that in the elections of 1936, the Communists, as extremists, had to secure 1.5 million votes to obtain seventy-two seats, whereas the Radicals, whose position was exactly centrist, won their 109 seats with 1.4 million votes. Furthermore — again as a result of the majority system — the non-Communist parties of the Popular Front had an over-all majority of the seats in the Chamber, making it unnecessary for them to accept Communist support except on their own terms. The Communists were aware of what P.R. meant to them and lost no opportunity to demand its adoption.

Rightist groups were placed under the same handicap by the majority system as the Communists. This applies, for example, to the *Action Française,* theoretically Royalist but practically similar to the Fascist parties which Europe was to know in the 1920's and 1930's. It was part of the celebrated doctrine of the *Action Française* not to participate in elections. The slogan of its master, Charles Maurras, was *Par tous les moyens* — "By all means." Thus, the right was claimed to use violence. When, however, P.R. was adopted in 1919, the *Action Française* immediately presented candidates. One of them, Léon Daudet, was elected. The percentage of the popular vote which he obtained leaves no doubt that he would have had no chance under the majority system. He subsequently claims that it was primarily due to his personal attacks on Briand that the policy of understanding with Republican Germany, which the latter was attempting to inaugurate as early as 1922, was defeated by one of the intimidating speeches which he made in the Chamber. Conditions in the French Chamber were such that the boast may not have been idle. The system of P.R. used at that time did, however, not provide for any transfer of surpluses from one constituency to the other and, as mentioned before, in most of the country the majority system applied. Therefore, the position of the *Action Française* was weak even under this system, and in 1924 all of their candidates were defeated.

More important than the *Action Française* were, from a practical point of view, the other Fascist or semi-Fascist groups founded in France after the First World War. Let us limit ourselves to the period of the 1930's, when the so-called *Croix de Feu,* led by Colonel de la Rocque, was the strongest. By 1935, the *Croix de Feu* was the largest political organization that France had ever known. The Colonel felt it necessary to influence the elections of the following year. He then came to realize, however, the difference between securing the support of a large number of Rightist voters, and translating it into victory under a majority system applied in single-member constituencies. In order to win he needed all of the Rightist vote, plus part of the independent vote, and this he had to do in hundreds of constituencies where there were already Rightist deputies who were entirely unwilling to yield to the newcomers presented by the *Croix de Feu.*

De la Rocqne acted like the fox in the fable who declared the grapes were sour when he could not reach them. He said that all he wanted was to act as the arbiter of the election. Several hundred candidates were endorsed, mostly the outgoing Rightist deputies. The Colonel found himself induced to support even members of the Left provided that they were members of the moderate Left and were threatened in their constituencies by candidates farther to the Left. Subsequently, explaining this policy in an interview he stated:

"Believe me, some of the candidates for whom I have invited my comrades to vote are not at all in sympathy with me. But the result comes first. We don't work in the skies. I told those who proved to be most scandalized: 'Vote, always vote; afterwards put your finger in your mouth and you will vomit. I shall probably do as you do.' " [13]

This quotation characterizes the position in which extremist movements find themselves under the majority system. They must support moderate candidates or face defeat. It goes without saying that the "New Freedom," which American supporters of P.R. praise as one of its major advantages, would have changed the situation entirely. De la Rocque could have presented lists of candidates all over France, and would have been certain to enter the new Chamber at the head of a strong, if not the strongest, party in the land. In combination with a large Communist bloc his votes might have sufficed to make positive action by the republicans impossible.

The effects of the majority system were, in the first place, that in most of the doubtful constituencies the endorsement of a candidate by de la Rocque meant his defeat. In spite of the gigantic mobilization of Rightist voters brought about by the Colonel, his principal accomplishment was to strengthen the Left, which he had set out to conquer.

Fate had more disappointments in store for him, however. The majority of the deputies whom he had endorsed subsequently claimed to be free in their political action. They had accepted the endorsement, but felt not constrained to make any political payment in return. Ultimately, the Colonel tried to found a parliamentary group of at least the thirty-five deputies who were members of the *Croix de Feu*. The thirty-five met, discussed the matter, and most of them refused to join his parliamentary group; ultimately only nine of them did so. This happened after the republican majority had used the clearcut popular victory which the majority system had given it to take action against the Rightist leagues; in June 1936 they were dissolved. The *Croix de Feu* felt it necessary to change its name to "French Social party," which was quite a humiliation for a group which had claimed to be a "movement" opposed to all parties.

The French republicans not only had a clear majority in the Chamber making such action possible but they were also certain of the moral backing of the country, because it was obvious to everyone that the election had meant the defeat of the opponents of the Republic, and that the government was only drawing the consequences resulting from this fact. We shall see later that conditions were entirely different in Germany when, under P.R., the government tried to dissolve the Nazi "Storm Troops" in order to make certain that no private armies existed in the country.

In conclusion, we must say, therefore, that if the Third Republic was weak, this weakness had, in the first place, clearly recognizable and remediable causes. In the second place, the weakness had its limits. In an emergency the republicans could always mobilize a majority. This means that the assaults directed against the Republic were defeated by the people themselves whom the majority system invited to group together for a clear decision.

Lastly, the governments of the Third Republic were not in every case as weak and unstable as they were during certain periods. The governments of Waldeck-Rousseau, Combes, Clemenceau and Poincaré governed for extensive periods and with a considerable degree of authority. With other unstable governments it always helped to know that if there was no clear majority for a government, neither was there a clear majority of obstructionists standing in its way. It was always possible in a few days, at the very most a week, to form a government which could begin its work with the confidence of the majority of the Chamber. These advantages were not sufficient to secure for France the safe political guidance which her people needed, but they constituted the minimum foundation on which reform could build.

Chapter 3. Negative Democracy and Dictatorship in Italy

Pre-Fascist Italy

Italy was one of the countries which adopted P.R. at the end of the First World War. Serious difficulties developed in short order. Parliamentary conditions, to be sure, had never been entirely satisfactory in the Italy before 1914. However, as in the case of France during the Third Republic the constitution was a living force, and in the case of Italy, it was gradually gaining in vitality. When P.R. was introduced, it destroyed strength where it had existed before, and replaced it by nothing but weakness.

The basic defect of constitutional life in pre-1914 Italy was, as in France, the absence of well-organized political parties. Only the Socialists at the extreme Left, and the Republicans at the moderate Left, had party organizations worthy of the name. Neither exerted any influence upon the formation of governments, standing aside as an irreconcilable opposition with which every government had to contend.

The bulk of the members of the Italian Chamber consisted of deputies with only a loose allegiance to their respective parties. In addition, since, in 1876, the so-called Historical Right had been defeated, no clearcut division between Right and Left existed. This constituted a disadvantage when we compare Italian with French politics, but there was the positive feature that in Italy nominally the king, and actually, the prime minister, had the right to dissolve the Chamber. This right was used infrequently, but its availability was not unrelated to the tendency to greater stability characteristic of Italian political life after the turn of the century.

The majority system of voting was largely responsible for the fact that parliamentary government in Italy was able to function as well as it did. Extreme Leftists, such as Socialists and Republicans, never secured as large a percentage of seats as of votes. Extreme rightist groups, if we may disregard the rather small Nationalist party which developed after 1906, hardly had a chance to make headway. In fact, one Italian observer remarked that all deputies not belonging to the extreme Left ought to be classified as belonging to the Center.[1] This must be taken into account when it is charged that there were about as many "parties" in Italy under the majority system as under P.R. A list of parties presented for this purpose by Mr. John H. Humphreys,[2] the late Secretary of the British Proportional Representation Society, for the Chamber elected in 1913, begins with a group called "Constitutional Ministerialists," credited with 291 members. In a Chamber consisting of 508 deputies this was an ample majority, quite apart from the fact that groups to which at least 100 additional deputies belonged were hard to distinguish from the "Constitutional Ministerialists."

The last elections held under the majority system were those of 1913. They were the first ones in which there existed a practically complete manhood suffrage. These elections were also characterized by a development which is typical of the integrating effects of the majority system. It concerns the Catholics who, since the new Italy had taken the Papal States by force, had abstained from any participation in voting. As new issues arose, an increasing number of Catholics voted, and in 1913 Catholics participated in the elections in a majority of the constituencies. There had been founded in 1906 the "Catholic Electoral Union," whose president was Count Gentiloni. This association submitted to the candidates for the 1913 elections a list of minimum demands concerning, for example, the problems of education and of divorce. Many candidates accepted the terms of the so-called *Patto Gentiloni,* and 228 of them were elected. A sufficient number of them formed an integral part of the government bloc to make it necessary for every cabinet to comply with their wishes.

The terms of the *Patto Gentiloni* had, of course, to be acceptable to both Catholics and non-Catholics. Such electoral cooperation has more than tactical importance. It brings the two partners of the bargain together on certain fundamental issues, and the psychological conditions for future cooperation between them are created. People coming from different groups who fight shoulder to shoulder in a campaign will know and appreciate each other's point of view. Such an understanding is then ratified by the voters themselves, which means that the people at large accept the terms of the compact and expect a government to be formed willing to act on this basis.

In the Italy of 1913 the *Patto Gentiloni* succeeded in freeing the political atmosphere from a great many conflicts and suspicions which would otherwise have poisoned it later. Thus it was demonstrated once again that elections held under the majority system constitute "a struggle with a tendency to integration." In spite of appearances to the contrary they unite rather than divide a country. Inevitably, the government found an overwhelming majority in the new Chamber.

P.R. in Operation

The first elections under P.R. took place in 1919, and immediately reversed the integrating process initiated by the majority system. Constituencies elected from five to twenty deputies each. Proportionality remained, therefore, somewhat limited, and the number of new splinter parties, such as the Economic party and the Veterans party, was kept to a minimum.

The real problem of the new elections is to be found in the nature of the parties which now emerged. Before the adoption of P.R. one of its prominent supporters had complained that under the majority system "the Clericals, Democrats, Republicans, and Socialists" were "Clericals, Democrats, Republicans, and Socialists only up to a certain point," [3] the reason being that none had been elected by the votes of their own partisans alone, but had to take the wishes of related groups into account. This had resulted in a "necessity for bargains," which prevented a policy based upon "clear ideas."

In this respect P.R. did in Italy what it was to do in France twenty-five years later: It completely and abruptly changed a political pattern which had existed for generations. Any party of adequate size was now able to elect candidates with votes of its own partisans alone. It no longer had to take other views into account, and was free to develop its own "ideas." These "ideas" soon developed into that mixture of pseudo-metaphysics and pseudo-politics which the Germans call a "political world outlook." Concrete issues were replaced by high-sounding "isms." Besides, the deputies elected by the new parties were dependent upon the party bureaucracy. They could not compromise with other groups, even if personally they would have preferred to do so.

When parties of this type arise it becomes clear that large parties are not desirable in themselves, but only to the extent that they serve the ends of integration. If they are to do so, they must be moderate as well as large. Otherwise, a condition is likely to develop in which none of several parties is large enough to prevent anyone else from forming a government.

This is what happened in Italy. There was, to be sure, a new phenomenon which required adjustments. Two "mass parties," the Socialists at the Left and Don Sturzo's Popular party in the Center, had arisen. Their share in political power was won at the expense of the groups which old-timers like Giolitti had been manipulating for decades. The "old guard" felt uneasy over the invasion of the Socialist legions, even though common anti-clerical views made them inclined to look with a measure of indulgence on the Socialist chiefs. The old guard were definitely annoyed, however, at those upstarts, the *Populari*, settling in what they had considered their own political backyard. That their populist leader, Don Sturzo, was a simple priest rather than a prominent churchman, did not make it any easier to yield to him a large slice of political power.

The mass parties presented their problems, but basically they were "what the doctor ordered." As mentioned above, when, after the electoral reform of 1867, British parties had to face masses of voters for the first time, their leaders, including Disraeli, the unwilling architect of reform, could not suppress a shudder. Yet, the masses gave to the British parties the popular foundation, and the stability, which they had lacked.

Let us assume, for a moment, that the majority system had been in operation in Italy in 1919. Giolitti, Sonnino and the other "old guard" leaders, of course, could not be expected to relish the invitation to move over and make room for the newcomers. They hardly had a choice, however. Since they needed the Christian Democratic vote, they would have had to pay the price. The price naturally meant a sharing of the available seats rather than the mere acceptance of certain demands, as was the case under the *Patto Gentiloni*. There was, however, no alternative. At the Left there stood a strong and militant socialism, at that time difficult to distinguish from bolshevism. Democrats and Liberals had a simple choice: cooperation with the Christian Democrats, or the prospect of a Socialist victory and an Italian Soviet state. They were sufficiently "bourgeois" to take refuge behind church walls, if need be, against the onrolling tanks of a socialism with a bolshevist tinge. They did, in fact, seek a coalition with the *Popolari* immediately after the new P.R. Chamber met. In that case an understanding was sought only after, during the campaign, both sides had developed their own peculiarities to the full, and made their dislike of each other the chief claim to the allegiance of their own followers.[4] Such trends cannot be reversed at will; all-out combat today is not easily followed by cooperation tomorrow. Cooperation, in fact, appears as treason to the followers of the respective partners.

The majority system does not permit the nonsense of "total" war between parties which fate has destined to govern jointly. They have to come to terms without delay or take the consequences. Party leaders are the first to submit to such necessities; they also are trained in the art of rationalizing tactical necessities into political principles. Thus the surgical operation which the appearance of the "mass parties" was bound to produce on the body politic of Italy would, under the majority system, have consisted of two parts. First, the old groups had to be cut off from the part of political power which was to go to the new ones. Second, so far as the *Popolari,* at any rate, were concerned, the new flesh and bone had to be joined to the old. The old and the new sections of the legs on which non-Socialist Italy was to stand had, perhaps, little time to knit before the elections. The campaign would, however, have provided for wholesome exercise: either the combination would manage to march on its new political legs, or it would have to accept defeat. No preacher or schoolmaster has ever developed a better device of political education than practical necessity. Besides, it does not seem undemocratic if the parliamentary coalitions of tomorrow are submitted for the approval of the voter in the campaign of today. In the long run, the stronger popular foundation was likely to increase stability, as it had done in England.

P.R. surgery left the Italian body politic not with two strong legs, but with three or four. There were the two mass parties, loudly and lustily marching into the political arena. There were Sonnino's Liberals and Giolitti's Democrats, whom, perhaps, we can count as one, if we accept Professor Salvemini's view that the latter "were politicians of a no less Conservative and nationalistic blend than the former, but more equivocal, and divided into groups and grouplets incapable of putting together any ministry that could have been supported by any majority whatever." Walking on these legs was likely to be uncomfortable.

The two mass parties, taken together, had a majority. Cooperation between them was, however, out of the question. Socialist radicalism did not permit it. Theoretically, a majority could have been formed of the Popular party, and the Liberals and Democrats, but the lack of timely integration stood in the way. During the campaign the old animosity between the Catholics and the others erupted, and everything on which agreement was reached in 1913 as a matter of course was a source of disagreement, magnified as the campaign progressed. Therefore, the atmosphere between the Popular party and the other centrist and rightist groups soon became charged with suspicion.

Nitti was the prime minister under whom the first P.R. elections were held. Under the majority system he might have secured a position similar to that which Giolitti had held since the turn of the century. Nitti was, however, unable to establish a working relationship with Don Sturzo and his party. As Don Sturzo later put it: "It was said that Nitti had the Popular party as his lawful wife and the Socialist party as his mistress; it was a *ménage à trois*." [5] The only common element between Nitti and the Socialists was Nitti's slight and the latter's strong tendency toward anti-clericalism. On all other issues their views were irreconcilable. Yet the issue of clericalism had become important enough to wreck what otherwise might have been stable coalition between Nitti and the (Christian-Democratic) Popular party.

The conflict between Nitti and the Popular party led to the latter's withdrawal of their ministers from the cabinet in March. At first, its deputies still voted for him in the Chamber, but they ceased to do so fifty days later. Thus, the cabinet was in the throes of a crisis as early as in January, almost immediately after the meeting of the first P.R. Chamber. As Professor Salvemini, who at that time was an unqualified supporter of P.R., put it: "In the new Chamber no single party had a majority. Nitti had to rely on a small section of the non-Socialist and non-Catholic deputies and on the half-hearted support of the Peoples party. He was able to remain in power until June 1920 solely because it would have been possible for no other man to gather around himself any majority whatsoever in the new Chamber." [6]

After Nitti's final resignation there was great confusion. An appeal was made to the pre-war leaders, like Orlando, Salandra, and Bonomi. It is interesting that none of the renovation of the political élite, which P.R. was supposed to bring about, had developed. Finally, it was necessary to appeal to Giolitti, then seventy-eight years old, who had virtually retired from politics in 1915, when Italy entered the First World War against his advice. His return to power intensified the then already almost general disillusionment, as it seemed to confirm that the war had been fought in vain.

Giolitti's method of government had, in the decades of his domination, been called "rimpasto." As a baker kneads and rekneads his dough to make a loaf, so Giolitti would take groups from the pre-war Chamber and shuffle and reshuffle them until he had a majority. He soon came to realize that in the P.R. Chamber there was none of the required flexibility. He had to deal with solid rocks rather than with soft dough. He was immediately challenged by Socialist obstruction; the Socialists opposed his clear-sighted attempts to balance the budget, end the inflation, and restore economic and political normalcy, by resorting to every obstructionist trick permitted by the rules of the Chamber. As a result the Chamber was, for several months, unable to consider other business, and Giolitti had to continue governing with decree laws, which he had meant to terminate.

Finally, the Socialists confronted Giolitti with "action" in the country. In August and September 1920 the workers, under Socialist leadership, seized the factories in northern Italy, and attempted to run them themselves. Giolitti did not use force against them, believing that the movement would automatically collapse. This it did, but only after having irritated the majority of the people to such an extent that the word *basta* —"it is enough"— was heard more and more frequently. Since the government proved unwilling or unable to put down violence when it came from the Left, people believed that it had to be put down by somebody else. Mussolini and his Fascists, who had been insignificant up to this point, seized upon the opportunity to gain adherents in large numbers, and to apply measures of violence against their opponents whenever and wherever they could.

The "old fox of Dronero," as Giolitti was named after his constituency, now resorted to an astounding policy. First, he reversed a lifelong stand of his and dissolved the Chamber before it had been able to do a substantial part of its work. Then, he allied himself with the Fascists. The latter were given places on joint lists presented by the two parties. In addition, the police provided the Fascists with guns, ammunition, and trucks, and looked the other way when Fascist gangs broke up the meeting of opponents, be they Communists, Socialists, or Christian Democrats. Truly, this was a policy of despair, adopted by a Giolitti who was determined to break the solid rock of opposition with the help of Fascist violence, since the flexibility characteristic of the Chamber under the majority system, which had enabled him to form majorities with more subtle methods, no longer existed.

The second P.R. election, held in 1921, did not fulfill any of Giolitti's expectations. The Socialists, to be sure, lost substantially in terms of votes, their percentage declining from 32.3 to 24.7. Even if we add the 4.6 per cent cast for Communists, who in 1919 had been united with the Socialists, there remains an appreciable decline. Giolitti says in his *Memoirs*: "Compared with the 1919 election those of 1921 showed a gain, on a total of eight million voters, of over half a million for the constitutional parties over the subversive elements. This proportion is quite considerable in view of the short lapse of time, and would under a majority system have sufficed to reduce Socialist, Communist, and Republican membership in the Chamber by more than half, whereas with the proportional system it only deprived the anti-constitutionalists of 30 seats." [7] Giolitti based this estimate on the well-known fact that, under a majority system, a small loss of votes can eliminate margins of victory in many constituencies. Under P.R., of course, the change in seats is likely to be inconsequential. Besides, Giolitti's cooperation with the Fascists had not improved his relations with the Popular party, without which he could not secure a majority. Finally, there were in the Chamber now fifteen Communists and thirty-five Fascists, including Mussolini, none of whom would have been elected under the majority system.

Giolitti at first thought of cutting the Gordian knot by abolishing P.R. through a royal decree, and submitting his act to the approval of a new Chamber elected under the majority system. However, as a French observer put it, "he found in this disorderly Chamber such a systematic opposition to this project that he resigned at the first occasion." [8]

Giolitti's successor was Bonomi, a Reformist Socialist. Personally able, he had the best of intentions, and tried to induce the Fascists to surrender their arms. His position was, however, so shaky that the application of force was impossible. He temporized and resorted to kindly persuasion which, of course, the Fascists did not take seriously. Bonomi had to resign on February 2, 1922.

The new crisis was disastrous. Giolittians and Christian Democrats had to cooperate if a new government was to be formed. The former wanted Giolitti's return to power, which the latter vetoed. Finally, after three weeks of wrangling a new government was announced on February 25, with Facta at its head.

The new Prime Minister had been selected, not on account of any strength but on account of the absence of any strength in his make-up. His very weakness made him the ideal compromise candidate for parties which were determined to compromise on nothing. The reason for Facta's selection was no secret. Mussolini greeted him in the Chamber with the words: "I wager that the person most surprised at your becoming Prime Minister was yourself!" [9]

Naturally, Facta was unable to give leadership to a country which was starved for it. In his cabinet, ministries and sub-ministries had, as is customary under P.R., been allocated to the various groups in proportion to their strength, the process requiring the kind of mathematical ingenuity which only party leaders under P.R. are able to develop. These ministers considered themselves only the delegates of their respective parties, to which, like diplomats representing their countries at an international conference, they would refer all important matters. Thus the cabinet could not act as a unit. Many anecdotes were passed from mouth to mouth during those days to illustrate the complete deadlock prevailing in the cabinet.

Facta knew that he was a stop-gap. He resigned in June, intending to go for good. Once again, however, the followers of Giolitti, and the Christian Democrats, vetoed each other's candidate for prime minister. In the end nothing was possible except to return Facta to power. Facta was unable, of course, to wield any authority whatsoever, and the struggle between Fascists and Communists, and often between Fascists and everybody else in the country, reached unprecedented heights. In the words of Professor Salvemini:

"While the forces which were to destroy democratic institutions in Italy were being massed and organized, the Chamber of Deputies was discrediting itself with inconclusive battles of words and trivial acts of violence. It finally reached a point where it was unable to create a cabinet that was worthy of anything but contempt.

"Decidedly, a disease was undermining the Italian political constitution — a parliamentary paralysis. And outside Parliament there was another disease at work — civil war. Either Parliament must recover its powers and put an end to the civil war, or parliamentary institutions would break down in Italy." [10]

Parliamentary paralysis — this is precisely the result which the deputy Alessio had predicted, when in a memorable speech delivered in the Chamber in the summer of 1919, he had warned against the adoption of P.R. Paralysis is indeed implicit in the premises of P.R., which attempts to set side by side a number of unrelated groups, none of which can expect to secure a majority of its own. In Italy this parliamentary paralysis prevented government action, when even a little action might have sufficed to end the menace of Fascism. The inflation was, thanks to the measures taken by Giolitti, about to be terminated, and economic conditions in general showed signs of improvement. It is strange indeed that Mussolini, like Hitler after him, and Napoleon III before him, should have come to power at a time when the economic depression — in the case of Italy the inflation, which produced social effects similar to the deflation characteristic of a depression — was about to end.

NEGATIVE DEMOCRACY AND DICTATORSHIP IN ITALY

There were, furthermore, signs of political improvement. The moderate Socialists split from the left-wing of their party. It was hoped that in the long-run they might be able to assist in forming a more stable government, although the very formidable obstacles standing in the path of such a solution must not be under-estimated. This applies in particular to the opinions which separated even the moderate Socialists and the Popular party on a number of issues, especially those related to religion, education, and the like.

Be this as it may, the paralysis lasted long enough to make government action impossible when it was needed. We must remember that Mussolini was able to say: "With this Parliament 30 crises could only result in 30 Factas." [11] An American writer, while more impartial, was no less explicit: "Meanwhile the press and public opinion were becoming daily more exasperated, until by fall Parliament had hardly a single friend in the country. The members themselves were disgusted with each other and the King was weary of selecting impossible prime ministers." [12]

It is small wonder that the Fascists deemed the moment ripe to strike. They did not, however, take any chances. On October 26, Facta was requested by certain Fascists to resign if he wanted to prevent an armed uprising. Facta called a cabinet meeting for the evening of that day, in the course of which his ministers placed their portfolios at his disposal. The Fascists, having been successful thus far, decided to push Facta a little farther. The next day they renewed their threat of uprisings unless Facta would agree to resign immediately. Whereupon, to quote Don Sturzo: "That excellent man that very evening tended to the King the resignations of the entire cabinet." [13]

After this, the Fascists knew that they could move without great danger. During the night of October 27, they started to occupy railroad stations, telephone and telegraph buildings, and the like, in northern and central Italy, and to converge upon Rome. The King was at first disgusted with a cabinet which had allowed things to go that far. As he told Facta that evening: "Rather than yield I will take my wife and son and go away." [14] Thereupon the cabinet, sure of the King's consent, but without having withdrawn its resignation, decided to proclaim martial law. While waiting for the King's signature, they instructed the prefects in the provinces to take the first measures for the application of martial law.

On the morning of October 28, Facta, the head of a cabinet which had already resigned, although its resignation had not yet been accepted, appeared before the King in order to secure his signature for the decree establishing martial law. To aggravate the situation, he told the King that he was still negotiating with the Fascists in the hope of a compromise. Professor Salvemini has described the events that followed in these words:

"The King clutched at these negotiations as a drowning man clutches at a straw: since there was hope of a peaceful understanding, why should he proclaim martial law? The cabinet would do well to reconsider the question. Facta therefore returned to the cabinet.

"The Ministers stuck to their first decision. When Facta, at ten in the morning, brought the decree back, the King refused to sign it. In the interval, a group of Nationalists had spoken with him and had assured him that the army would refuse to fight the Fascists. The news that the Duke of Aosta was among the Fascists, ready to take up his cousin's crown as soon as the King should let it fall, gave the final push." [15]

Thus it was the Nationalists who defeated the request made by Facta's cabinet. They hoped to secure the prime ministership for a Rightist leader such as Salandra. Like the German Nationalists in 1933, however, they were made to realize that the forces for which they had opened the way were not willing to be bought off with minor concessions. Mussolini, who had been hiding in the vicinity of Milan, refused to come to Rome unless and until he was assured of the prime ministership. Finally, the King consented, and the "Duce" started his "March on Rome" in a sleeping car. When it became known that the King had refused to sign Facta's decree, law and order broke down all over Italy. The Fascist Blackshirts filled the streets, and dealt summarily with all opposition, the police no longer making any attempt to resist.

On one point there can, however, be little doubt: Had there been serious resistance to the Fascists by a legitimate government the Fascist movement would have collapsed. General (subsequently Marshal)

NEGATIVE DEMOCRACY AND DICTATORSHIP IN ITALY

Badoglio had declared several weeks earlier that "five minutes of gunfire" would suffice to end fascism.[16] Professor Salvemini has expressed the view that it would have been sufficient to let the Fascist groups, camping on the barren hills in the vicinity of Rome, at a total strength of about 8,000 men, run out of supplies. The regular contingents in Rome amounted to 12,000 men and could have dispersed the loosely-organized Fascist groups at any time.[17] Fascist writers, such as Volpe,[18] the official historian of the party, and Pini and Bresadola,[19] express in different words what amounts to essentially identical views.

Everything, then, depended upon a show of resistance by the legitimate government. About the head of this government Professor Salvemini said: "Facta — one of the biggest idiots of all times and countries — hesitated more than the King." [20] Facta was a personal embodiment of the deadlock caused by P.R. No other system of voting could have produced such a prime minister. We can, therefore, understand it when, on a subsequent occasion, Lord Curzon was able to make the following statement:

"During the last three or four years I have been confronted with the phenomenon of a series of unstable Italian governments, seldom lasting for more than a few months, and depriving their representatives at Allied Conferences of that power which derives from stability of institutions. I think I have put the same question to every succeeding Italian Minister, be it Prime Minister or Foreign Minister, with whom I happened to be associated, and on every occasion I have had the same reply: 'The weakness of our institutions and the instability of our Governments is due to Proportional Representation and Proportional Representation alone.' " [21]

The views of Lord Curzon's informants contain an over-statement. Italy's post-war difficulties had their share in the rise of the Fascist movement as well as in its final success. Yet Professor Salvemini groups all these difficulties together under the heading of "post-war neurasthenia" and concludes that they had passed their peak months before Mussolini came to power. The latter event presupposed, in Salvemini's terminology, "parliamentary paralysis," and for that P.R. is to blame.

BETWEEN DEMOCRACY AND ANARCHY

OBJECTIONS[*]

It may be useful to stop for a moment and consider the major objections which have been raised against the above arguments. In the first place, it is emphasized that factors other than P.R. were responsible for the collapse of parliamentary government in Italy. Reference is made in particular to those which Professor Salvemini summarized under the heading of "post-war neurasthenia": the feeling of "mutilated victory," the agitation over Fiume, the inflation, the land seizures, and the like.

One or Many Causes

As will have become plain from the above discussion, we readily admit the influence of these factors. It often happens that a certain effect is produced, not by one but by a number of causes. Economists have to face this problem when they deal with what they call the theory of "imputation." All factors of production, commonly listed as land, labor and capital, must, as a rule, cooperate to produce a certain good. If two factors are given and the third factor is added, the economist will "impute" the entire product to the last factor, since without it there would have been no production. The presence of the first two factors would have been insignificant. On the other hand, the roles in this game can be reversed. The factor which was the last one to be added might, in a different case, have been present from the start. In fact, every one of the variables in the equation might have assumed the role of the independent variable. In our discussion, we were dealing with the political aspect of the Italian crisis, and therefore we selected the independent variable from this field. Had we been concerned with economic history it would, within limits, have been possible to treat economic, in particular financial, factors as the independent variable.

Form and Matter in Politics

A word of caution is needed, as not all factors share equally in producing a certain historical result. We must, with Professor Rudolf Smend,[22] divide all factors into two categories: those related to "mat-

---

[*] Most readers may wish to omit this part. On the other hand, those interested in additional details will want to consult the author's *Democracy or Anarchy? A Study of Proportional Representation*. Notre Dame 1941, pp. 198-211.

ter" and those related to "form." In certain situations matter prevails over form; in others form prevails over matter. We might, however, add that, so far as political decisions are concerned, matter never acts by itself. It must assume a particular political form, and it can prevail over form only in the sense that it rejects the form not suited to it, and causes it to be replaced by a different one.

As long as a democratic constitution finds a social material to which it is at all adapted, the system of voting is the most important part of its political form. What makes or breaks a democracy is the spontaneous action arising from the people, an action which, if it is to be orderly and successful, must express itself through the medium of political parties. Parties assume an entirely different shape under the two principal systems of voting, serving the purpose of integration in one case, and the purpose of disintegration in the other. Signor Alessio, in a speech made to the Italian Chamber of Deputies before the adoption of P.R., expressed himself in these words:

"What is the function of P.R.? It consists in . . . creating an elected Assembly, in which the forces of the different parties are distributed in the same proportion in which they exist in the nation.

"But that, gentlemen, is absurd. Parliament is confused with the nation. The nation, gentlemen, has continuity of existence; it has permanence. . . . Parliament has a duration of five years. In this short time it must carry out a program and support a government or replace it. Its purpose and action cannot be accomplished without a majority.

"Now, what is the result of P.R.? To create not a majority, but a collection of minorities, often incompatible with one another, with ideas which are mutually contradictory. . . . The nature of the minorities which we get with this system of P.R. excludes the possibility of a coalition in parliament, whereas the passion for power's sake, which is so strong among the Latin peoples, leads to paralysis and destruction . . .

"The application of this system under present conditions would lead to a very bad functioning of the Chamber, would make it impossible to form a lasting cabinet, and would bring about in the long run a paralysis of public life." [23]

Signor Alessio's remarks could be reworded to the effect that P.R. ignores the difference between the state and society. Society is characterized by what John Locke terms "the variety of opinions and the contrariety of interests which unavoidably happen in all collections of men." [24]   It is the specific task of the state to rise above these differences, and to establish unity in the sense of a unity of action — action designed to keep the various elements of society from harming each other, and to promote their common welfare. To assume that such unity arises spontaneously out of society, simply by "representing," on a smaller scale, whatever social differences exist, means accepting the basic tenets of anarchism — no longer, of course, those of the old-fashioned anarchism looking upon individuals as social units, but those of group anarchism, which is one of the basic characteristics of our age.

It is interesting to note that St. Thomas Aquinas was clearly aware of the need of basing the state on a factor transcending the multiplicity of society. In his words:

"If therefore it is natural for man to live in the society of many, it is necessary that there exist among men some means by which a group may be governed. For where there are many men together, and each one is looking after his own interests, the group would be broken up and scattered unless there were also someone to take care of what appertains to the commonweal." [25]

St. Thomas saw the unifying factor in a monarchy. Living during a time when one city democracy after the other collapsed and gave way to tyranny, he saw in monarchy the only way to secure what he termed "the unity of peace" in a manner compatible with human freedom. Locke, closer to our time, realized that decision by majority could perform the same function, although it was too early for him to realize that majority decision had to be combined with the institution of political parties in order to achieve its final purpose.

If we apply these principles to the concrete situation in which Italy found herself at the end of the First World War, we must conclude that the problems besetting Italian society at that time became so grave because there was no state strong enough to undertake their solution before they had passed the stage of effective control and plunged the country into near-anarchy. The state — democratic in intention — was paralyzed because its central organ, the government, was weak, and this weakness was so closely related to the essence of P.R. that Signor Alessio was able to predict this paralysis. As mentioned above, the inflation, which was the source of so much secondary social friction, could have been ended at an early date through the means which Giolitti proposed when he became prime minister. In the P.R. Chamber, however, he held a position without power, and the evil which he intended to stem stayed in the social organism long enough to make the timely recovery of constitutional life impossible.

The King and the Intriguers

Similar considerations apply when the argument shifts to the contention that Mussolini's victory was due to his appointment by the King, rather than to the effects of P.R. The facts leave little doubt indeed that if Victor Emmanuel had signed the proclamation of martial law, this would have meant the end of fascism. Few would argue, however, that fascism could have grown to the point which made the "March on Rome" possible without the paralyzing effects of P.R., or that, with just about any other political leader at the head of the government than the typical P.R. product, Facta, the King would have done what he would personally have preferred to do, i.e., sanction the action against the Fascists. Victor Emmanuel had, ever since his accession to the throne, been a strictly constitutional monarch, anxious to appoint prime ministers in conformity with the wishes of a presumptive parliamentary majority. But, where was the democratic majority in October 1922?

It is hardly necessary to discuss in detail the argument which places the principal burden of the rise of fascism upon the Nationalist intriguers surrounding the throne, whose activities were decisive for Mussolini's appointment. There are intrigues and intriguers in all countries and at all times. In a well ordered democratic state, however, power is in the hands of majorities and their leaders. Only the absence of such majorities, so clearly stemming from P.R., can create the kind of vacuum which — in Italy as later in Germany — intriguers could rush in to fill.

Matter versus Form

A last objection arises, which is potentially formidable. Italy was a country with widespread illiteracy. In the south and in the islands, in particular, large groups of the population knew so little about the functions of their government that Italian political scientists spoke of them as "the absentee masses." Under such conditions, the question is whether Italy's social material was adapted to the forms of parliamentary government. If we place this objection last, it is because the forces which undermined parliamentary government in Italy — we do not speak of an Italian democracy — have no tangible relation to illiteracy. The strongholds of the extreme Left, as well as of the extreme Right, were in northern Italy, and in parts of central Italy where the literacy rate was comparatively high. The south and the islands, on the other hand, provided the various governments of the post-1919 period with such reliable support as they had, being still controlled by the old "political class." In this respect, conditions were quite different after the reinstitution of parliamentary government in Italy at the end of World War II.

Chapter 4. P.R. and the Triumph of Hitler

Nowhere have the consequences of P.R. manifested themselves as disastrously as in Weimar Germany. One reason was the typical German thoroughness with which the P.R. system had been carried almost to its logical conclusions. Constituencies were large, a national list took care of surpluses, and even very small parties were able to succeed. Besides, the actual and potential strength of the country made the collapse of democracy and the rise of tyranny in Germany more significant than it had been in Italy.

Before considering the effects of P.R. we must briefly mention the argument that the number of parties was as large in Germany before the adoption of P.R. as later. Those who raise this objection[1] make the statistical mistake, in the first place, of including national minority parties in their comparison. These originated in areas which formed a part of Germany before, but not after, the war. Had the areas in question remained a part of Germany after 1918 those parties would certainly not have disappeared. Secondly, not all of the small groups listed as pre-war parties were separate parties in the true sense of the term. The campaign alliances which the majority system necessitates had caused practically all national minority parties to associate themselves more or less closely with the Center party. The same applies also to the Guelphs, who in fact belonged to the parliamentary group of the Center party throughout this entire period, but are listed as a separate party.

Lastly, Germany, like France, did not have the plurality system. The second ballot took, in the German case, as mentioned above, the form of run-off elections, in which only the two candidates with the highest vote in the first ballot were admitted. This system is preferable to the French system, which had admitted everybody in the second ballot who was willing to run. Still, a part, at least, of the multiplicity of parties is due to the run-off elections.

P.R. was introduced in German national elections by "The Council of Peoples Commissars," which had been established by the revolution of 1918. It consisted entirely of Social Democrats. The Social Democratic party had adopted a plank favoring P.R. in its famous Erfurt program of 1891,[2] and had subsequently been instrumental in having the Second International endorse that system of voting. At that time all Socialist parties were handicapped by the majority system, as they constituted as yet a comparatively small left-wing minority. In Germany the Social Democratic party suffered from the particular disadvantage that the apportionment of seats for the Reichstag had not been changed since 1871. Subsequently, the industrial cities, in which the Social Democrats were strong, had increased greatly in population, without a new apportionment having done justice to this fact. Since in 1918 the Social Democrats were in full control of the government they had the power to institute a fair redistribution. There is agreement that had they used it, they would have done better under the majority system than they did under P.R.

When, in 1919, the Weimar Constituent Assembly considered the issue of voting systems, a memorable warning was expressed by Friedrich Naumann, the President of the Democratic party. Naumann declared in the Constitutional Committee of the Assembly that: "The consequence of P.R. is the impossibility of forming a parliamentary government." He was too ill to press his point orally. In a letter to one of his followers, however, he raised the issue even more sharply:

"I do not believe that we shall get to a satisfactory solution of the problem of forming a majority, but I fear that we are creating a condition, which can be remedied only by a later *coup d'état*. However, I know well that I am alone in my far-reaching pessimism on this question. Since one does not want to endow the President with strong governmental rights of his own, one ought to take care that there is a natural majority in Parliament. That is what is not being done and what, so far as I am able to see, is not accomplished by the way chosen. Therefore, the new Constitution lacks a state-forming organ." [3]

Subsequent developments make us less inclined than Naumann was to see any advantage in giving independent powers of government to the head of the state under a parliamentary system. His warning as to the consequences of P.R. is all the more pertinent. He had no doubt that a thoroughgoing system of P.R. meant taking an utterly negative view in regard to the problem of government in a democracy, and that the consequence would be an impasse of a kind that excluded the possibility of a peaceful solution.

P.R. AND THE TRIUMPH OF HITLER

The history of P.R. in Weimar Germany, which was to bear out Naumann's warning so fully, may be divided into three periods. First, there is the period of the National Assembly, from 1919 to 1920, during which it was the principal effect of P.R. to prevent the Social Democrats from securing an over-all majority. The second period extends from 1920 to the elections of September, 1930; this is the time of what came to be called the "Pluralist Parties State." There followed the totalitarian revolution in the political system, extending from September, 1930, to January 30, 1933, when Hitler was appointed Chancellor.

In the elections for the National Assembly the so-called majority Social Democrats obtained 37.9 per cent of the total vote. Under a majority system they would have secured the support of most of those who, under P.R., supported their former left wing, the so-called Independent Social Democrats. It is not certain that a Social Democratic majority would have developed, but a number of competent observers regard this as probable. The question arises: What would such a majority have meant for Germany?

Surely the result would not have been a Socialist dictatorship. The German Social Democrats were orthodox Marxists and believed in automatic evolution toward Socialism rather than in abrupt steps in that direction. They had been moderate when confronted with practical issues, and when a small minority among them, the so-called *Spartakisten,* tried to set up a German Soviet state, the Social Democrats allied themselves with the remnants of the army to suppress this attempt at real revolution.

Last but not least, a Socialist election victory would have swept a great many Social Democratic candidates to victory who owed their margin of success to non-Socialist voters. Such deputies are rarely inclined to support revolutionary policies, in particular when they entertain moderate views themselves.

For these reasons this writer is not one of those whom the prospect of a Social Democratic election victory would have frightened. Had it materialized, the Socialists would either have had to adopt a responsible course, or they would have had to face defeat in the elections to the new Reichstag, due within a space of less than two years. On the other hand, the threat of a Socialist victory was bound to act as an incentive for the non-Socialist parties to unite, and a desirable tendency in the direction of a two-party system would have developed. Who can deny that such a result would have been preferable to the type of coalition government which had to be resorted to later on and which often tried an impossible blending of socialism and capitalism?

The Period of Pluralistic Stagnation

Beginning in 1920 the German election system followed the so-called automatic type, which has been discussed above. There was from that time onwards an almost unlimited utilization of surpluses, and a number of minor parties were successful which, under the majority system, would have fallen into the category of the "also-rans." A further result was the immediate destruction of the Weimar majority. In the elections to the first Reichstag of the Republic there was, as a result, no Republican majority; the "Republic without Republicans" had been born. This would have been impossible under majority elections.

The first new group to benefit from the liberalized system of P.R. was the Communists. It is interesting to note that their dependence on P.R. is admitted by the leading proponents of P.R. in the United States, Messrs. Hoag and Hallett, who write:

"We do not doubt that the rise of new parties, extreme as well as moderate, is often facilitated by P.R. In Germany in the P.R. election of May 4, 1924, the New Freedom Party of General Ludendorff (Hitler's party), which could scarcely have made a creditable showing under a majority system, elected 32 members to the Reichstag. In the same election the larger Communist minority electd 62." [4]

The elections of May 1924 represent the high tide of radicalism in Germany before 1930. If the extremist parties had failed under a majority system in these elections, they would have stood no chance at any other time.

So far as the Communists are concerned, it is possible that Hoag and Hallett conceded too much. They were rather strong in certain industrial areas, and might, as a result, have elected a few of their candidates, although hardly more than a dozen. In May 1924 the German Communists secured 12.6 per cent of the total vote. One is inclined to compare them to the French Communists of 1928, who at that time secured eleven per cent of the total popular vote, but only 2.3 per cent of the seats in the Chamber of Deputies. The German Communists might have achieved similar results in May 1924, electing about two per cent of the deputies. They would, however, have lost some, if not all, of the seats gained in May, 1924, when new elections took place in December of that year, and their percentage of the total popular vote had declined to nine. Certainly, under a majority system, the Communists could not have successfully opposed the Social Democrats in all parts of the country, ever ready for a demagogic exploitation of the responsible attitude of the latter.

The above quotation from Hoag and Hallett covers the National Socialists even more explicitly than the Communists. This group was at that time represented by one major party, under the leadership of Ludendorff, who took the place of Hitler, then in jail, and two minor ones. The combined percentage of these groups was 7.6, enough to give them twenty-six seats in the Reichstag. They did not enjoy local strongholds comparable to those of the Communists, and because of this it is doubtful whether they could have elected a single deputy.

What would have been the effect of continued electoral defeats on Hitler's party? Hoag and Hallett add to the above quotation:

"But we do not regard the just representation of such parties as a disadvantage. . . . Representation does give them a hearing. . . . Sometimes extremists are needed to oppose existing wrongs. . . . The just representation of an extreme party also has the wholesome reaction on the party itself: it tends to make the party less bitter and more responsible." [5]

The two authors add that if such a party is deprived of all representation, it may be driven underground, and attempt a revolution.

The last argument can be taken up briefly. The Nazis did try a revolution; it took the form of the beer hall putsch of November, 1923. One volley fired by the Bavarian police sufficed to end it. During the years which followed Hitler insisted strongly that his followers act in outward compliance with the law. His opponents, in the darkest days of the Republic, hoped and prayed that he would reenter the path of open revolution. Bruening was no Facta; he would have acted without delay, with utter collapse of the whole Nazi movement as the inevitable result.

Nor do we, at this time, have to procceupy ourselves with the argument that parliamentary representation might have made the Nazis moderate and responsible. They have answered that argument themselves, as have the Communists, not only in Germany, but also, more recently, in France and Italy.

On the other hand, the opportunities provided to the National Socialists by P.R. assisted them greatly. First, the party's candidates never had to fear the objection that voting for them meant wasting one's vote. Under the majority system they would, in almost all constituencies, have stood no chance. As a result their popular vote might soon have dwindled into insignificance. The party could hardly have survived the experience for long, and Hitler might have found it more profitable to resume the profession of a house painter.

Second, successful participation in elections gave the National Socialists enormous chances to secure publicity. Hitler, in *Mein Kampf*, expressed himself bitterly about the lack of publicity during the early days of his movement. He concluded: "If in those days people had attacked us, had they even taken the trouble just to laugh at us, we would have been glad either way." [6] As soon as the National Socialist lists were entered successfully in political elections, there was no danger of their being ignored. They could receive votes in every hamlet, and every other party had to be on its guard against them everywhere, countering their actual and potential attacks, thus providing them unintentionally with nation-wide publicity.

Third, Hitler's party profited financially from having members in the Reichstag and in the parliamentary bodies of the Laender. The National Socialist deputies had to hand over a part of their indemnities to the party treasury which, in lean years, could not have survived without this assistance provided by the taxpayers of the Republic. Likewise, the so-called *Freifahrkarte*, which enabled all deputies to travel on all railroads first class, without payment, made it possible for the National Socialists to go from one corner of the country to the other. The Nazi deputies, of course, took no interest at all in the positive work of their respective parliamentary bodies and, in fact, were professional agitators paid at the public expense.

P.R. AND THE TRIUMPH OF HITLER

Dr. Goebbels has expressed his appreciation of the benefits derived by his party from parliamentary representation in these words:

"We enter Parliament in order to supply ourselves, in the arsenal of democracy, with its own weapons. We become members of the Reichstag in order to paralyze the Weimar sentiment with its own assistance. If democracy is so stupid as to give us free tickets and salaries for this bear's work, that is its affair . . ." [7]

A German jurist, Dr. Huber, expressed himself on this subject in similar terms:

"The parliamentary battle of the NSDAP had the single purpose of destroying the parliamentary system from within through its own methods. It was necessary above all to make formal use of the possibilities of the party-state system but to refuse real cooperation and thereby to render the parliamentary system, which is by nature dependent upon the responsible cooperation of the opposition, incapable of action." [8]

Dr. Huber was right. The National Socialist deputies in the Reichstag did more than make speeches. Their mere presence, always combined with the possibility of voting together with the Communists against any democratic government, sufficed to make the operation of parliamentary government difficult. We can only conclude that parliamentary representation, as made possible by P.R., was a vital element in the final success of the Nazi party.

A few words must be said about the other parties whose success was made possible by P.R. The interest groups were particularly significant. They included the "Economic Party of the German Middle Classes," plus two, and sometimes three, Farmers' parties. The former could, under the majority system, never have elected a single deputy. One or two of the latter might have elected an occasional candidate, but such deputies would have entered the Reichstag as independents rather than as representatives of a new group.

The interest groups were significant not only because they complicated the task of forming a majority, but also because they brought about a general decline of the intellectual and moral level of the Reichstag. The middle class party would naturally nominate merchants, artisans and the like, and the Farmers' party farmers or paid employees of farmers' organizations. In the one case in which the Economic Party of the German Middle Classes nominated a university professor its orators hastened to add that he was placed on the party's list only because he was also a landlord, and that he represented the interests of the landlords.

The presence of interest groups meant that all of the larger parties had to fill their lists of candidates with representatives of economic groups. The Catholic Center party, for example, would, in a typical constituency, begin with either a farmer or a Catholic trade union leader, depending upon circumstances. Then would follow an artisan, a civil servant, a representative of the middle classes, and after that the farmers and the trade unions would secure additional places on the ticket. It was no better with the Democratic party as long as this left-wing liberal group was large enough to elect more than one deputy from a P.R. constituency. The result has been indicated clearly by Max Weber, who predicted in 1919 that the Reichstag would eventually be "a Parliament of idiots, utterly incapable of providing material for the selection of cabinet members." [9]

Among the other effects of P.R., let us mention only the doctrinal rigidity and the bureaucratization. In the words of Professor Alfred Weber: "The Germans regard political parties as though they were denominational groups, whereas they should only be regarded as helps toward the achievement of certain definite political goals." [10] Nebulous "isms" took the place of concrete issues.

Bureaucratization naturally followed from the above tendencies. Parties had to be organized for large districts, where the work, which in the single-member constituencies was carried on mainly by amateurs, required professional employees. The latter, together with a few party leaders on the provincial level dictated the composition of the party lists. The individual deputy knew that unless he would do the bidding of this group, he would stand no chance of reelection. An illustration of the extent to which this dependence of the deputy upon the party organization was carried is provided by developments within the German Nationalist party. When Alfred Hugenberg assumed control of this party in the late 1920's, he and his henchmen were able to eliminate even the best known leaders of their party from its tickets. As soon as the leader of the parliamentary group of the party,

Count Westarp, took an independent attitude toward the cabinet of Dr. Bruening in 1930, the chairman of the party committee in the province from which he came — a man whose name had not been mentioned in the national press before, and was not to be mentioned there later — was able to wire him that he would not be renominated. It was, of course, always possible for such deputies to establish a new party to compete with a party which acted in this manner. However, the establishment of an effective party organization under P.R. requires large amounts of money which are not likely to be available to people whose principal characteristic is their desire to preserve their intellectual integrity.

It is hardly necessary to add that the young generation was more repelled by this condition than the older voters. The bureaucratization of parties meant that a small group of insiders controlled the party tickets, and they operated on the basis of a mutual reinsurance system, which provided little chance for newcomers. Besides, young people were repelled by the type of "cow-bargaining" which was the normal way in which the P.R. parties reached their compromises. The Economic Party of the German Middle Classes, for example, mindful of its landlord support, offered to vote for the Young Plan if the rents were raised. Youth is idealistic and resents such practices. The National Socialists and the Communists, on the other hand, whatever else was to be said against them, did not participate in such bargains, which was one of the reasons why they attracted young people as strongly as the older parties repelled them.

The formation of governments became more and more difficult during this period. Professor Brecht, who witnessed these developments as a high official in the German Department of the Interior, has drawn attention to the fact that for two-thirds of the period between 1920 and 1932, a total of eleven minority governments were in power.[11] These governments depended for their survival on the assistance of either Rightist or Leftist parties, which could shrug off their responsibility at any time and play with the government like a cat with a mouse. For four and a half years majority cabinets were in office. These were either Rightist cabinets, which in that case extended from ardent monarchists at the Right to determined Republicans at the Left; these cabinets were always threatened by disagreements on constitutional questions. Or cabinets of the so-called "Great

Coalition" were in power, extending from Stresemann's "German People's party," the party of big business, to the Social Democrats, the protagonists of socialism. These cabinets were always threatened by disagreements over economic issues, and it required super-human efforts to hold them together. Stresemann died on the evening of a day which he had spent in an effort to prevent the coalition from disintegrating.

The conditions prevailing during the period of pluralistic stagnation have been well characterized by Count Westarp, a moderate monarchist who would have made good material for a German Tory democrat in case German democracy had been worthy of the name. Count Westarp complained that after the blockade during the First World War had made the German people accustomed to *ersatz* for foodstuffs, the Weimar Republic had managed to accustom them to *ersatz* in politics. A number of minority cabinets were substituted for cabinets enjoying a solid majority. The minority cabinets, in their turn, substituted for the confidence of a majority, which was anticipated by the constitution, the failure of the opposition to gather a majority for a vote of censure. Only the heterogeneity of this opposition induced it to acquiesce for a while in a government which it could easily overthrow, and which it would overthrow eventually. Thus, Count Westarp added, the political parties were characterized "not by their joining of forces for the purpose of discharging a clear responsibility, but by their craven shrinking from any parliamentary responsibility whatsoever." [12] This criticism of party behavior during the period under consideration is severe but just. It explains why German democracy repelled rather than attracted former opponents.

Totalitarian Revolution

The period of totalitarian revolution is characterized by political polarization. Pluralistic stagnation means primarily that the process of integration is ended, whereas polarization reverses it. Integration leads to a mutual assimilation of two major parties, or of two major groups of parties, both of which come under the common influence of the marginal vote in the Center. Polarization implies that the two rival forces of political attraction develop at opposite poles. In Germany, the National Socialist and the Communist parties became the two poles, with most of the intermediate groups either pulverized, or reduced to impotence. It goes without saying that polarization is a reaction to pluralistic stagnation, and follows from it in the manner in which, as Plato emphasized more than 2000 years ago, in politics as in other fields one extreme creates the other. Thus, stagnation was followed by revolution. The fact that in this process the number of parties that mattered was reduced to five is irrelevant. These parties were entirely unable to perform the integrating function which was their *raison d'être*. A number of small, but comparatively moderate, parties is preferable to a few large, but immoderate, parties, none of which can expect a majority of its own.

An event outside the political field, the world economic crisis, was the occasion for polarization to follow stagnation in Germany. Such German prosperity as there was in the 1920's was largely based upon loans from abroad. The lowest level of unemployment was reached in October 1927. Afterwards, unemployment rose almost without intermission, and as early as in 1930 it assumed near catastrophic proportions. Hopelessness and despair spread all over the country, in particular among the young generation, and the extremists used the ample opportunities given them by P.R. to exploit it to the full.

Polarization became manifest for the first time in the elections to the Reichstag of September 14, 1930. One hundred and seven National Socialists and seventy Communists were elected. From this moment onward, a normal functioning of parliamentary government was impossible. Right after the elections the then Prussian Prime Minister, Otto Braun, demanded a "coalition of all reasonable men." By this he meant that all parties between the National Socialists and their Nationalist allies on the Right, and the Communists at the Left, should form a coalition. His recommendation was not accepted in this particular form; instead, Dr. Bruening's government, consisting of elements of the moderate Right and the Center, remained in office, being supported indirectly by the Socialists, who would vote against all Rightist or Leftist votes of censure, or any demands by the extremists to invalidate Dr. Bruening's decree laws. This negative majority was termed the "majority of toleration." Under prevailing conditions, it represented the only possibility of preventing an immediate collapse of the Republic.

Yet, this solution had great and vital disadvantages. A "coalition of all reasonable men" is altogether too reasonable, in the sense of being too rationalistic. Human nature abounds in irrational elements, and unless a political system leaves a safety valve for this irrationality, it will not be healthy. This safety valve normally consists in the availability of a democratic opposition. Those who blame the government of the day for everything which they dislike, depressions in particular — as American voters have done ever since they defeated Van Buren in the aftermath of the panic of 1837 — can vote for the opposition, and therewith bring it into power, without in any way affecting the stability of their country's democratic institutions. The latter may, in fact, be strengthened in the process, as the change from the "outs" to the "ins" may relieve a group worn out by the burden of office, and give a younger and more vigorous team its opportunity. All countries with majority elections, including the United States, France, and England, showed the operation of this process in the course of the world economic crisis. In Germany, however, after September 14, 1930, the safety valve of a democratic opposition no longer existed. Instead the opponents of democracy received a monopoly of opposition, and its proponents a monopoly of responsibility. In times of economic stress, such a burden is too great to carry.

Still, as late as in September 1930, after eleven years of P.R., the majority system would have led to a victory of the democratic parties. This becomes clear if we divide Germany into 400 approximately equal single-member constituencies, and calculate the percentage of the votes obtained in them by the respective political parties.[13]

The first result is that neither National Socialists nor Communists received as much as forty per cent of the votes cast in a single one of these constituencies, and the National Socialists in none. Both parties were much stronger in the twenty to thirty per cent bracket. If we want to investigate their chances under the majority system, we must, however, take into account that their principal opponents — at that time, the Social Democrats, the Center party and its ally, the Bavarian People's party — were in a much better strategic position. To begin with, they secured a plurality in 296 of the 400 constituencies. In the second place, they had the advantage of being *buendnisfaehig* — they could easily form campaign alliances, and gain votes from related

P.R. AND THE TRIUMPH OF HITLER

groups even without formal alliances, attracting additional support from from the Right and from the Left. National Socialists and Communists could make such gains only on one side. Furthermore, in the constituencies where their prospects were best, they would have encountered the opposition of Nationalist or Social Democratic incumbents, who would hardly have been inclined to look with favor upon the invitation to step aside in favor of National Socialist or Communist newcomers.

It is interesting to note that the percentage of the total vote which the National Socialists secured in September 1930 was 18.3. This compares with the 16.2 per cent received by LaFollette in the American presidential elections of 1924. In comparing these figures we must bear in mind that LaFollette's ticket could not be entered in a number of states on account of certain legal requirements directed against small parties, whereas the National Socialist ticket could be entered, and was entered, in all German P.R. constituencies without any difficulty whatsoever. LaFollette, competing under the plurality system, received only the thirteen electoral votes of his native Wisconsin, constituting 2.4 per cent of the total. The day after the elections discontent among his followers was so great that the third party, which they had been planning to establish, fell apart before it was founded. LaFollette's voters took their places again among the major parties from which they had come and by which they were reassimilated without any apparent effort. Hitler, on the other hand, received his full share of seats in the Reichstag. Together with the Communists, whom P.R. had similarly favored, he was in a position to encircle the democratic majority and to prevent it from operating under normal conditions. The world economic crisis gave further assistance, omissions and commissions outside as well as inside the country made their contribution, and in little more than two years Hitler was the master of Germany.

OBJECTIONS

The rise of national socialism to power resembles, in many details, that of fascism. It is, therefore, natural that the objections to our arguments should follow a similar course. For the same reason, the reply can be brief.

The World Economic Crisis

In the first place, more than one factor was responsible for Hitler's as well as Mussolini's rise, and it is proper to assign its share to every one of them. In the case of Hitler, our attention turns immediately to the world economic crisis, which performed an even greater service for Hitler than the Italian inflation performed for Mussolini.

Yet, those who assert that "the true reason" for the victory of nazism was the world economic crisis, make the unconscious assumption that democracy is a fair-weather form of government, unable to withstand a serious blow. The depression was as severe in the United States as it was in Germany; in fact, in the two countries, all curves of economic activity, beginning with unemployment, show an amazing parallelism until the end of 1932. In the United States, however, the very large, and very angry, protest vote created by the depression could turn only in one direction; the system of voting left, next to the party in power, but one other large party which had a chance in a presidential election. There were, of course, Socialist, Communist, and other presidential candidates. In fact, in 1932 people in Germany expected that Norman Thomas would poll a large vote. He failed to do so for the simple reason that, under the plurality system, those desirous of protesting against the Hoover administration knew that the best way to reelect Hoover was to vote for Norman Thomas, and that the one way of making certain of Hoover's defeat was to ensure Roosevelt's victory. They acted accordingly, and American splinter parties never fared worse than they did in 1932, and likewise in the elections which were to follow.

In this connection it must be borne in mind that economic and political factors were closely interrelated in the course of the world economic crisis. What made the crisis so severe was the monetary panic of 1931. That it reached Germany was not unrelated to the political uncertainty resulting from the P.R. elections of September 1930. Credit requires confidence, and foreign investors found it difficult to retain their confidence in Germany's future after the rapid rise of the extremists.

Intrigues and the President

Next, we come to the intrigues of Nationalists and others, which brought Hitler into power at a time when his party was on the downgrade. As in Italy they were important only because they filled a political vacuum, caused by the absence of a majority. In fact, when the intriguers found it difficult to persuade old Hindenburg to entrust the government to the same Hitler whom, a few months previously, he had received without offering him a chair, their clinching argument was that only Hitler could relieve Hindenburg of the need to govern by decree, since only Hitler had a chance to secure a majority. In the words of Konrad Heiden: "Hitler came to power because he seemed the only man who could restore to Germany a parliamentary government, such as Hindenburg had demanded in August, and even more in November (1932)." [14]

Had the German Republicans possessed a clear majority, Hindenburg could have done little against them even if he had wanted to do so. The head of the state under a parliamentary system, be he king or president, must secure the counter-signature of a responsible minister for all his acts, and he cannot stay in office for long without being in agreement with ministers who command a parliamentary majority. The first case to prove this occurred in France in 1877. After MacMahon had caused a cabinet to resign which enjoyed the confidence of the Chamber's majority, the Republican leader, Léon Gambetta, told him: "Listen well, Mr. Marshal, after the people will have made their sovereign voice heard, you will either have to submit or to resign." The majority system made it possible for the people of France to speak with a clear voice; they returned the Republican majority, and MacMahon first submitted and, when continued submission went contrary to his sense of honor, he resigned. Subsequently, two other French presidents (Jules Grévy in 1887, and Alexandre Millerand in 1924) were shown that a simple refusal of the majority in parliament to cooperate with them can leave a parliamentary president no alternative except to resign. Two kings (in Norway in 1905 and in England in 1937) had to step aside for the same reason.

In Germany, there was no clear majority to express the will of the people; a number of parties cancelled each other out with their rival claims. Small wonder then that the aged President (as Victor Emmanuel had done before him, and King Leopold after him) took it upon himself to determine what the people wanted.

In this connection reference must be made to a political factor other than P.R. Had the president been elected by parliament rather than by popular vote, it is unlikely that Hindenburg would have been the choice. Popular election appears to be the democratic solution, but if a country is too large for the people to know the candidates, they will vote for the legend rather than for the man. Under a two-party system, there are safeguards. A party man will usually be selected, and if an outsider, such as General Grant in the United States, wins, he will have to act within the framework of the two-party system. Under a multiple-party system, the choice of an outsider is, as Professor Brecht has pointed out, logical since he will have a wider appeal than a candidate who is a member of a particular party himself. (The analogy of the United States is, of course, deficient because the American president constitutes the executive himself and does not have to search for a prime minister capable of securing a parliamentary majority.) We shall later see that France did well when, in her new constitution, she entrusted again the selection of her president to a parliamentary body.

A few words must be added on the role played in Germany by the army and by the large estate owners, the so-called *Junkers*. The army, through General von Schleicher, had a fateful share in overthrowing Dr. Bruening in 1932, although it did not want Hitler in 1933, von Schleicher doing all he could do prevent the latter's appointment. The large estate owners had their share in both events; their fear of bankruptcy drove them into accepting Hitler as it had driven them into seeking the dismissal of Bruening. Both factors could, however, become operative only to the extent that President Hindenburg was able to fill a political vacuum. When, in 1927, General von Seeckt, the organizer of the Reichswehr, disobeyed an order of the then Minister of Defense, Gessler, and permitted a son of the Crown Prince to take part in maneuvers, he was summarily dismissed. In other words, as long as Republican cabinets had some measure of authority, they could make their decisions prevail. Dr. Bruening could be overthrown so easily because everyone knew that in new elections he would not secure a majority, and the same applies to General von Schleicher in 1933. Everything is, of course, possible in a democracy whose defenders — General von Schleicher, and the army with him, had indeed become would-be defenders of democracy in January 1933 — cannot expect to secure a majority in new elections.

Politics and the Class Structure

The next objection will have to be considered in greater detail, because it has a far-reaching influence upon the nature of the entire discussion. It is stated that political life in general, and German political life in particular, is shaped by the class structure. On two occasions, when this writer attempted to bring the significance of systems of voting to the attention of American officials, he was told that the class structure determined the course of politics; constitutional provisions of any kind, including systems of voting, were "irrelevant." This view originates in the economic interpretation of history as developed by Karl Marx and Friedrich Engels. In a less consistent form it underlies a great deal of the Liberal thought in this country.

We readily grant that the economic interpretation of history can be helpful if it is regarded as a tool of analysis, to be used where it is adapted to the material, and to be discarded otherwise. In the above discussion, reference has been made to economic factors, in connection with the social consequences of the Italian inflation of the 1920's and the German deflation of the 1930's. Furthermore, economic factors were taken into account indirectly, insofar as they were reflected in the shifting distribution of votes, which is particularly large when depressions create a huge protest vote. We also emphasized that there is a difference: Under the majority system, the protest vote is forced into relatively safe channels; under P.R. it is attractd by the political extremes, and this process may go so far as to replace the integration characteristic of the majority system by the polarization which represents the extreme consequence of P.R. The social fate of the German middle classes, which is so often mentioned by writers stressing economic factors exclusively, is significant to our problem mainly insofar as it intensified the protest vote.

Proponents of the economic interpretation of history often state their views in general terms, without attempting to relate them to concrete political developments. For them, apparently, the truth of their major tenets is so firmly established that concrete proof of their applicability is not needed, but it is a natural reaction that this attitude should have been criticized under the heading, "Historical Mysticism." [15]

Our own thesis (that the majority system of voting can act as a sufficient agent for controlling disruptive forces in society) grew out of concrete experience, which has been discussed above, as well as in more detail upon a previous occasion. From the point of view of the economic interpretation of history, however, the mere suggestion of such a possibility is anathema. This only proves that the underlying theory is a-political. Friedrich Engels left no doubt that for him the state (relations to which makes actions "political" in the specific sense of the term) had no existence, and no functions, of its own; it was but "a product of society in a certain stage of development." Lenin filled in details when he wrote: "The state is the product and the manifestation of the irreconcilability of class antagonisms." [16] The bourgeoisie created the state as a weapon to oppress the proletariat; the victory of the latter will do away with the state, there being no need for what in the above discussions has been called integration. With the class struggle its product, the state, will "wither away," to be succeeded by the "society of the free and equal."

Critics have not failed to note that the latter prediction was basically anarchistic; we must add that this conclusion was implied in its premise. Marxism does not just end up with the prediction of a future in which no coercion is needed; it represents an a-political approach to the problems of politics — what in Germany is termed *Die Politik der Unpolitischen* — "the politics of the unpolitical."

Against this background the advocacy of P.R. is natural. The majority system, and whatever else is required to complete the apparatus of political form, is related to the creation of a *state;* P.R., on the other hand, in theory at least (i.e., as long as the "dynamic consequences" of that system of voting do not appear), leaves society as it is, without subjecting it to transformation by political agencies. Socio-economic groups[17] can share in the distribution of the seats in a parliamentary body without becoming a genuine political party, namely, an instrument of integration. For Socialist parties, this accords well with tactical requirements. They claim to be but the reflection of a social class. Under a majority system they would almost immediately be forced into compromises with voters from other social classes, and risk succumbing to what Communists in later years called "bourgeois opportunism." Better then to remain small, if necessary, as long as class purity is retained.

Thus, more than considerations of "justice," or faithfulness to a stand once taken, was involved when Socialist parties (as the German

Socialists did in 1918-19 and the French Socialists in 1945) maintained their allegiance to P.R. at a time when the majority system of voting would have given them a larger number of seats. These Socialist parties, by sponsoring P.R., attempted to remain the mere reflection of a social class. Inevitably, political life took its revenge; in the large countries of Continental Europe — Italy, Germany, France — where P.R. was adopted, socialism remained politically sterile. In England, on the other hand, a non-Marxist version of socialism prevailed. Its first national leader, Ramsay Macdonald, discussed, in his book *Socialism and Government*,[18] the problems of political power in their proper political terms, in full awareness of the importance of political form in general and systems of voting in particular. British socialism is now synonymous with political success, and Continental socialism with political failure.

German parties could not, even under P.R., entirely escape the integrating tendencies which are the *raison d'être* of political parties, even if P.R. was ultimately to develop disintegrating features of its own, which outbalanced the rest. Thus, the Center party consisted of workers and industrialists, members of the urban middle class, and peasants. Stresemann's "German People's party," in which the industrialists of the Ruhr Basin were the most characteristic element, derived its voting strength principally from white-collar voters, who defied Marxist analysis by refusing to merge with "the proletariat." The left-wing liberals (first called the Democratic party and later the State party) were generally looked upon as the party of the large banks; yet, they also relied on the urban middle classes and white-collar workers for mass support. Socialists and Communists, to be sure, found their large voting batallions among the industrial workers, but assiduously courted middle class elements, not to mention the rich sprinkling of intellectuals among their leaders. The mere fact, of course, that what according to Karl Marx was to constitute the one social class of the proletariat, was politically divided into two parties, sufficed to deprive the Marxist theory of any claim to political validity. In addition, we should bear in mind that the continued existence of a separate middle class, assigned so large a part in Marxist attempts to explain fascism and nazism, would, had logic held its sway, have led to an abandonment of the Marxist scheme, rather than to attempts to "adapt" to it conditions with which it was incompatible.

German political history during the Weimar period was, on at least one occasion, determined by political decisions which clearly cannot be explained in terms of the class structure. Thus in the second ballot of the 1925 presidential elections, von Hindenburg, the candidate of the Rightist parties, was elected with 48.3 per cent of the total vote; the Republican candidate, Marx, had 45.3 per cent, and the Communist, Thaelmann, 6.4 per cent. Purely political decisions could have changed the result in one of three ways. Had the constitution left the election to the Reichstag, von Hindenburg would have stood no chance. Had even the plurality system been used in the popular vote, it is quite unlikely that Hindenburg would have risked his candidacy; only after the naturally inconclusive first ballot had shown that he, and only he, had a chance of carrying the Right to victory, was he prevailed upon to accept. Finally, had the Communists supported Marx rather than Thaelmann, Marx would have won. Certainly, the class structure had nothing to do with the fact that one "proletarian" party was ready to support the Catholic and Republican candidate and the other was not; in fact, had the policy of "saving the remnants of bourgeois democracy" been in force in 1925, as it was ten years later, the Communists would have helped to defeat Hindenburg, thus eliminating an essential link in the chain of events which brought Hitler to power.

Chapter 5. Negative Democracy in Smaller Countries

The Austrian Tragedy

Republican Austria adopted P.R. with the same eagerness — and with the same lack of public discussion — as had Republican Germany. The results were equally disastrous.[1]

Austria had, between 1919 and 1934, two major and several minor parties. The major parties were the Socialists at the Left and the Christian Social party at the Right. The minor parties at first were the so-called Great Germans, who favored a union with Germany, and the Agrarians; in 1930, the *Heimwehren* presented lists of their own. The smaller parties usually elected between ten and twenty per cent of the deputies. This was to a considerable extent due to the limitations imposed upon P.R. Austria admitted only a limited utilization of surpluses, and had no national list. The Austrian Nazis, who secured five per cent of the total number of votes in 1930, did not elect a single candidate.

Thus, the large parties combined were able to control between four-fifths and nine-tenths of the total number of seats. Neither of them, however, secured a majority, although the Christian Social party elected, in 1923, 82 out of 165 deputies — one less than a majority. A coalition between the major parties was formed immediately after the revolution, when an attempt was made to carry the principles of P.R. into the executive. Naturally, the attempt failed, and afterwards governments were formed by coalitions between the Christian Social party and the smaller parties. These coalitions were not stable; the fact that the smaller parties were so much weaker than the Christian Social party only caused them to insist the more upon their indispensability. Therefore, much jealousy and friction existed in all the Rightist coalitions. The total number of governments between March 5, 1919, and March 4, 1933, the day when parliamentary government came to an end, was no less than twenty, with ten different chancellors.

This record of instability is all the more remarkable because there can be no doubt that under a majority system one of the major parties would, under normal conditions, have enjoyed an over-all majority, and have been able to form a government of its own. There were only a few areas where the smaller parties were strongly enough concentrated to make a serious bid for the election of one of their candidates; the best they might have accomplished would have been the election of a few individual deputies, who from a practical point of view would have entered the so-called National Council as Independents rather than as representatives of a political party.

It has been held that in Austria a two-party system would have meant an earlier outbreak of the civil war, which ultimately occurred in 1934. Those who make this assumption overlook the dynamics of the majority system. Neither of the major Austrian parties had a following strong enough to give it a majority; both needed the marginal vote which, in Austria as well as anywhere else, adhered to the middle of the road. This dependence implied a premium on political moderation, which did not exist under P.R. Furthermore, the centralized control of the major parties which developed early in Republican Austria, would have been difficult to establish under a majority system. In that case conditions in the 165 single-member constituencies would have been decisive. They were too small to develop a bureaucracy of their own, and too independent to accept the dictates of a central bureaucracy.

It is, therefore, likely that the majority system would have seen more moderation in the large parties than actually existed. Besides, the radicalizing influence of groups like the *Heimwehren* would have been a good thing to miss.

So far as the Socialist party was concerned, its intermediate position between democratic socialism and Russian communism, characterized by the term "Austro-Marxism," was a comparatively late development. The party had been fairly moderate until the end of the First World War, and it remained moderate a while longer, under the leadership of Karl Renner. After the effects of P.R. had manifested themselves fully, "Austro-Marxism" was able to develop. In parliament the Austrian Socialists added the weapons of obstruction to those of opposition, just as the Italian Socialists had done before the rise of fascism. It is well to bear in mind what Professor Jászi has said about this type of socialism: ". . . A mass movement based on orthodox Marxist theory makes an evolutionary politics impossible. It is catastrophic in its nature. It excludes all reasonable compromise." [2]

In the Christian Social party government responsibility reduced tendencies toward radicalism, but it became possible for Monsignor

Seipel to take, in 1930, the ill-advised step of an alliance with the semi-Fascist *Heimwehren*. Faced with Socialist failure to play the rules of the game in the National Council, he yielded to the same temptation to which Giolitti had yielded in Italy in 1921. Both overlooked, however, that alliances with anti-democratic groups set a chain of consequences in motion which it is not possible to arrest at will. In Austria, the result was to introduce elements into the National Council, and into the government, which were opposed to any compromise with the Socialists where it might have been attainable. This applies in particular to the then Minister of the Interior, Fey, who in February, 1934, gave the police the order to search the headquarters of the Socialist party in the city of Linz, where they were received with machine gun fire. The Socialist uprising in Vienna followed.

It serves little purpose to blame persons for these developments. The difficulty was institutional rather than personal, and the unsatisfactory manner in which these institutions operated was clearly shown in the tragi-comic sequence of events which led to the end of parliamentary government. The cabinets formed in the National Council elected in 1930 had to rely on a majority of one, or even upon the provision of the rules according to which a motion was lost in the case of equality of votes. Austrian cartoonists had a field day in dealing with the incidents which this situation provoked; the situation was typical for P.R. parliaments (as shown in this country by the first city council elected under P.R. in New York City, which was divided 13:13).[3]

The end of the Austrian National Council ran true to form. On March 4, 1933, the government was under attack on account of the measures which it had taken against a railroad strike. A resolution directed against the government had been passed by a vote of eighty-one to eighty. It was then discovered that a Socialist deputy had erroneously used the ballot of his neighbor, and a general tumult resulted. The speaker, Dr. Renner, resigned in order to cast his vote with his fellow Socialists. The two deputy speakers, however, did not want their party to lose their votes either, and resigned one after the other. After the second deputy speaker did so he forgot to adjourn the meeting. When the deputies realized what had happened, they looked at each other in bewilderment, and just went home.

New elections would, at this stage, only have benefited the Nazis and Communists. Both extremist groups were certain to secure a substantial number of seats, as the provincial elections of 1932 had shown. The only other certain result was the defeat of the government, which no possible combination could have replaced. That is the reason why, after Hitler's victory in Germany on March 5, 1933, Dr. Dolfuss decided to govern without a parliament. The dictatorship, once established, could not turn back. On the other hand, new elections under the majority system would, at any time before Hitler's march into Austria in 1938, have led to a defeat of the extremists.

When, in February, 1934, the Austrian Socialists chose to fight rather than lose their arms and face a later dissolution of their party, they did not any longer have a positive goal. They simply preferred death to submission. Everybody will admit their heroism. Still, their death was no longer a death for a cause. P.R. had destroyed the spirit of Austrian democracy before its body was buried.

Poland

Poland was one of the countries in which the existence of the "material" conditions for democracy was doubtful. Widespread illiteracy prevailed, in particular in the provinces which had belonged to Tsarist Russia. The phenomenon of the absentee masses, which was mentioned in the case of Italy, was also characteristic of Poland. It alone sufficed to render the operation of democratic government difficult.

On the other hand, the Polish provinces which had been a part of pre-1918 Germany and Austria, had comparatively high educational standards. Besides, many of the political difficulties which developed in Poland in the 1920's were so typical of the effects of P.R. that the relationship between that system of voting and the early collapse of Polish democracy has to be discussed.

Like all other new republics which came into existence in Europe at the end of the First World War, Poland adopted P.R. without even discussing it; in the field of political theory the victory of P.R. was, at that time, almost complete, although the older democracies, in particular England, steadfastly refused to give up the majority system. For the election of the Polish Constituent Assembly the so-called d'Hondt system of P.R. was used, which provides for a fixed number of seats in every constituency.[4] These constituencies were comparatively small, which reduced the chances of small parties. Still, P.R.

made possible the success of twelve Polish and two national minority parties, none of which secured as much as thirty per cent of the total membership in the national assembly. Ultimately there were fourteen Polish and eight national minority parties; during the entire period of the Republic (until May, 1926, when Marshal Pilsudski established his dictatorship) no less than eighty parties sprouted up, though not all were in existence at the same time. Some of these parties would also have existed under a majority system, and Poland could not have expected to witness the development of a two-party system. Still, it suffices to compare the results of the elections held under the majority system before 1918 in the Polish parts of Imperial Germany with those held in the same provinces subsequently under P.R. in order to realize that much of the splitting up of Polish parties is due to P.R. Also, it is probable that under the majority principle a system of two blocs would have developed, which in many ways would have functioned like a two-party system.

It is not surprising that the multiplicity and heterogeneity of parties as produced by P.R. made the formation of governments an almost impossible task. There were 16 cabinets during the period from November 18, 1918, to May 14, 1926, which gives an average duration of five months and twenty days. For one-half of this period cabinets were formed by civil servants, which indicates that it was impossible to establish a formal coalition of parties. The first such government had to be resorted to in 1920, which means that, like Germany, Poland had a "Republic without Republicans" right from the start.

The attitude of the Polish parties soon after the adoption of the constitution exhibited during this time all the short-sighted selfishness which is known to the student of P.R. from a long list of other countries. At one time Mr. Thugutt, one of the leaders of the Radical Peasant group, declared in an open letter that the parliament "while not without a capacity for sacrifice in moments of crisis, was afflicted with a probably incurable impotence." [5] He continued: "In Poland everybody desires to be in the opposition, but nobody is willing to take responsibility. Poland cannot prosper by criticism alone." [6] So far as the period immediately before Pilsudski's *coup d'état* is concerned, Machray says: "Many Poles, too, had by this time lost all faith in the Sejm (the parliament) — the Executive as well as the Legislative power; indeed, its general impotence, owing to party strife with all its extraordinary bitterness in Poland, was seen and known to all men. Added to its futility was the fact, which came to the surface now and again, that it was tainted with corruption, bribery, 'wrangling' of offices and posts in and under the administration and concession hunting." [7] Pilsudski used even more vigorous language when he said that the Sejm was "a sterile, jabbering howling thing that engendered such boredom as made the very flies die of disgust;" it was comparable, he said, to "a locomotive drawing a pin." [8] For years, after he established his personal rule, Pilsudski nevertheless did not disband the Sejm. A contributor to the (London) *Tablet* gives the following reasons for this course of action: "Pilsudski, wiser than Mussolini, did not abolish the elected assembly.... He calculated rightly that if the Sejm was allowed to go on with its party struggles in the public eye, it would lose any hold on the public affections, and so it did." [9] This was indeed the case, but it would be hard to find a parliament elected under the plurality system about which the same thing could have been said. Pilsudski neither in 1926 nor later held a majority in the Sejm. He failed in the elections of 1930 in spite of the strongest administrative pressure brought against the opposition; this included the arrest and, some say, the torture, of leading men of the opposition in the fortress of Brest-Litovsk. Again he demonstrated that a dictator, once in power, will maintain himself whether he has a parliamentary majority or not. The Sejm was finally abolished in 1935, and the people did not seem to be unduly disturbed over its demise. They may have felt like R. L. Buell, who said that Pilsudski's regime "probably prevented the growth of anarchy." [10]

Czechoslovakia

Czechoslovakia presented a more favorable soil for the growth of democratic government than did Poland. Only in Slovakia and Ruthenia did widespread illiteracy exist, and these provinces contained less than a fourth of the total population. The country as a whole must be judged on the basis of the rather advanced conditions prevailing in Bohemia and Moravia.

Czechoslovakia's principal domestic problems arose out of her multi-national character. The country has often been called an "Austria-Hungary on a minor scale," since it contained Czechs, Slovaks, German-speaking former Austrians, Hungarians, Ukrainians, Poles and Jews. It has been claimed that P.R., by giving "fair representation" to all groups, helps in solving such minority problems. Actually, P.R. can easily become a disturbing factor, because it will make it unnecessary for the leaders of either majority or minority groups to win the support of a cross section even of their own nationality. They can be elected with the support of the more radical elements within their own national group. The principal difficulty under the majority system is to secure a fair apportionment. If this is done, candidates would first have to appeal to a cross section of voters among their own national group. In constituencies with a mixed population, members of national minority groups might be able to turn the scales, and wield an influence out of proportion to their numbers. If that is the case — in Czechoslovakia it would have been the case at least to some extent — the majority system can operate as an integrating agent, as the cross connections established in this manner will, in the course of time, promote cooperation among all national groups.

It seems clear that P.R. encouraged the more radical group among the Sudeten Germans. To be sure, in the 1935 elections, Konrad Henlein's party obtained a majority of all the German votes. This party came to serve Hitler's aims perfectly, although the original Nazi party had been banned by the Czech government, and Henlein's party proclaimed loudly that it was not Nazi, and loyal to Czechoslovakia, demanding only provincial autonomy for the Sudeten Germans. Still, Henlein's party was more radical than the older German parties which it brushed aside in 1935.

In this task, it was greatly assisted by P.R. In the first place, because the older German parties had, as a result of P.R., become centralized, impersonal, discredited by participation in multi-party coalitions and, therefore, unpopular. Then, it is one thing to displace old parties under P.R., when it is only necessary to enter lists in a few large constituencies, and something else again to do this under a majority system, where the incumbent deputies have a strong personal following in their single-member constituencies, and must be dislodged one by one. American attempts at "purges" have shown us how strong the position of an incumbent is in such a case. Also the application of the "leadership principle" within the Sudeten German party was greatly facilitated by the power which the system of voting gave to the central party committees.

Czechoslovak political life was so definitely characterized by the typical effects of P.R. that their adequate description would require a volume.[11] A system of "rigid lists" prevailed; party committees would present lists of candidates for one of which the voter had to vote without being able to make any changes. Individual members of parliament were almost slaves of their party leaders. Before they were nominated they had to sign a declaration that if they left their party they would resign their seats. According to the jurisdiction of the electoral court, whose members were appointed by parliament (which means by the party leaders) exclusion of a deputy by his party would practically deprive him of his seat. As a result, party discipline was even more severe than in Republican Germany, where it was already too severe to be compatible with the requirements of party democracy and party vitality. There were many charges of corruption, and public opinion forced parliament, in 1924, to pass a law which was to prevent the close association between deputies and private economic interests. The law was practically not enforced.

The splitting up of parties was considerable from the beginning, and was later intensified. When this became apparent, the electoral law was modified; a party was to obtain seats on the national list only if it obtained seats in the local constituencies. The votes for which the small parties could not obtain seats of their own were not simply disregarded, but — a unique feature — attributed to the large parties. Also, the city of Prague was artificially divided into two constituencies in order to make the success of small parties more difficult. Later some of the small parties learned how to circumvent these provisions by technically cooperating with one another or with larger parties; in parliament, however, they formed groups of their own. Thus while, in 1929, only sixteen party lists secured seats, they actually constituted twenty-four different parties.

It goes without saying that this multiplication of parties made the formation of governments[12] a difficult task. Coalitions followed one another, and several cabinets of civil servants became necessary. Eventually the coalitions proved unable to maintain the normal process of legislation, and "acting under sweeping enabling laws, the government ruled more and more by decrees under the ultimate control of the parliament." [13] It is obvious, however, that no matter how lumbering the operation of Czech democracy had become, it still worked better than the one in Poland. National sentiment was strong in Czechoslovakia; it was embodied in such non-political organizations as the Sokols (athletic groups) which did much to unite what the P.R. parties had artificially separated. Also, there was the almost legendary figure of the first president, Masaryk, who patiently brought the parties together again and again and often succeeded in reconciling the irreconcilables. His successor, Benes, was involved in more controversy than Masaryk, but was still a much more powerful factor than the head of the state normally is under the parliamentary system.

Still, during the last years of the Republic symptoms of crisis were abundant, and it was deemed necessary to take some of the steps which Professor Lowenstein has summarized under the heading of "Militant Democracy." [14] In 1933 a law was passed empowering the government to suspend and dissolve any group which, in the government's opinion, was "apt to endanger the constitutional unity, the integrity, the republican-democratic form of the state, or the safety of the Czezchoslovakian Republic." The law at the same time enabled the government to restrict the freedom of press, speech and assembly. The essential feature was, of course, that such sweeping powers were given to the executive, which in their use could not help but be influenced by considerations of partisan policy. This, of course, is not what we understand by democracy in Anglo-Saxon countries, and the then Czech Premier, Dr. Milan Hodza, admitted as much in an interview given to the Communist newspaper, *Izvestia,* in which he said: "For the time being I see in Europe three types of democracy: the liberal French democracy, the chief characteristic of which is liberalistic freedom; further, the traditional English democracy which by way of an individualistic citizen tends toward a rigid voluntary discipline. In Czechoslovakia there has developed a third type, a co-ordinated democracy." [15]

Commenting upon this, Dr. Pergler writes: "Just what Dr. Hodza means by a 'coordinated democracy' he never explained. Certainly he must differentiate it from English voluntary self-discipline, and if he does, then he, of course, means an imposed discipline. Who shall impose it?" [16] The reply is, of course, the government, which again means that one group of parties is given somewhat arbitrary powers over other parties.

Also, it is doubtful whether this policy was really successful. The

Czech Fascist and Communist parties were allowed to exist, although both of them came within the meaning of the law. The original German Nazi party had been dissolved by an administrative act before the law was enacted. When later Henlein founded his Sudeten-German party he was careful to comply with the provisions of the law, and yet he proved to be an even more efficient tool of Hitler's policies than the original Nazi party had been. On the other hand, there is little doubt that the legitimate aims which Czech "coordinated democracy" sought by means at variance with democratic traditions could have been accomplished without discrimination against anybody by the majority system. There would have been no chance for the Czech Fascists, only a slight chance for the Communists (who were not divided according to nationalities), no chance at all for the original Nazi party, and, for the reasons mentioned above, Henlein might have found the going rather hard if with his Sudeten-German party he had tried to dislodge the incumbent German deputies from single-member constituencies in which most of them would have been firmly entrenched. Also, there would have been less disintegration so far as the moderate Czech parties are concerned; for such groups as the "Small Traders Party" there is simply no place under a majority system. Therefore, the position of the Czech government would have been stronger and more secure — without any law giving it discretionary powers against anyone.

The question arises whether the results of "coordinated democracy" did not have something to do with the surrender at Munich. To the present writer it has always seemed that the right of self-determination has much more in its favor than its critics admit, but it is not necessary to go into that matter here. When Hitler took the Sudeten districts he did not do so in order to give self-determination to their inhabitants (who immediately passed under the rule of the Gestapo), but in order to take it away from the Czechs and, as soon as possible, from just about everybody else. It is incomprehensible why the Czech government did not see this. To be sure, they were under strong pressure on the part of France and England, but then, why did they yield to this pressure? In fact why did they allow themselves to be maneuvered into a difficult tactical position by admitting Lord Runciman? If Dr. Gallup had at that time been operating an Institute of Public Opinion in Czechoslovakia, he would have found a tremendous majority in favor of rejecting Hitler's demands. The mood of the people left no doubt about this. However, throughout the negotiations the government, fortified by the powers of "coordinated democracy," severely restricted the freedom of the press and of assembly. Ultimately they issued the order of mobilization and placed the country under martial law. The people thought that this was done to prepare for military resistance, whereas the actual purpose was to make surrender easier. Just how much the results of "coordinated democracy" had to do with this is, of course, impossible to tell. But there will probably be agreement on the point that in such a situation the will of the people should prevail rather than that of the government, and that the people should have the fullest opportunity to express their will.

After the Second World War,[17] elections were held on May 26, 1946. The Czech Communists secured 93 out of 300 seats, and the Slovak Communists, who had combined with the Slovak Socialists, 21. Communist voting strength was, with thirty-eight per cent of the total, larger than it was in France at its peak. Still, the Czech Communists insisted on P.R. They were aware of the difference between even a very large minority and a majority; nothing serves as much to unite all non-Communist elements as the prospect of a Communist victory. P.R., on the other hand, did nothing to render Communist "Trojan horse" tactics difficult.

The final Communist victory came in February 1948. New elections were scheduled; under an impartial government they were likely to show substantial Communist losses. Thereupon the Communists provoked a cabinet crisis, and used all methods of intimidation at their command. Finally, on February 25, President Benes allowed Premier Gottwald to install a Communist-dominated cabinet.

Dr. Benes was under severe pressure; if, during the preceding years he had shown a surprising willingness to accept Russian terms, it must also be said that the Western powers did little to establish a closer relationship to Czechoslovakia. Still, when Benes submitted to Gottwald it must have been clear to him that, as in the days of Munich, he made a decision which deprived the remainder of his countrymen of their last chance to fight for freedom. The concessions which he made in both cases gave unlimited power to the enemy. One cannot help but wonder whether the failure of Czech politics to infuse the fighting spirit into its leaders which the majority system fosters, did not have its share in the new surrender, as well as in the old.

Greece

In the case of Greece, as in the case of Poland, we must refer to a large degree of illiteracy. The 1928 census put the average illiteracy of men at forty-one per cent of the population, and the average illiteracy of women at fifty-eight per cent.[18] Such percentages are all the more significant because they mean that in many cases people have been counted as literate whose schooling was rather sketchy. As the English expressed it on the basis of their experience in India, education will not "stick" with pupils who, when they return to the environment from which they came, find little use for the written word. Conditions were, of course, better than average in the city of Athens, which is definitely a part of modern civilization, than in the remainder of the country where conditions remain primitive.

Greece suffered, in addition, from the problems of what — rather euphemistically — was called the "population exchange" with Turkey. The Greeks from Asia Minor were expellees whom, on account of their numbers and their destitution, European Greece never assimilated. They remained an element of instability; both the leaders and the fighting members of the Communist guerilla forces, which arose after the Second World War, consisted largely of expellees and descendants of expellees.

If, in Greece as in Poland, the "material" conditions for democracy were deficient, it is nonetheless true that some of the effects of P.R. have manifested themselves in such a typical manner that they must be discussed. C. M. Woodhouse expresses himself in these words:

"Because too, Greece usually elects its Parliament (when it has one) by proportional representation, there is a chance for any number of splinter-parties to obtain representation. Because there is little danger of these having to form a Government by themselves, they need not bother with a social programme; or with any sort of programme beyond the slogan, 'Down with everyone else!' Even absolute power never corrupted so absolutely as absolute irresponsibility." [19]

The last pre-war elections were held in January, 1936, and gave to the parties belonging to the former Royalist bloc 48.14 per cent of the votes, and 143 out of 300 seats. The parties belonging to the former Republican bloc secured 44.54 per cent of the votes, and 141 seats. The Communists, with 5.87 per cent of the votes, had 15 seats. One Independent was also elected. Thus, the 15 Communists turned the scales between the 143 Rightists and the 141 Leftists.[20] Let us again quote Woodhouse on the events that followed:

"The election of January 1936 finally exposed the bankruptcy of democracy as conducted by these men, by leaving the balance of power in the House in the hands of fifteen Communist members. In April the House prorogued itself, and was replaced by a Committee which reproduced its proportions and defects; in the same month Metaxas became Prime Minister through a process of elimination by death. The deadlock precipitated his *coup d'état,* and left in the hearts of many Greeks the feeling that it was about time too." [21]

The "feeling that it was about time too" filled the hearts of many people also in other countries where the wrangling brought about by P.R. was finally ended by dictatorship. To be sure, to quote again Woodhouse, the methods of Metaxas, "eliminated the evil of the electoral system of representation (meaning P.R.) by eliminating Parliament. . . . In all this Metaxas might be compared to a doctor whose only cure for a headache was decapitation." [22] Few of us would welcome such a cure, in particular since the evil could have been remedied at the point where it entered the body politic. As long as no correct diagnosis of the evil is made, however, the unsatisfactory results of P.R. will always redound to the disadvantage of democracy.

New elections were held in 1946, after the liberation, while civil war was raging in the country. An Allied commission had been appointed to watch the elections; Allied influence had its share in the retention of P.R. Greece, it might be noted, is one of the countries where the evils of that system have been recognized long since. The elder Venizelos was its chief opponent once he had seen it in operation in the elections of 1926.[23] In 1928 he actually did what Giolitti had been advised to do in Italy in 1921, but did not feel strong enough to do: he abolished P.R. by decree. In the P.R. elections of 1926 there was no workable majority, and governing proved impossible after the experiment of an all-party coalition had been tried and failed.

The new elections, held under the majority system, showed, however, that in a country in which the shift in the popular vote is as strong as in Greece, the majority system has drawbacks which could, and should, be corrected. The seven parties following Venizelos secured sixty-six per cent of the votes and ninety-one per cent of the seats. The resulting weakness of the opposition was perhaps not as serious as the mere figures indicate, as the strength of an opposition rests as much on its moral prestige as on the number of its representatives in a parliament.

There could, on the other hand, be no objection to securing for the opposition a number of seats large enough to make it possible for it to oppose the majority vigorously in parliament. A number of devices are available by which this could be done. It might, for example, be provided that whenever a particular party or group of parties secures more than sixty per cent of the seats, the total number of the membership of that particular parliament would be increased by a certain number, such as forty, or thirty, or twenty-five per cent. Among the defeated opposition candidates, those would be attributed the extra seats who secured the highest percentage of the votes cast in their respective constituencies.

To avoid misunderstandings, it might be noted that such an arrangement would differ from the use of the limited vote in Spain where, after the 1936 elections, the Rightists charged that the number of seats assigned to majority and minority in the multiple-member constituencies had been arranged to their disadvantage. The claims of the Spanish Rightists are open to challenge, but it would be wise to make their repetition impossible. Under the above plan, votes for both majority and minority would be added up nationally, excluding any new type of gerrymandering. It is hardly necessary to add that in the older democracies, where violent shifts in the distribution of votes do not occur, no arrangement of this type would be needed.[24]

When the 1946 elections were held, the 85-year-old Prime Minister, Sophoulis, claimed that P.R. had to be used because the law of 1936 which established it was still in force; observers referred to the fact that the fraction of the Liberal party which he headed might have fared badly under the majority system. Both the Populists (Monarchists), and the Liberals who followed the younger Venizelos, came out strongly in favor of the majority system. The die was cast when Sophoulis succeeded in having the Regent sign a decree ordering elections under P.R. which, incidentally, was also favored by the Western Allies. The prevailing civil war mentality led, however, to a political crystallization around the Populists who received, with a bare majority of the popular vote, 206 out of 354 seats in the Chamber. Since the civil war continued, a party government seemed inadvisable; various governments were formed on changing foundations.

Shortly before the next elections were held in 1950, the coalition between Populists and Liberals, which had been in power since June, 1949, broke down because Mr. Venizelos charged his Populist allies with premature electioneering. The official resignation took place on January 5. The King appointed a caretaker government headed by the Speaker of the Chamber, Mr. Theotokis, who had left the Populist party in November. This government considered restoring the majority system by decree, but bowed to protests pointing out that, after the dissolution of the Chamber, which had taken place on January 7, any change of existing laws would be unconstitutional. It was certain that under P.R. no party would secure a majority, and Mr. Venizelos, among others, expressed the view that the new Chamber might have to be dissolved again after a short time, and new elections held under the majority system.[25]

The elections resulted in the almost equal strength for Tsaldaris Populists, the Venizelos Liberals, and General Plastiras' National Progressive Union; there followed the Democratic Socialist party (which, like the Venizelos and Plastiras parties, is an offshoot of the old Liberal party), and the Democratic Front, which was generally believed to have benefited most from the votes of the outlawed Communist party. Finally there were, with a strength almost equal to that of the Democratic Front, the Independents, an extreme Rightist group, led by former associates of General Metaxas. Five minor parties constituted the remainder of the Chamber's membership.

The first government formed was headed by Venizelos, who expected to rely upon the support of the Populists, to whom the election had brought a great defeat. American pressure was one of the reasons why Venizelos resigned; the American Ambassador implied strongly that this government, whose composition hardly did justice to the election results, would not be able to carry out the needed reforms. Thereupon General Plastiras formed a coalition consisting of the three groups sharing the heritage of the old Liberal party. The new government had every appearance of being the logical solution, but it had its weaknesses. As A. C. Sedgwick wrote in *The New York Times* of April 15, the coalition parties had "the not-substantial majority of 136 in the 250-member Chamber." There had been considerable animosity among the three groups, which made support of the government by all the deputies of the coalition doubtful. General Plastiras was often accused of harboring Communist sympathies and of having received Communist support, Moscow having ordered the Communists to vote for the Democratic Front in the cities and the National Progressive Union in the rural areas.[26] Finally, there was the heterogeneous opposition, consisting of the Populists and the Independents at the Right, and the Democratic Front at the Left, with the Communist party remaining banned.

It is difficult to estimate the effects which the majority system would have produced in the Greek elections of 1950. Yet, the general trends observable under that system indicate a weakening of the extremists, and the elimination of the smallest parties, with the combination of the remainder into two blocs with common principles and common leadership. C. L. Sulzberger reported: "There are political experts here (in Athens) who are predicting that the next government may not manage to gain a majority of the Center; that, if it succeeds, it cannot last long; that new elections on the majority system, instead of proportional representation, are, therefore, likely this autumn." [27]

The Plastiras cabinet did secure its parliamentary majority, but in August it collapsed over the issue of cabinet solidarity. This led to a revival of plans to abolish P.R., difficult of realization as these may be in a parliament elected by that system of voting.[28] There were, of course, reasons for keeping this parliament alive in order to inaugurate, if possible, the essential reforms pointed out by the American Ambassador. Yet, one wonders how Greece can, in the long run, bear the burden of P.R. in addition to so many others. On March 5, Mr. C. L. Sulzberger reported to *The New York Times* what, under P.R., is likely to be a permanent situation:

"When the present campaign began there were more than ninety contending parties. It is still possible that 250 legislative seats may be shared among twenty-six political machines.

"Most of them, indeed, will be limited to one, two or a handful of deputies. But when it is remembered that no single party is likely to obtain a majority and that therefore the coalition formula will remain an administrative necessity, it can be seen that these fragmentary groups may well be in a position to foment political ruckuses and occasionally play decisive roles." [29]

Even if, as was the case on this occasion, such prospects are only partly realized, Greek democracy cannot be expected to prosper as long as they last.

Chapter 6. Positive and Negative Democracy

in Smaller Countries

The smaller countries discussed in this chapter have not experienced a collapse of democracy. It has, in fact, been claimed that they demonstrate the success of P.R. Several of them in particular have played a part of considerable importance in the history of P.R. The first country to adopt P.R. for national elections was Belgium, which inaugurated this system of voting in 1899. Until the end of the First World War one party, the Catholic party, maintained an over-all majority, forming stable one-party cabinets. Belgium's relative success with P.R. came to an abrupt end after 1919. Its role as the model P.R. country was then taken over by Ireland, in which a fair degree of stability was preserved. Proponents of P.R. will also refer to Switzerland, and since the middle 1930's to the Scandinavian countries. Therefore, the basic aspects of the P.R. experience of these nations will be considered in this chapter.

Belgium

In Belgium P.R. had been adopted because, before 1899, elections were held under the majority system in multiple-member constituencies. In the larger ones, in particular, a shift in a small number of votes could throw a considerable bloc of seats from one party to the other. It would have been possible to remedy this situation by the introduction of single-member constituencies, but P.R. was adopted instead.

At first P.R. seemed to justify the expectations of its supporters. The Liberal party which, in the late 1890's, had found itself in the same position as the British Liberal party since the end of the First World War, came, as its followers had hoped, back to life. This fact did not, however, interfere with the over-all majority of the Catholic party, and was for that reason not commented upon adversely. Only one minor party, the so-called "Dansistes," secured seats during this period. On the other hand, there is agreement among proponents and opponents of P.R. to the effect that under the majority system a clear-cut two-party system would have developed during this period.

While P.R. did not prevent the over-all majority of the Catholic party, this was secured with a minority of the popular vote. For example, for the two elections of 1906 and 1908, which are comparable to a single election, because in each of them only one-half of the Chamber was renewed, the Catholics should, according to the computation of the British Proportional Representation Society, have received only 80.7 instead of 87 out of 166 seats.[1] In this case they would have lost their majority and coalitions would have become necessary. The advantage of the Catholics was brought about by the lack of proportionality of the Belgium system, which did not provide for any transfer of surpluses. Furthermore, there was "plural voting;" people who fulfilled certain types of educational or property requirements received additional votes. In general, this circumstance also resulted in an advantage for the Catholic party.

During the period in question the Catholic majority was, however, small. A prominent Belgian authority on constitutional problems[2] has expressed the view that the small size of this majority was the reason why so little was done to solve the conflict between Flemings and Walloons before a critical stage had been reached. The Catholic party was afraid of losing a few crucial votes in the Walloon part of the country; therefore, against the better knowledge of its leaders, no adequate measures were taken in order to fulfill the legitimate demands of the Flemings.

After the First World War, two changes were made. Plural voting was abolished and a utilization of surpluses within the same province was permitted. The Catholic party lost its majority in the first elections held under the new provisions. Subsequently, the relation of strength among the three major parties remained fairly well stabilized. This meant a more or less permanent deadlock. In addition, new parties developed, all of which owed their success to P.R. The first was the party of the Flemish Nationalists, which expressed the views of the radical minority within their own group, the moderate majority continuing to support the Catholic party. Next was the Communist party, which has elected deputies since 1929, although at first only a few. The pre-war peak of nine seats was reached in 1936. The latest comer was the Rexists, a pro-Nazi party which developed in French-speaking parts of the country under the leadership of Léon Degrelle.

Thus, the older parties were threatened by the demagoguery of the new and more radical ones. In addition, the influence of economic interest groups became strong within the two largest parties, the Catholics and the Socialists. The former had to undergo the influence of farmers' and similar associations, and the latter the influence of the trade unions and the cooperatives. This lowered the quality of the political personnel, and at the same time led to charges of corruption, since the deputies related to these organizations were accused of promoting the interests of their respective groups. Furthermore, it was difficult to replace older deputies with younger candidates. One newspaper said: "It is the system of 'earned rights,' no matter how mediocre or even how unworthy may be its beneficiary." [3]

There followed ever-increasing difficulties in the formation of governments. Sometimes the Catholics and the Liberals would combine to form a cabinet, which was always threatened with dissension over matters pertaining to problems such as education. In 1926, a government of the three large parties was formed, which found it necessary to replace the ordinary process of legislation largely by government decrees. Subsequently, such three-party coalitions were in power between 1935 and 1940. They were formed only after protracted negotiations and remained divided by deep antagonisms from the first day to the last. Important measures were often enacted by decree. No serious objection was made to these decree laws; most observers agreed that there existed what Edgar Ansel Mowrer has called the "semi-paralysis" of Belgium's legislative bodies, and that the vacuum had to be filled.

The vacuum created by P.R. was, also, to an increasing extent, filled by the King. Leopold III ascended the throne in 1934. During his reign he never witnessed clear majorities and governments with any real authority of their own. The four cabinets preceding World War II, beginning with that of Van Zeeland, were almost "royal cabinets" in the same sense in which the government of Dr. Bruening in Germany was a "presidential cabinet."

A real crisis broke out in Belgium in the middle 1930's. The elections of 1936 saw the spectacular rise of the Rexists, who on this occasion elected twenty-one of the 202 deputies of the Chamber. Together with the sixteen Flemish Nationalists they formed a formidable

Right-wing opposition, generally supported by the nine Communists at the Left.

It suffices to read newspapers for this period to realize how serious the condition of Belgian democracy was regarded. One article in *The New York Times* carried the headline: "Dictator Likely Belgians Believe." [5] The article went on to speak of the prospect of a dictatorship by Prime Minister Van Zeeland, rather than by the Fascist leader, Degrelle, but emphasized that fear of the collapse of democracy was general. A Belgian deputy gave an interview to a French newspaper in which he said: "We are exactly in the situation where Italy found herself in 1922. The Italian government possessed a strong majority, but its members were not able to find the basis for an agreement." [6]

The Belgian political scene showed some improvement immediately before the outbreak of World War II, since in the 1939 election the Rexist vote declined by more than half, and on account of the peculiar features of the Belgian system of voting their number of seats in the Chamber declined from twenty-one to four. The formation of cabinets remained, however, as onerous as ever. King Leopold had, with great difficulty, succeeded in constituting a cabinet headed by Pierlot on February 21, 1939. He had to reconstitute it on April 18 and September 5 of the same year, and once again a few days before the invasion of his country in May, 1940. Whatever authority this government had was derived from the King, without whose constant intervention it could not have existed.

These events form the background of the Belgian royal crisis. The general public has been so much impressed by more spectacular charges and countercharges concerning the King's actions during the war that the deeper causes of the conflict were overlooked. Leopold was inclined to take a high view of his own powers, for the simple reason that the power of the cabinets which attempted to govern during his reign was so weak. It was perhaps not unnatural that he should have developed a low opinion of the country's party system, and of the majority of its politicians, who seemed to him to be intriguing against each other rather than acting in concert for the common good of the country.

Open conflict between the King and his ministers ensued when the King took his constitutional function as war-time Commander-in-

Chief of the Armed Forces literally. He personally decided upon the surrender of the Belgian Army, claiming that for this act he did not need the counter-signature of a responsible minister. At the same time, he refused to heed the cabinet's request to join it outside Belgium in order to continue the war, in which Belgium continued to play a part not only in the hope of final liberation, but also because her rich colonial empire continued to be under Belgian administration. The case for the cabinet and against the King was extremely strong when we consider the spirit rather than the letter of the constitution. Still, the moral authority of the cabinet hardly existed in the eyes of the King who had patched it up time and again, and who felt that in a time of emergency it was his personal duty to act on behalf of the country. There is, in such a case, little use in moralizing. The power of the King of the Belgians had increased for the same reason for which the power of King Victor Emmanuel in Italy and of President von Hindenburg in Germany increased. It is difficult to imagine Leopold acting the way he did had he been King in a country with clearcut majorities and homogeneous cabinets able to function under recognized leadership from the beginning of a particular parliament to its end.

The same factors which had established the background of the Belgian royal crisis before the Second World War presented its timely solution afterwards. New elections took place on February 17, 1946, and June 26, 1949.[7] The political picture had been simplified by the fact that both the Flemish Nationalists and the Rexist parties were banned as collaborators. Most of the voting strength of these two groups went to the Christian Social party, the successors of the former Catholic party. A complicating feature was the increasing strength of the Communist party, which secured twenty-three seats in 1946 and twelve in 1949. The Christian Social party, which had won ninety-two seats in 1946, fought under the slogan, "absolute majority," in 1949, only to fall short of the goal by two seats, electing 105 out of a total of 212 deputies. The fact that this was a gain over the ninety-two seats which the party had held in 1946 (with a total Chamber membership of 202), provided little comfort.

The political situation had been confused before 1949 when just about all possible combinations were tried, beginning with Catholic-

Socialist-Communist coalitions, followed by Socialist-Liberal coalitions and Catholic-Socialist coalitions. That the Christian Social party had, in 1949, come close to an absolute majority did not assist them in the task of forming a government. The Liberals had increased their voting strength from eighteen to twenty-nine seats, and were determined to exact as high a price as possible for their share of government responsibility. The negotiations for the formation of the new coalition, which crippled Belgium for six weeks, ended when the 44-year-old Gaston Eyskens, a Christian Social leader, secured the cooperation of the Liberals in forming a cabinet in which they received eight seats as compared with the nine seats of the Christian Social party, whose strength in the Chamber was more than three times larger than the strength of the Liberals.

The inconclusive result of these post-war elections blocked the road to a solution of the royal question. Few doubted that any solution could be a real solution unless it was adopted quickly and without too much popular discussion. Had the Christian Social party enjoyed a majority they would have brought the King back immediately. In the face of a clear majority Leopold would have had to play the part of a constitutional monarch, and would have been forced to exercise this function in conformity with the rules of the game of the parliamentary system. A Socialist majority would have forced the King to abdicate. Inasmuch as neither the institution of monarchy nor of dynasty was involved in controversy, the Socialists being willing to have the elder son of the King take over, this also would have represented a workable solution.

When no party secured a clear majority, no solution could be found. The decision to submit the matter to an advisory popular vote, which was held on March 12, 1950, meant that Belgium got the worst of both worlds. A King is, under a parliamentary system, a symbol of political unity. This unity is denied when the person of the monarch becomes the object of a heatedly fought popular consent, which inevitably fills the air with charges and countercharges. If, in such a case, the monarch wins, enough of the charges will survive to make it difficult for him to fulfill his functions again. If, on the other hand, the minority compels his abdication, the majority will feel embittered. Its members will feel that they conducted the battle on a clearcut issue, that they won, and that all the rules of the game were violated when they had to submit to the minority.

Leopold had agreed to abdicate if he should secure less than fifty-five per cent of the popular vote. With 57.68 per cent, he secured only slightly more than the minimum. His opponents hastened to call this a moral defeat, and demanded his abdication; his supporters pointed out that the details of the vote were rather favorable to the King,[8] as only the two industrial provinces of Hainaut and Liège had yielded substantial majorities against him. The fact that in leftist Brussels the opposition did not rally more than 51.80 per cent, was regarded as a moral victory for the King.

The New York Times commented as follows: "The results of the Belgian plebiscite on the return of King Leopold III are little short of tragic. The vote has settled nothing; it has merely proved that the nation is hopelessly and bitterly divided . . ."[9] The *Times* felt that abdication of the King could alone solve the problem; this is a solution which his supporters, just emerging from a battle in which they had to take their share of blows, would have regarded as desertion. Negotiations for a compromise, doomed to failure, began immediately, soon to coincide with a cabinet crisis, which it proved impossible to solve. In the end, the cabinet Eyskens was reactivated, after everyone had believed it dead; under its leadership, though with vigorous protest from its Liberal members, the Chamber was dissolved. The Christian Social party could not forget the 57.68 per cent cast for the King in a country in which any hope for some kind of positive majority seemed to have been abandoned. The popular vote had, of course, necessarily led to that consolidation behind a clearcut answer, which P.R. elections made impossible. The Christian Social party felt that after the popular vote had brought about this result, the ground was prepared for their securing that absolute majority in new elections which they had missed so narrowly in 1949. Their opponents regarded this as a partisan trick, but if so, it was the kind of trick which the situation invited.[9(a)]

In any event, a festering sore developed to which the proper remedy could not be applied. In view of the fact that all of this had arisen out of the lack of clearcut parliamentary majorities, one cannot but recall the warning with which the Catholic leader, Woeste, had concluded a speech against P.R. before the adoption of that system of voting: "I resume this discussion with the cry, 'unfortunate government, unfortunate country!' " [10]

Ireland

P.R. was introduced into Ireland by British legislation, which according to its supporters was intended to give the religious minority in each of the two parts of the country a fair chance to express its grievances. Irish observers held that the true motive was the intention to divide and rule. As one Irish politician put it:

"P.R. has been administered to us by the English in 1917, while they were still the masters of the country. . . . They installed it in our country in order to permit the small minority of Protestants and the small minority of Unionists to be represented. To put it otherwise, when, in order to govern us more easily, they felt the need to divide us more, they discovered that P.R. was the best procedure." [11]

It will be seen later that whatever the intention of the British was, it was not realized.

In discussing Irish P.R. we must first bear in mind its lack of consistency. The constituencies were small, seldom electing more than five deputies, and since no transfer of surpluses from one constituency to another was possible, large parties inevitably gained a great advantage over small ones. In 1932, for example, Fianna Fáil, the party of De Valera, obtained on an average of one seat for 7,867 first preference votes, whereas the Labour party had an average of 14,040 votes.[12] These figures are typical. The advantage accruing to the major parties greatly facilitated the success of, first, Mr. Cosgrave, and then Mr. De Valera.

In the first period of Irish government the characteristic fact was the absence of De Valera's followers from the Dáil, which they did not enter because they refused to take the oath of loyalty to the British King. Thus, Mr. Cosgrave, whose party never secured a majority of all seats in the Dáil, was able to govern with a clear majority in the rump parliament. In 1927, De Valera changed his tactics and asked his followers to take the oath and regard it as a mere formality. On August 16, 1927, a vote of censure against the government was rejected with seventy-one votes for and seventy-one against it, the vote of the Speaker deciding the issue in favor of the government. The hostility between the two major parties being what it was, at the time, Irish government could not have been continued on this basis. Mr. Cosgrave was, however, able to restore the position of his government by new elections, in which the strength of his party increased sufficiently to make it possible for him to govern in conjunction with the Independents and the Farmers' party. The escape from chaos was narrow though, and Professor James Hogan wrote: "We can thank our lucky stars that Proportional Representation did not get the chance of plunging the country into Mexican politics, perhaps for a generation." [13]

Mr. De Valera assumed control of the government in 1932, not to relinquish it until 1948. At first, he relied upon the support of Labour, but secured an absolute majority of one vote in 1933. In 1937, Fianna Fáil elected exactly one-half of the membership of the Dáil, although during the following year De Valera was able to restore the balance by new elections, in which he secured 77 out of a total of 138 seats. In 1943,[14] he again lost his majority, only to regain it in 1944, having once again utilized an issue in the field of foreign affairs in order to dissolve the Dáil at a favorable moment. In the case of complete proportionality between votes and seats, he would have had to be satisfied with sixty-nine seats, exactly one-half of the total.[15]

During the last months of 1947, De Valera was faced with opposition on the part of the new Republican party led by Mr. McBride, which in December won two out of three bye-elections. De Valera decided to hold new elections before the Republican organization would be fully developed. In the new Chamber he secured, however, only 68 of a total of 167 seats. His party was still by far the strongest single force in the Dáil. Yet, contrary to all expectations, the entire opposition gathered its forces to form a cabinet under Mr. John Costello. For this purpose it was necessary to combine Fine Gael, the Labour party, the National Labour party, the Farmers, the Independents, and the Republicans, — in other words, six different groups.

These developments make plain what a more detailed analysis of election figures indicated from the outset. The relative stability of Irish politics was not due to P.R., but to extraneous forces. First, the so-called "treaty issue" tended to divide the country into two major groups, those who favored and those who opposed the treaty with England. Whenever this issue moved into the foreground, more divisive forces, such as economic interests and parties formed on that basis, were sufficiently pushed into the background to strengthen the major parties. The treaty issue was succeeded in 1944 by the issue of neutrality, which assisted De Valera in a similar manner. In 1948, when no such issue arose, a more "normal" development took place, and the splitting up typical of P.R. was clearly discernible.

It may be well to consider the election results since 1943, as set forth in the following table:

PARTIES	1943	1944	1948
Fianna Fáil (De Valera)	67	76	68
Fine Gael (Cosgrave; Costello)	32	30	31
Labour party	17	8	14
National Labour party	..	4	5
Farmers	14	13	7
Independents	8	7	12
Republicans (McBride)	..	..	10
Totals	138	138	147

The figures for 1948 make it plain that the Costello government presents the unusual picture of a combination of all parties against the largest party. Such a situation has all the appearances of a combination of opposites. The Fine Gael party, for example, was known as the Conservative party in Ireland. It is represented in the same cabinet by the two Labour parties, both of which advocate socialism, and the Republican party, which also presents a radical left-wing program. Similarly, Fine Gael was traditionally in favor of continued association with Great Britain and the Commonwealth. This time it cooperated with the Republican party, which as its name indicates, wanted from the start a republic in form as well as in substance, whereas even De Valera, who had split with Fine Gael over this issue, taking what was then regarded as the radical side, had been ready to accept the shadow as long as he had the substance. When the cabinet was formed, its participants were aware of these differences and, therefore, the cabinet was officially designated as an "inter-party government" rather than as a coalition government. Naturally, in the ensuing debate in the Dáil,[16] De Valera's spokesmen asked whether this name was to imply that the parties from whose ranks the ministers were drawn were unwilling to assume responsibility for the government's policies.

Strains did develop in the Costello government, but the will to overcome them was so strong that they were kept under control. As is likely to happen in such a case, the most extreme group, McBride's Republican party, prevailed over its more moderate allies. A Republic was formally proclaimed, and Ireland's association with the Commonwealth ended. This is a policy which, in the elections of 1948, only the Republicans demanded, and which all other groups, in particular Fine Gael, rejected. Apparently, however, the ten seats of the Republican party proved more influential than the sixty-nine seats of the other coalition parties. When the issue was presented in the Dáil, De Valera had been outflanked and was forced to concur in the decision reached.

The question arises whether the proclamation of the Republic conferred any advantage on Ireland. The immediate result was to create active antagonism in those sectors of British public opinion where a benevolent attitude had prevailed previously. Thus, *The Manchester Guardian* commented: "Mr. Costello, in tearing up his election pledge, was moved by party considerations. He wanted to dish Mr. De Valera's anti-partition campaign by doing something even Mr. De Valera had never done — cut the Commonwealth painter. It was rather sordid Irish politics."[17] Actually, the procedure was typical P.R. politics. As no major party had a majority, the one of the minority parties whose cooperation was the most difficult to secure had to be allowed to call the tune. Similar cases of minority rule have occurred repeatedly under P.R., even if it is natural that *The Manchester Guardian*, a proponent of that system of voting, should prefer the alibi of "sordid Irish politics."

In this connection, it must be borne in mind that if the formal establishment of a Republic was all Mr. McBride, the Foreign Minister, wanted, he could have obtained it and yet remained within the

Commonwealth by waiting only a few months. After India had set a precedent, Ireland could safely have followed it. As it was, Great Britain undertook the redefinition of her relationship to Ireland in the Ireland Act of 1948, which sensibly left to Irish citizens the privileges which they had enjoyed in England previously, and did not provide for any retaliation. On the other hand, the act contained for the first time an explicit assurance that no change in the separation of the six counties around Belfast from the remainder of Ireland would be undertaken, except with the consent of the parliament of the six counties. That consent was not to be expected. On the contrary, the proclamation of a Republic and Dublin's secession from the Commonwealth gave the Northern Irish government the welcome chance of dissolving its own House of Commons and holding new elections, in which its top-heavy majority was returned more strongly than ever.

Whatever the ultimate consequences of the proclamation of the Irish Republic and of Ireland's secession from the Commonwealth may be, the immediate reaction on both sides was a hardened attitude on the partition issue. Sir Basil Brooke, the Belfast Prime Minister, had more strings to his propaganda bow than ever. Dublin had broken the remaining ties with "King and country"; the bastion of Catholicism had refused to join the Atlantic Pact, intended to erect a wall against communism. Mr. McBride, the Dublin Foreign Minister, had declared that Ireland could not join the Atlantic Pact as long as the six counties remained separated from the rest of the country; his action tended to confirm that separation.

Recent developments do not, however, justify the original separation of the six northeastern counties from the twenty-six remaining counties. When that step was taken there was no proper analysis of the issues involved. The separate government for the six counties was deemed necessary for the purpose of protecting the 800,000 Protestants who formed a majority of two to one over the Catholics in this area, and were supposed to be defenseless under an all-Irish government. Yet, there are some 200,000 Protestants in the twenty-six counties who enjoy full equality with their fellow citizens. Had there been a joint government for all thirty-two counties, under a majority system of voting, the million Protestants in a united Ireland would have provided close to twenty-five per cent of the electorate.

POSITIVE AND NEGATIVE DEMOCRACY IN SMALLER COUNTRIES

The major Irish parties could not afford to ignore, let alone antagonize, such a large voting group. The Protestants would not only have been in a strategic position to defend their own interests against infringement, but they could also have turned the scales in regard to Ireland's foreign policy. It is difficult to see how, under such conditions, a party unwilling to continue a close association with England could have secured a majority. It is, in fact, likely that with the entire country united under one government there would have been no serious opposition to close association with England from any quarter. The friendly spirit with which Parnell greeted Gladstone's first Home Rule bill might have arisen again. Therefore, had the six counties in 1922 remained a part of Ireland, the result would not have been to deprive England of all of Ireland, but to make all of Ireland a close and reliable friend.

It might be mentioned in passing that for the Catholic and Nationalist minority in the six counties, conditions were equally unfavorable during the period when P.R. was used, and after the reestablishment of the majority system. Permanent minorities derive little comfort from occupying a number of seats in a parliament whether that number be proportionate to their voting strength or not. They are certain to be voted down on every issue which matters from their point of view. During the period in question, the Irish Nationalists illustrated their lack of appreciation for the seats gained under P.R. by failing to attend the sessions of the Northern Irish Parliament. When P.R. was abolished, the loss of seats sustained by the Irish Nationalists — from twelve to eleven or nine, depending upon the circumstances of a particular election — was insignificant. What does matter is the considerable degree of gerrymandering which prevails in the six counties. It is particularly relevant in the county councils of Fermanagh and Tyrone, and in the city council of Derry, where a Nationalist majority was rendered unable to elect a majority of the councillors. The remedy for unfair apportionment is, however, a fair apportionment rather than P.R. The latter, incidentally, does not necessarily exclude gerrymandering.[18]

The future of Irish government cannot be judged on the basis of the 1948 elections, and of the comparatively successful cooperation among the components of the Costello government. Only one consideration brought these disparate elements together: the fear of De Valera. De Valera had, for a number of years, opposed P.R., which he rightly held responsible for the threat of instability hanging over Irish politics. During the campaign of 1948 he had consistently refused to promise that, if he were returned to power, he would not seek the abolition of P.R. That step would have been fatal for the minor parties, and by this time Fine Gael had developed a minor party psychology. Therefore, the parties joining in the so-called "inter-party" government felt that their cooperation was the only way to assure their continued existence.

The question remains to what extent such an assumption is justified. While the majority system would have led to a regrouping of parties, it would have brought gains as well as losses. The opposition to Fianna Fáil totaled more than fifty-five per cent of the total popular vote, and under a majority system it would have found a way to assert itself. It seems likely that Fine Gael would have been the principal beneficiary in terms of votes and seats, although it would have had to adapt itself to the new forces in Irish politics. There is a strong probability that the majority system would tend to produce a two-party system in Ireland, which would make it possible for the voter himself to decide on the formation of governments, rather than have the party leaders arrange for a solution which no one anticipated during the campaign, as happened in 1948.

Recent Irish history seems to confirm what a prominent Irish observer, who had been deputy prime minister in Cosgrave's cabinet, told this writer in Dublin in 1937. P.R., he said, was boding no good for the country's democratic future, but it had created so many vested interests that its abolition appeared impossible. At present, these vested interests are stronger than ever. P.R. is endorsed not only by those parties which actually depend on it for their political survival, but also by those who would be likely to gain from its abolition, though at the risk of a complete political reorientation. It is a strange fact that when a party either has a majority or is within striking distance of a majority, it can see the advantages of stability and the disadvantages of P.R. very well. During the crisis of 1927, prominent members of the Fine Gael pointed to P.R. as the cause of their party's and the country's misfortune, and demanded its abolition. Some of them, like the gentleman referred to above, — since publicly identified by an Irish journalist as Mr. Ernest Blythe — and Mr. Desmond Fitzgerald, the one-time Minister of Defense and of Foreign Affairs in Cosgrave's government, remained faithful to their earlier attitude. Mr. Fitzgerald emphasized in conversation with this writer that he did not care if his party lost a few seats as a result of the majority system while it was in a minority anyway, as long as there was a prospect of its securing an adequate majority again when the political tide turned. This is a farsighted and statesmanlike attitude which, however, is rare among political leaders.

The Scandinavian Countries

The Scandinavian countries have, since the middle 1930's, often been referred to as a proof for the beneficial effects of P.R., because in certain elections the Social Democratic parties of Sweden and Norway secured over-all majorities, which formed the basis for stable governments. This fact must not, however, make us overlook that there were periods in which the splitting up of parties led to serious difficulties. Nor should we ignore that, if conditions were good under P.R., they would have been no less good under the majority system. The latter was certain to simplify the party structure and prevent the rise of extremists.

So far as Denmark is concerned, no one party ever secured an over-all majority under P.R. The Socialist party came closest to this result in 1935, when it obtained 68 out of a total of 149 seats. Therefore, coalitions were always necessary, unless minority governments were formed. On the other hand, there can be little doubt that in view of the rising Socialist strength the majority system would have encouraged consolidation of the non-Socialist parties, several of which were so small that the majority system would not have permitted their separate existence. Also P.R. gave opportunities to extremist parties, such as the Communists and the National Socialists which, while their numbers remained small even under P.R., would have elected no deputies under the majority system.[18(a)]

In Norway, the adoption of P.R., in 1919, was at first followed by a considerable splitting up of parties. In the last elections under the majority system, held in 1915, one party enjoyed an over-all majority. Under P.R. this condition did not recur until 1945, when the Labor party secured 76 of a total of 150 seats, thereupon forming a one-party government, and in 1949 when its strength rose to 85. In both cases the majority of the seats was obtained with a minority of the votes, amounting to forty-two per cent in 1945 and forty-eight per cent in 1949. Limited proportionality is a feature common to the election laws of all three Scandinavian countries. Small parties are unable to use many of the votes cast for them, and large parties benefit correspondingly.

In Norway the splitting up of parties never went as far as in Denmark, and as a result the concentration of parties, which the majority system would have necessitated, would not have been as important. The Labor governments which have been in power since 1945 pursued a moderate and constructive course, which had popular consent even if the parliamentary majorities were obtained with a minority of the popular vote, just as may happen under a plurality system. As long as P.R. is retained it is always possible for a relapse to occur to the conditions prevailing in 1932, when Dr. Braunias wrote: "The consequence (of the introduction of P.R.) was that no party obtains a majority any longer, and that the Storting (the Lower House of Parliament) is split in a number of groups. Since all power is concentrated in the Storting, its weakening through this splitting up of parties reacts on the entire life of the state." [19]

Sweden adopted P.R. in 1909. The party line-up changed at first but slowly, but since the end of the First World War a definite political splintering has taken place. During the 1920's one minority government after the other had to be formed, and the basis of such governments was often narrow. Thus, the cabinets headed by Mr. Ekman governed from 1926 to 1928, and 1930 to 1932, with the direct support of only the twenty-eight deputies belonging to the Liberal group, whereas the Lower House of the Swedish Parliament had a total of 230 members. During this period there developed considerable criticism of parliamentary government. As Professor Sandelius put it: ". . . Politicians together with their critics in the Swedish community begin, rather generally, and of nearly all parties, to consider that the responsibility of their political leadership is not sufficiently concentrated to withstand very well the threat of chaos. If, eventually, it should prove unable to do so, then as theretofore, it will be followed by absolutistic reaction . . . the thought of Fascism —

though in a very small kernel, to be sure — has appeared in Sweden, too." [20]

Conditions took a definite turn for the better in 1932, when the upsurge of the Social Democratic party began. On that occasion it secured 104 out of 230 seats, and was able to form a stable coalition in combination with the Agrarian party. The carefully planned social and economic policy inaugurated by this government is too well known to require discussion. The Social Democratic party continued to grow until 1940, when it obtained 134 seats and therewith an over-all majority. In 1944, it elected exactly half of the Chamber's membership, 115, which incidentally was accomplished with 46.6 per cent of the total popular vote. The 1948 elections brought a further slight decline of the party's strength to 112. Social Democratic cabinets continued to exist in spite of these political declines, and as yet no serious consequences have developed. On the other hand, there can be little doubt that the majority system would have led to a political consolidation. Likewise, the cause of political moderation would have been furthered by the elimination of the Communist party from the Chamber which, in 1944, elected fifteen deputies, and in 1948, eight. Certainly, the country would have nothing to lose by the transition to the majority system, as certain gains were unlikely to be offset by any losses. Under P.R. a return to the conditions prevailing between 1920 and 1932 is not impossible.

The Netherlands

The Netherlands had, before the adoption of P.R. in 1917, a multiple-party system of related parties, several of which would combine in an election to obtain a majority. If they succeeded, they had direct popular backing for the cabinet which they formed. The first result of P.R. was to make campaign alliances unnecessary, and popular endorsements for governments impossible. Several new parties developed which could hardly have been successful under the majority system, and the formation of the governments encountered at times all but insuperable difficulties. Coalitions were formed among the various Rightist parties, which were separated by denominational and other issues. In 1925 the coalition between the Catholic and the two Protestant parties broke down on account of the refusal of the Protestant parties to continue the diplomatic relations of The Netherlands with the Vatican. It took three months to form a new cabinet, and for fifteen years conditions were never again satisfactory. Between 1925 and 1940 no formal party coalition commanding a majority could be formed. Therefore, on the eve of World War II, conditions were almost as bad in The Netherlands as in Belgium. The cabinets headed by Colijn and by DeGeer were characterized by little positive action, but provided the occasion for a number of disquieting headlines in American newspapers.[21]

P.R. also led to the rise of radicalism, making possible the success, even if a limited success, of the Communist and National Socialist parties. No election was held at a time when these parties were at the peak of their strength. Therefore, the drawbacks resulting from the parliamentary representation of these parties were largely limited to disturbing scenes which they were able to cause in parliament.[22]

At the end of the First World War,[23] the political situation was simplified by a fundamental change at the Left. The old Socialist party combined with other elements to form the "Partij van de Arbeid," which was, as the name indicates, based on the example of the British Labour party.[23(a)] Less doctrinaire than its predecessor, it was able to enter the government and form relatively strong combinations first with the Catholics, and later with the Catholics and two minor parties. This meant a noticeable improvement over pre-1940 conditions.

It is hardly necessary to repeat that The Netherlands would have been unlikely to experience, under a majority system, the very strained conditions under which their democratic institutions operated for a full fifteen years before the Second World War reached their shores. If conditions have been better since the liberation, few would want to claim that this development, which may be temporary, bears any relationship to P.R. The mere fact that under a majority system the Communist party would be unlikely to secure any electoral success, and that no Fascist party could ever rise again, would offer political assurances which P.R. is unable to give.

Switzerland

The Swiss experience with P.R. has now moved into the center of the argument presented on behalf of P.R., so far as the practical results of that system of voting are concerned. Thirty years ago,

Belgium ceased to be a commendable example, and the formation of a six-party coalition in Ireland in 1948 renders P.R. in that country less attractive than it was under the one-party governments of Cosgrave and De Valera. What happened in these two countries has made it increasingly difficult to deny that P.R. tends to destroy one-party majorities; English political history after the First World War adds its weight to the argument as, with the exception of the election of 1931, which is obviously not comparable, no party ever secured a majority of the popular vote.

Swiss experience seems to show the way out of the difficulties to be expected under a multiple-party system. Switzerland has a National Council roughly corresponding to the American House of Representatives, and a Council of States corresponding to the American Senate, though it is less powerful. The two parliaments jointly elect the members of the Federal Council, which constitutes the executive. Members of the Federal Council are elected for four years. Custom decrees, however, that they be reelected as long as they are willing to serve. Nor are they expected to resign if the parliament or the people (the latter by means of plebiscite) reject a law which they have recommended. The result seems to indicate that Switzerland has shown how to secure political stability in spite of a multiplicity of parties. There are no cabinet crises and Switzerland's government functions better than that of any other democratic country in Europe with the exception of England. It has often been recommended that countries which adopt P.R. should avail themselves of this experience, and base their constitutions on the Swiss model.

The question arises whether it is possible to adapt Swiss experience to the political life of other countries. In the first place, Switzerland's population is small. With approximately 4.5 million, it is comparable to that of a large city such as Paris, London, or New York, rather than to that of a large country. If comparatively small size means fewer problems, a similar effect follows from Switzerland's traditional policy of neutrality. Switzerland has avoided participation in two world wars, and has not been exposed to the problems resulting from these wars, in particular to that of inflation. If we consider how severely the governments of France, Italy and Germany had to suffer from post-war inflations, it will become apparent that this is a major consideration.

Similar consequences arise from the fact that Switzerland is divided into twenty-two states, called cantons. These retain a considerable degree of self-government, and the scope of activities reserved to the federal government is correspondingly lessened. Thus the burden placed on the Swiss national government is a great deal lighter than the burden which even a country like Belgium has to carry, not to mention the major European nations.

Nor must we overlook that initiative and referendum play a large part in Swiss constitutional practice. The decision of the people naturally takes place on the basis of majority rule. This factor induces a tendency on the part of the political parties to unite for the purpose of securing a majority in the electorate, which is very jealous of its privileges.[24] This is not the place to investigate whether initiative and referendum are generally commendable in national government. In Switzerland they have, on the whole, worked well enough and brought about a type of cooperation by the P.R. parties, which would hardly have developed had not this outside pressure been constantly borne in mind.

Finally, it must be taken into consideration that the composition of the Federal Council (the executive) is not *as* dissimilar to the composition of a government under the parliamentary system as it might appear. Until 1892, all federal councilors were members of the so-called Radical Democratic party which, at that time, had an over-all majority in parliament, although not in the electorate. In 1892 the Catholics were given a share, and in 1929 the Peasants' party. During this period, the Federal Council had the appearance of a non-Socialist coalition, which held a majority in the federal parliament as well as in the electorate. This coalition was not, however, threatened by a swing of the pendulum; it was a permanent majority. Had this not been the case, but had, for example, the Socialist party secured a parliamentary majority backed up by a majority of the electorate in referendum, this would have been likely to entail wholesale changes in the composition of the Federal Council.

In 1943 the continued growth of the Socialist party did have the result that one of its members was elevated to the Federal Council. In this body he has not, however, attempted to make a Socialist policy, but, like the remainder of the Federal Council, limited himself to the role of an administrator of current affairs, in this case of financial policy. It would hardly seem likely that such an attitude could be continued if the Socialist party should ever win an over-all majority. In that case pressure for a Socialist policy would be so great that it would have been difficult for non-Socialist members of the executive to carry on.

Swiss P.R. was introduced by a popular referendum as a result of a coalition of minorities; it immediately destroyed the parliamentary majority of the Radical Democrats. The subsequent splitting up of parties was limited by the fact that each one of the twenty-two cantons forms a constituency of its own; no surpluses can be transferred from one of the cantons to the other. The smallest canton elects only one member of the National Council, and, of course, it does so under the majority system; likewise, the members of the Council of States are elected by majority vote. True P.R. can, on the federal level, be seen in operation only in the elections to the National Council in the larger cantons.

Among the new parties which developed under P.R. the Peasants' and Citizens' party was the largest. It had enough local strongholds to be a factor even under the majority system, although success would have been on a much more limited scale. Besides, the party would have had to emphasize a general (rather than a specific interest) appeal, and to present candidates acceptable to a cross section of the voters at least in a rural constituency.

A number of small parties developed whose success is a result of P.R. The height of the splintering process was reached in the election of 1935, when the total number of successful parties was fourteen. In these elections the Communists elected two candidates, and the more or less Fascist National Front, one. Neither of the extremist parties could have expected any seats under the majority system. It might be added that the National Front was banned during the War, and that the Communist party was banned temporarily. More recently, the Communists combined with left-wing Socialists to form the so-called Labor party, which elected seven candidates in 1947 and would also have been a doubtful entry under a majority system.

Returning to the 1935 election, we find a party called "Independents," led by the merchant Duttweiler, whose surprising political strength lay in his appeal to the consumer, as well as to those tired of the party system as it had become under P.R. This party could hardly have developed under a majority system. After P.R. made it possible to force the initial breach the party has now, in some areas, developed considerable strength. Mr. Duttweiler himself was elected to the Council of States in the canton of Zurich. — The remaining parties are too small to require specific discussion.

During the 1930's Switzerland was strongly affected by the world economic crisis. A political crisis[25] developed in its wake, which could assume its particular form and intensity only on account of P.R. There was general dissatisfaction with the existing party system, which was blamed for its bureaucracy and mediocrity, and the "low level" which it introduced into the National Council. The country's leading newspaper, the *Neue Zuercher Zeitung,* in fact, in an article published on November 12, 1935, spoke of the possibility that P.R. might lead to conditions in which neither the parliament nor the executive would be able to fulfill their functions.[26]

During the 1930's several members of the executive left office for political reasons. Thus, Mr. Haeberlin resigned when the law providing for emergency powers to maintain order had been rejected. A little later Mr. Musy resigned because he could not conduct Swiss financial policy as he deemed necessary. Finally, Mr. Schulthess, the head of the Department of Commerce, resigned after twenty-three years in office. He too was unwilling to remain the nominal head of his department while a policy was pursued which he could not approve.

In Switzerland then, as in other countries, men of real worth will not long continue to hold office if they are expected to carry out a policy which they consider radically wrong. It is, of course, the purpose of parliamentary systems to tie "men" and "measures" together, and bring about a change in the "men" if there is a substantial change in the "measures." The limited problems to be solved by the Swiss national government have so far not led to a complete change in "measures" and, therefore, a complete change in "men" has not been necessary. It is, however, difficult to see how this experience could be duplicated in other countries, where the national governments have more comprehensive tasks, and where a swing of the pendulum may bring about a complete shift in basic policy. Who, for example, would have expected Mr. Churchill to remain in a cabinet which had to carry out Labour's program of nationalizations?

We can only conclude that if the Swiss political system has proven itself well adapted to Swiss conditions, there is no reason to expect that it could be successfully imitated in any large country. Besides, the Swiss system operated more smoothly under the majority system than it does under P.R., even if the power of the vested interests connected with the latter makes the chances of any attempt to abolish it appear dubious.

Finland

Finland might have been treated as a Scandinavian country; this is often done, although reasons have been given why Finland should be regarded as a Baltic nation. Actually, the country shows political traits of its own, which do not conform to any general pattern. This is the reason why we did not follow any geographic consideration in discussing P.R. in Finland. P.R. was adopted in 1906, and maintained in 1919 when the parliamentary system was instituted. The Finnish constitution differed from the usual picture by giving to the president rights which exceed even those of the president of the Reich under the Weimar Constitution. Thanks to the prevalence of weak governments, these rights have been effectively exercised, and this has been done in the interests of democracy and stability.

So far as the specific effects of P.R. are concerned, suffice it to quote Dr. Braunias, who, in 1932, referred to them in these words: "Thus, all cabinets were coalition cabinets which carried the germ of disintegration in themselves. Temporarily, governments of civil servants were formed as transition governments (as that of Mr. Cajander), but more frequently minority governments were resorted to. No government existed for more than a year, and the average duration was 10 months." [27] After 1932, there were a few governments with longer tenure, but in the main conditions remained as Dr. Braunias described them. The cabinet of Mr. Kekkonen, formed in March 1950, was the thirty-third, if we begin the count with November, 1917, when the country became independent.

Finland, well known for her trials in the field of foreign affairs, suffered from considerable difficulties also in the domestic field. In

1930, there developed the so-called Lapuan movement, which Professor Loewenstein rightly characterizes as semi-Fascist.[28] It arose in reaction to the Communist party, which in the 1929 election had, thanks to P.R., secured a large representation in parliament, preventing the latter from enacting widely advocated constitutional reform measures. The Lapuans similarly demanded an end to the political instability, and a strengthening of the executive. Under their pressure, a few reforms were adopted, one of which provided that parties aiming at a forcible change of the political and social order be banned. In the words of Dr. Loewenstein:

"When, however, after the elimination of the Red danger, the Lapuan movement became increasingly overbearing, and also resorted to lawlessness and terrorism against the constitutional government, the acting cabinet, under the presidency of the 'liberator' of Finland, Svinhufvud, invoked against the Lapuans the same laws by which Communism had been crushed. In December 1931, the Lapuans, in the Maensillae uprising, tried to seize power by armed rebellion, but the movement collapsed immediately, when it encountered, in March 1932, militant application to the extraordinary powers. Additional legislation was adopted to curb the activities of the Fascist movement." [29]

In this way Finland was able to prevent a victory of the extremists, but her parliamentary life did not become a model of stability.

The following quotation from a dispatch by George Axelsson to *The New York Times* of March 12, 1950, is characteristic of a situation in which the country found itself repeatedly: "Finland's cabinet crisis is now in its second week, and the possibility has been raised that unless President Juhov K. Paasikivi is able to form a government soon he may dissolve the Diet and call parliamentary elections sixteen months ahead of schedule." [30] On March 18, a coalition cabinet of three Centrist groups was formed which did, however, command only 75 seats in a Parliament of 200 members. Conservative support, to be arranged from case to case, was expected to bring its strength to 108 votes.

Finland is used to such crises, and in the long run she has always been able to overcome them. Nobody will, however, want to contend that a democracy of this type is a tower of strength. Certainly, under the majority system, the people of Finland would find a clearer and more effective expression for their will to freedom.

POSITIVE AND NEGATIVE DEMOCRACY IN SMALLER COUNTRIES

Additional Countries

Only a few supplementary remarks can be made in regard to other countries. The fact that the Russian Constituent Assembly of 1917 was elected [31] under P.R. would not have to be mentioned here except for one reason. Proponents of P.R. always claim that what they call "full expression of the popular will" by P.R. makes a parliament more respected by the people, and less subject to the attacks of violence. The Russian Constituent Assembly, to be sure, met after the Communist revolution had taken place, and therefore the frustration of the attempt to establish a democracy in Russia cannot be laid to P.R. Yet, when the Assembly had just begun its deliberations, a few ignorant sailors were able to order it to terminate its work as soon as it had become clear that a majority was opposed to the Bolshevist dictatorship. It would be easy to quote at length from the publications of the proponents of P.R. in the United States, in 1917, as well as in Great Britain, to show that they took great satisfaction in the establishment of P.R. in Russia, and claimed that this would go far toward assuring Russian democracy of success. The United States and England were chided for their failure to imitate this progressive example.

Brief reference might be made to the small Baltic country of Latvia, which in 1922 acquired the unique distinction of establishing full proportionality between votes cast and seats obtained. The result was a splitting up of parties for which there is no parallel. Thus, in the election of 1931, when proportionality had already been somewhat limited, no fewer than twelve parties secured one each of the 100 seats in the Chamber. Only two parties obtained more than ten seats (one of them fourteen, and the other twenty-one), and the total number of parties winning seats was twenty-seven. There were seventeen parties which failed to elect candidates, making a total of forty-four parties in a country with a population of less than two million.[32]

In conclusion let us mention just a few figures. The countries which adopted P.R. in which democracy failed (excluding Russia) are Italy, Germany, Austria, Poland, Latvia, Lithuania, Estonia, Bulgaria, Greece, Yugoslavia and Czechoslovakia. The total population of these countries was (as of 1937) 198 million. The nations which have P.R. and in which, up to the outbreak of the war in 1939, democracy had survived, are Ireland, Belgium, Luxembourg, The Netherlands,

Switzerland, Denmark, Sweden, Norway and Finland. Their total population, as of the same date, was 40.6 million. That is a ratio of almost five to one. To be sure, this enumeration yields nothing but a statistical correlation. Enough has been said above, however, to take the mortality rate of eighty per cent, which this comparison reveals for a period of not much more than half of one generation, as a fair indication of the political effects of P.R. Compare with that the long duration of democratic institutions in countries with a plurality system, such as the United States and Great Britain!

Section II

POSITIVE AND NEGATIVE DEMOCRACY AFTER WORLD WAR II

Chapter 7. France

Resistance and Reconstruction

France was the first country to undertake the task of democratic reconstruction after the war. Much thought was given to this topic by the leaders of the Resistance, who were aware that much of the weakness of pre-war France was due to a fragile constitutional framework. The question was how to effect the transition to a more stable constitution in a manner which would be democratic and yet avoid extensive squabbling over constitutional issues during a time when all the energies of France were required for the purpose of economic reconstruction. It seemed that a solution might be found by devising a new constitution which General DeGaulle could, after his return to France, put into effect by decree. A year or two after the Liberation, the new constitution was to be submitted to the voters for ratification.

The major non-Communist Resistance groups entrusted the problem of constitutional reform to the so-called "General Committee of Studies" (French abbreviation, C.G.E.). This Committee called upon young Michel Debré for a draft. Debré secured opinions from interested experts, and submitted a draft which a majority of the "General Committee of Studies" accepted with minor changes.[1]

The background of the new draft was set forth by Debré in a clandestine publication in these words: "The French Republic of yesterday . . . was feeble, incoherent, and incapable of maintaining French power; it has led us to defeat and to the regime of Vichy. The Republic which France expects must be strong, organized, even authoritarian." [2] Debré was aware that some of his associates were in favor of copying the presidential system as it exists in the United States; there was even the demand for modifications of the American system, designed to strengthen the power of the executive. Debré rejected this solution, and advocated a revised form of parliamentary government which, in all essentials, was inspired by the English example. He defended himself against the charge that the parliamentary system was a specific English form of government, emphasizing its French precedents, and adding that the logical requirements of democracy were the same in all countries.

Debré concentrated first on the position of the president of the Republic, which he wanted to strengthen through election by a special college composed of representatives of provincial, local and other assemblies, as well as of the members of parliament. His term of office was to be twelve years without the possibility of reelection. The most important point on which, under Debré's constitution, the position of the president would have differed from that of the president of the Third Republic was to be an unlimited right of dissolution. This right was, in fact, to be exercised by the prime minister, and to be used only for the purpose of deciding a conflict between the government and parliament by means of an appeal to the people.

Debré paid special attention to the system of voting, of the crucial importance of which he was keenly aware. He wanted to ban the second ballot which, in his opinion, led to shameful political bargaining, and had been invented by Napoleon III in order to multiply the means of intimidating and bribing the electorate. At the same time he wanted to eliminate the old system of voting in single-member constituencies which, on account of the absence of organized parties, had led to the election of too many local celebrities. Furthermore, he opposed P.R. unequivocably, stating that it "provokes the multiplicity of parties, which falsifies the meaning of the parliamentary system by not permitting it any majority, — in other words, by not permitting any policy to develop within a parliament." He proposed that elections under the plurality system he held for each *département,* with the seats in the particular *département,* usually four or five, going to the candidates with the largest number of votes. This system, he contended, was simple and clear.

Debré also intended to adopt a number of other reforms which, for example, would have limited the duration of parliamentary sessions, the possibility of "interpellations" of the government by deputies, abolished permanent committees, and the like.[3] One is inclined to conclude that some of these provisions might have introduced into the French constitutional system a measure of the rigidity which Debré himself wanted to avoid. At the same time, however, it is obvious that, in all essentials, the plan was workable. Minor details could have been ironed out on the basis of practical experience. Under a constitution of the proposed type a clear parliamentary majority, and its leadership by a government capable of governing, were likely to develop. Where these two conditions are granted, there exists the driving power needed for further reforms.

Debré had not reckoned with one particular factor. In the words of Gordon Wright: "The C.G.E.'s hopes were quickly wrecked on the hitherto submerged rock of Communist opposition." [4] At that time the position of the Communists on constitutional problems was not known. The French Communists had regarded attention to the problems of political form as un-Marxist, since in their view the social structure determined political life. Still, they knew how to appraise political facts when they encountered them. Debré's constitution was certain to strengthen the executive. It might, in the long run, have succeeded in giving France a two-party system, and a government comparable to the British in stability. No matter how popular the Communists were during that period they knew that they could not attain a parliamentary majority themselves. Therefore, it was likely that the advantages of a strong government would come to rest in the hands of their opponents. Hence it seemed wiser to reject the plan for a strong executive, and in particular the plan for a system of voting favoring a clearcut popular decision, which, when it came, could not favor the Communists.

Early in 1944, a Communist underground publication contained an article by the party's leading journalist, Georges Cogniot, which demanded what was later called "government by assembly." [5] France was to have a unicameral parliament, elected by P.R. and in full control of the country's policies. It was obvious that the assembly would not govern by itself, and that P.R. would create a typical condition of political pluralism, within which bargaining among parties and party leaders would determine whatever common policy would emerge. Such a situation might be bad for France, but it maximized the opportunities of the Communists. The weaker the executive, the stronger the Communist forces inside and outside parliament. Under P.R., the Communists were certain to send a powerful bloc into the parliament, which, as long as their cooperation was deemed essential by other parties, would give them a veto power comparable to that later inserted into the provisions governing the Security Council of the United Nations Charter.

At about the same time, DeGaulle decided to turn away from the Resistance with which he would have preferred to work, and to shift his support to the old political parties, purged as much as possible of collaborators. When constitutional discussions were placed upon this level, the victory of weak government was certain. So was the adoption of P.R. The Communists and the Socialists were committed to P.R., as was most of the French Right. The newly-constituted Popular Republican Movement (M.R.P.) decided in favor of P.R. in the hope that this system of voting would do most to facilitate its rapid rise to the status of a major political party. Its leaders were, at that time, probably not aware of an article contributed by Jacques Maritain, whom the Popular Republicans regarded as their principal political philosopher, to the New York magazine, *La République Française,* in December 1943, in the course of which he said:

"In order to eliminate, in addition, every attempt to introduce the 'Trojan horse' of proportional representation into the democratic structure, let us note that just as the common good is not a simple sum of individual goods, so the common will is not a simple sum of individual wills. Universal suffrage does not have the aim to represent simply atomic wills and opinions, but to give form and expression, according to their respective importance, to the *common currents* of opinion and of will which exist in the nation. The political line of a democracy must frankly and decidedly be determined by the majority, while the parties composing the minority play the part, also fundamental, of the *critical* element, in an opposition which is not destructive, but as much as possible constructive and cooperative. Thus the majority and the minority express the will of the people in opposite, but conplementary and equally real, fashions."

This argument of Maritain disposes, of course, also of the claim that P.R. is just. To assume that it is, means to assume that the common will does not exist, and that the expression of particular wills is the only purpose of the act of voting.

De Gaulle's decision in favor of reliance upon the reconstituted political parties was, to a large extent, due to his desire to overcome the impression that he intended to govern as a dictator. Such charges were numerous, in particular in England and in the United States, where the requirements of constitutional reconstruction were ignored in regard to France as they were ignored in regard to every other country. In addition, the desire not to see a continuation of Pétainism under another name had the result not only of reestablishing the Third Republic with its major weaknesses, but of adding sources of weakness from which the Third Republic was free. Thus, the tall figure of Pétain cast its shadow across all constitutional discussions. Negative democracy developed in a form which can only be called "frightened democracy."

The spring and the summer of 1945 brought the most important decisions in regard to France's constitutional future. It was ultimately decided that the voters were to be offered the choice between a return to the Third Republic and the election of a Constituent Assembly. Similarly, they were to decide whether the new parliament, if it was to act as a Constituent Assembly, would have to follow certain rules in regard to the executive. These rules received much attention at that time, but they merely anticipated the ineffectual restrictions on the right of the assembly to overthrow the cabinet, which were to form part of the constitution of the Fourth Republic.

Debré stated later that the decision relating to the system of voting practically predetermines the essential features of a democratic constitution. He would have agreed with what Professor Dawson said: "Parties lie beneath the discussion of almost all governmental activities like the postulates underlying a book of Euclid; they provide the fundamental assumptions which are essential to the validity of the argument." [6] Political parties provide, in other words, the dynamism without which the entire machinery of democratic government would lie motionless. Democratic constitutions cannot determine the actual method of integration; all they can do is to leave the way open for it.[7] "The people," whom the constitution calls upon to rule, cannot act by themselves; they need to be organized into large political groups of an extra-constitutional nature before they are capable of any coherent action. These groups we call political parties.

Everything, or nearly everything, depended upon the type of parties which would operate the French constitutional system, and the parties were bound to be shaped by the system of voting. There had been ample warnings as to the type of parties which P.R. would produce before the war, and Debré as well as René Capitant repeated them to DeGaulle after the Liberation. Yet, DeGaulle felt that he had to accept the party leaders' preference for P.R. Besides, he felt that a Constituent Assembly "was a special kind of body which ought to reflect as faithfully as possible all the main currents of opinion in the country." [8] The latter argument also played a part in the Italian discussions. It suffers from the obvious defect that a Constituent Assembly must have a majority in order to function. Without a majority it cannot sustain a government. It will even find it difficult to write a workable constitution since the kind of compromise which P.R. parties conclude usually consists of meaningless formulae, which is unlikely to be conducive to effective government.

Lastly, it must be borne in mind that P.R., once instituted, will perpetuate itself; it can no longer be rejected at will. Those parties which owe their existence or strength to P.R. will not vote for its abolition; neither will the party leaders want to relinquish the power over their fellow party members which they enjoy under that system of voting. In the struggle between reason and vested interests the odds favor the latter.

Two Majority Elections

Before French national elections took place under P.R. an effective contrast was provided by two elections held under the majority system. The first were the local elections held in April and May 1945, and the second the provincial elections (élections cantonales), held in September.[9] These were local elections, to be sure, but they were the first elections after the Liberation. The political parties made every possible effort to assert themselves in order to establish their national strength, and to get their organization into shape for the election to the Constituent Assembly. Local factors did assert themselves on occasion, in particular in the municipal elections. If, however, we take the result of the whole, especially in the provincial elections, there was general agreement that the result reflected the national party trends.

Both elections showed strong losses of votes on the part of the Right and the Radical Socialists. Rightist groups were strongly compromised by collaboration during the war, as were to a lesser extent the Radicals. Some of the seats and votes lost by the rightist groups accrued to the M.R.P.; the remainder went to the Left, which was stronger than ever before. Communists as well as Socialists gained by comparison with the last provincial elections under the Third Republic, held in 1937. Yet, as in the preceding municipal elections, the Socialists gained much more than the Communists. The Socialists secured a total of 811 members of the provincial councils, the Radicals 607, the Communists 328, and the M.R.P. 230. The remainder went to smaller parties. Léon Blum said, without being contradicted, "We have the wind in the sails." [10] And the French journalist, Leduc, began an article with these words: "In the light of the result of recent cantonal elections, France seems likely to be the next big country in Europe where a conspicuous trend to democratic socialism will triumph." [11] It was generally assumed that this trend would continue in the elections to the Constituent Assembly, and that the French Socialist party might, even if at some distance, follow in the footsteps of the British Labour party which, a few months earlier, had won an absolute majority in the House of Commons.

Those who harbored such expectations overlooked that what happened under the majority system was different from what was certain to happen under P.R. The number of votes obtained by the Socialists and their allies was about twenty-five per cent of the total, only slightly, perhaps by about two per cent, larger than the percentage obtained by the Communists. Yet, as mentioned before, the Socialists secured 811 seats and the Communists only 328. Even at that time, when the prestige of the Communist party was at its peak, the vital requirement of campaign alliances operated against the Communists. This results also from a comparison between the Communist and the Radical positions. The Radicals, standing exactly in the center of French politics, secured about fourteen per cent of the votes but, with 607 seats, almost twice as many as the Communists obtained with about twenty-five per cent of the total popular vote.

P.R. Enters the Picture

The elections to the Constituent Assembly on October 21, 1945, were the first ones to be held under P.R. That system of voting was subsequently used for the elections to the Second Constituent Assembly of June 2, 1946, and for the election of the First National Assembly under the new constitution, held November 10, 1946.[12] (National Assembly is the name of the approximate equivalent of the Chamber of Deputies during the Third Republic. The powers of the National

Assembly were, of course, greater than those of the Chamber of Deputies.) The following table gives the results for the parliamentary groups rather than for party lists; this was done because the presentation of joint lists by certain parties does not indicate the relative strength of the partners:

Distribution of seats in the two Constituent Assemblies, and in the first National Assembly chosen under the new constitution (the groups are listed as they sat from left to right, with their strength as it stood in each session. For the National Assembly, figures are given as of July 1947).[13]

	First Constituent Assembly	Second Constituent Assembly	National Assembly
Communists	152	146	168
Union of Republicans and Resisters (M.U.R.F.)	9	7	15
Triumph of Democratic Liberties in Algeria (Messali)	..	..	5
Algerian Manifesto (Abbas)	..	11	..
Socialists	143	129	105
U.D.S.R.	29	21	27
Radical Socialists	28	32	43
Algerian Moslems (Bendjelloul)	7	..	6
M.R.P.	150	169	167
Peasant group	10	9	8
Independent Republicans	19	23	28
P.R.L.	35	35	35
Madagascar Nationalists	2	2	3
Unaffiliated	2	2	8
Totals	586	586	618

The most striking feature of the election to the First Constituent Assembly is the shift in the relative strengh of Socialists and Communists. Whereas the Socialists had been clearly in the lead in the elections held under the majority system, P.R. caused them to drop immediately, first to the second, and then to the third place. The Communists were, thanks to P.R., no longer dependent upon campaign alliances. All votes cast for them could, without difficulty, be turned into seats. The Socialists, on the other hand, found themselves in the middle of a crossfire between the Communists at the Left and the other parties, in particular the M.R.P. in the center. The time was to come when the Socialists seemed in danger of losing their major party status.

Still, the Socialists were at first inclined to declare themselves satisfied with the result. Their leader, Léon Blum, wrote an article shortly after the election to the First Constituent Assembly, in which he congratulated himself on the results of P.R., since the expected splitting up of parties had not occurred.[14] The concentration of political strength in the three mass parties of Communists, Socialists and M.R.P., he believed, would facilitate the task of governing. He overlooked that the slight success of small parties was due, not to P.R., but to a deliberate limitation of the proportionality between votes cast and seats obtained. Elections were held within each *département*, and the larger ones were subdivided, in order to prevent the election of more than nine deputies in any one constituency. The average number of deputies to be elected per constituency lay between four and five. There was no national list, and whatever votes had not been utilized in the *départements* were lost. This factor alone meant a sharp reduction in the chances of small parties, which were further handicapped by certain technical provisions in regard to the distribution of seats.

M. Raoul Husson, the author of the widely-known volumes on the elections of 1945 and 1946, has shown in detail how small, or comparatively small, parties suffered from these provisions.[15] The percentage of votes cast for the party, which could not be utilized for seats, rose in the case of some smaller groups to 65.1. The Radicals who, during the Third Republic, had been the leading party, saw, in October 1945, 56.6 per cent of their votes unutilized. They tried to prevent this result by forming common lists with other groups, which in 1945 included the Communists. They also decided not to present lists of candidates where their chances were too small. As a result, they were able to reduce the percentage of unutilized votes, in November, 1946, to 29.5. Yet, they were angry with the election law, and referred to it as "a bastard system." It might also be mentioned that in the elections of November, 1946, the number of votes needed to secure a seat oscillated between 31,000 for the Communists and 62,000 for an unofficial DeGaullist group.

The question arises whether such provisions against small parties make the consequences of P.R. more tolerable or not. They certainly improve statistical appearances, and the proponents of P.R. are proud of them. On the other hand, small parties, such as the Radicals, who suffered so much from the limitations of proportionality, were better equipped to assume their share in carrying on the government of the country than some of their larger rivals. The Communists, who were always the chief beneficiaries of the limitation of proportionality, eventually ceased to be eligible for government participation. Therefore, it would have been a great deal wiser to have adopted an undiluted system of P.R., with the inevitable result of assisting the formation of smaller parties, than to have a system whose principal political effect was to strengthen the position of the party which was soon to form the biggest stumbling block for French governments.

The effects of the deliberate limitation of P.R. could have been foreseen. There were, for example, discussions in Germany between 1930 and 1933, which had the purpose of establishing a majority in the German Reichstag in spite of P.R., which was prescribed by the Weimar Constitution. It had been proposed to divide Germany into constituencies with three seats each, and not to permit any utilization of surpluses. The suggestion was rejected because at that time it was already obvious that the National Socialists and the Communists would have derived considerable advantage from such a provision. There is little use in promoting a concentration of political strength upon large parties if these parties are radical and unable to perform the integrating functions of a political party. Under a majority system, large size and moderation go hand in hand. The dependence upon the marginal voter in the center forces all parties to emphasize their moderation during the campaign, and to live up to it subsequently. P.R. created in France the typical picture of a multiplicity of unrelated, even though comparatively large, parties. If such parties emphasize nothing but their dissimilarity during the campaign, and minimize anything which might unite the country, they only demonstrate that they are agents of disintegration rather than of integration.

Judging the results of the first election under the new system, the authoritative yearbook, *L'Année Politique,* rightly stated that they had led to "great modifications in French political traditions." [16] If ever proof were needed for the tenuous character of political traditions it was provided by the abrupt political change France witnessed in the fall of 1945. The political observer had some difficulty in deciding whether he was in the France of the ancient tradition of political individualism, or in the Germany of the Weimar Republic. French political life showed all the characteristics of the "pluralist parties state." The parties had developed into "monolithic" political structures. The individual deputies, once inspired by the feeling that every one of them was a king, had become mere pawns. As the correspondent of *The Manchester Guardian* put it: "The deputies, once elected, will follow the party leaders for fear of losing their places on the lists of candidates." [17]

Nor was the basic condition much better so far as the individual voter was concerned. In the words of Michel Debré: "With us, in order to become members of a political party it is first necessary to make a profession of faith, and to abandon one's critical spirit." [18] Inevitably, there followed a doctrinal petrification of the parties. As later developed, seasoned observers, such as Léon Blum, who for so long had demanded P.R. for the very purpose of strengthening the element of "doctrines" in political life, were appalled by this process. They had a feeling comparable to that of Goethe's "magician's apprentice," who first was proud of having succeeded in summoning the spirits which his master used to conjure up, but then terrified when he could not get rid of them. Naturally, what was correct "doctrine" was determined by the party bureaucracy, which decided whether a particular candidate was to be given a safe place on the party's list or not.

The individual voter had lost as much under this multiple system of unrelated parties as the deputy. Before 1940, each election had ended with a clearcut victory of either the Right or the Left; as mentioned before, what destroyed the results of this clear popular decision was primarily the fact that the government, in case of conflict with parliament, was not able to renew its contact with the people by dissolution of the Chamber. Under P.R. the French voter could do nothing except join one of the rival party columns, all of which were marching off in different directions. Political confusion was the inevitable result. A report sent to *The Chicago Sun* shortly after the elections to the First National Assembly under the new constitution carries the headline: "Who Won? France Asks After Vote." [19]

What the individual deputy and the voter lost was not gained by the National Assembly. French experience once again demonstrates that "government by assembly" is impossible. When decisions were made, it was done by political parties, which, however, were rarely able to agree among themselves. Governments were coalitions on the Weimar model. The parties "delegated" certain ministers to the government; they "instructed" these ministers, they expected all important decisions of the cabinet to be referred to them for final disposal and, when they decided that it was opportune to do so, they "withdrew their ministers from the government." France had become what was called "The Republic of Parties," to give the title of a book which discusses the phenomenon in detail.

Uneasiness developed soon even in the ranks of sincere supporters of democratic government. Thus, the weekly, *Temps Présent,* which expressed the views of the M.R.P. intelligentsia, wrote (in its issue of July 5, 1946):

"The French government has presented itself to the Chamber.
"It has received 517 votes.
"One knew that in advance.
"One knows everything in advance with our prefabricated automatons of deputies.
"The principal argument of the partisan of a bicameral system is that a single and sovereign Chamber might easily be carried along by passion.
"*Mon Dieu!* Our single Chamber Constituent Assembly does not show more passion than conserved veal in the can."

Similarly, in March 1947, Henri Defournel commented as follows on the widely-held hope that P.R. would lead to a rejuvenation of the political élite:

"Unfortunately, one must admit, that for its debut the Fourth Republic has put on the shoes of the Third. Not only has it collected people for its leading positions who almost all belong to the formerly leading group of the past regime — that one could admit, and it is not forbidden to appeal to the experience of those who are without blame, as is the case with several of them. The most grave fact is, however, that parliament has created the appearance of wanting to renew the worst traditions of the past regime, and that the Byzantine bargains to which the struggle for the positions of presiding officers of parliament have led, are not apt to rehabilitate the prestige of the parliamentary system. 'The Fourth Republic is dead,' thus one has already proclaimed. It would not take many weeks like the one which has just passed in order to cause public opinion to return to an anti-parliamentarism, which would lead it straight to the acceptance of a dictatorship." [20]

FRANCE

Additional features developed which did not make the new version of parliamentary government more popular. There arose, for example, what French writers called "the new feudalism." When, at long last, enough parties had agreed to form a coalition, they did not do so in order to act as a unit. The principal reason why they were willing to join was the power to be derived from control of the ministries assigned to their members. They would administer them as a kind of feudal fief, appoint their own followers to all positions, and pursue their own policies. This condition was particularly grave as long as the Communists were members of the government, but the basic difficulty continued after they had been expelled.

A feature of similar interest is the growing importance of the president of the Republic. The constitution had limited his functions strictly; in particular, he was no longer able to appoint the prime minister and the cabinet. He could merely designate a candidate for the position of prime minister, who then would first confront the National Assembly alone, in order to receive a vote of confidence, which required a majority of all the members of the Assembly. Subsequently, the designated prime minister could select his cabinet, and the formal appointment was made by the president. The clumsiness of this procedure should have been clear from the start. Prime ministers who, like Queuille and Bidault, were aware of the nature of the political situation, circumvented part of these provisions by selecting their prospective cabinet members, and making them agree on some of the outstanding issues of the day before they presented themselves to the National Assembly. So far it has always been possible for someone to secure an absolute majority of the votes in the Chamber, but it was not difficult to foresee a condition under which this would not be feasible. During the Third Republic a majority of those who voted had sufficed. If at any time in 1948 and 1949, new elections had been held under the prevailing system of P.R., it would have been unlikely that any government would have secured a majority of those who voted, let alone a majority of all the deputies in the National Assembly.[20(a)]

Vincent Auriol, the Socialist leader who had been elected President of the Republic, soon became, contrary to his own expectations, the "guardian of the constitution." He did not and could not interpret his functions literally. Instead, he regarded it as his duty to support various prime ministers in the task of securing and maintaining a cabinet to the best of his ability, and to enable this cabinet to function. He took a bold step in May 1947, when the Communist members of the cabinet Ramadier contended that they could vote against the government and yet retain their ministries. Such behavior completely jeopardized cabinet solidarity. Ramadier could have resigned and formed a new cabinet without the Communists. There was, however, a general feeling that it would not be wise to make this concession to the Communists. Instead, the Prime Minister and the President agreed on a declaration that the Communist ministers had left the cabinet. Simultaneously, the President of the Republic, upon the recommendation of the Prime Minister, assigned other ministers to the task of taking charge of the ministries which had been in the hands of the Communists.[21] The constitution contained no authorization for this step. Yet, it seemed to be a political necessity and, apparently, Auriol succeeded in establishing a precedent. His prestige rose considerably when French public opinion supported his action.

A new occasion for the President of the Republic to assert his authority arose after DeGaulle's victory in the municipal elections of October 1947. There was a feeling of crisis and uncertainty in France, and the General demanded that the National Assembly be dissolved and new elections be held. The only legal way to do so would have been, at that time, for the Chamber to shorten its term of office by law, a power which was implied in Article 6 of the Constitution. This, of course, the Assembly was not willing to do. The President of the Republic declared that it was within its right, and that its continued existence was absolutely legal. On May 31, 1948, he made a speech at Quimper in which he emphasized that while he was not the president of a political party, he was the President of the Republic. As he put it: "I beg you to believe that I would not watch the death of the Republic without taking up again, if necessary, the fight for the Republic in the ranks." As President of the Republic, he reemphasized that he did not desire to be involved in party conflicts, but added: "It is necessary that I should intervene in the name of the public good to appease passions and smooth out difficulties."[22] These events demonstrate once again that political developments under P.R. have a logic of their own. As in pre-Fascist Italy, in Weimar Germany, or in monarchist Belgium, the head of the state attempted to fill to the best of his ability the vacuum which the destruction of clear majorities by P.R. had created.

A third characteristic of the French political situation was a widespread condemnation of "the regime of parties." General DeGaulle had condemned wholesale; others were tempted to justify without qualification. In the case of political parties this was done, in particular, in a brilliantly written article by Maurice Schumann[23] (the well-known journalist of the M.R.P., who must not be confused with Robert Schuman) within which it is emphasized that also in countries like the United States and England, to which General DeGaulle frequently referred in terms of commendation, political parties occupied a decisive position. It is, of course, true that democracy cannot work anywhere except through the medium of political parties. Yet (if for the purposes of comparison we limit ourselves to England, which has the parliamentary system in common with France), we see that English political parties are means to an end rather than ends in themselves, as parties tend to be under P.R. In England the voters will, as a rule, give an over-all majority to one of the major parties and thereby determine the nature of the government themselves. The principal function of the parties is to organize the electorate and to make it possible for it to function. Ultimately, the people choose the government, and the latter is able to govern on a semi-plebiscitary basis.

In France a similar condition might develop if there were a majority system combined with an unrestricted right of parliamentary dissolution. In that case also the parties would merely be intermediate agents of political action, i.e., devices created for the purpose of assisting the people in choosing the government themselves. French political parties, as created by P.R., are, in fact, so dissimilar from political parties as they exist in the Anglo-Saxon countries, that one is inclined to apply to them the term faction, in the sense in which Madison used it in Number 10 of *The Federalist*. Certainly, if there is to be a clearcut political discussion in France — which alone could lead that country out of its constitutional impasse — it is vital that the true function of political parties be understood. DeGaulle is right if he condemns French parties as they are; likewise, his opponents are right when they emphasize that without political parties democracy cannot exist. It should be made clear that parties under P.R. are one thing, and parties under the majority system, combined with a workable right of dissolution, something else. The latter would give France what she needs, a combination of the parliamentary and the plebiscitary principles, as it has existed in England ever since the electoral reform of 1867.

Formation of Government

It was natural that in France after the Liberation at first all major parties should have attempted to cooperate, including the Communists, who at that time pretended to be wholeheartedly devoted to the reconstruction of France. Besides, the Communists had tremendous power within the trade unions and their good-will was as valuable as their open opposition would have been detrimental. It goes without saying, however, that these cabinets pushed the heterogeneity of coalition cabinets almost to the point of absurdity. The French journalist, "Pertinax," [24] reported that the meetings of General DeGaulle's coalition cabinet were characterized by clashes between Communists, Socialists, and M.R.P. ministers, which ended in complete confusion. The General would step in and impose a solution of his own. This would be accepted, but as soon as the ministers had left the meeting-room, they would follow the instructions of their respective parties and pursue a policy of their own. By January 20, 1946, General DeGaulle was so disgusted by these conditions that he resigned, and temporarily withdrew from public life.

After DeGaulle's resignation the Socialist leader, Gouin, and the popular Republican leader, Bidault, successively continued to combine the functions of the head of the state and of the prime minister, as the new constitution, providing for their separation, had not as yet been adopted. The government which they headed consisted again of Communists, Socialists, and the M.R.P., occasionally with the support of smaller parties. It is hardly necessary to add that these coalitions did not coalesce. The elections to the First National Assembly, under the new constitution of November, 1946, led to a two-week deadlock during which no coalition could be formed. To the surprise of everyone, a Socialist minority cabinet was formed under the leadership of the veteran Léon Blum. This was unexpected not only because it was a minority government, but also because the Socialist party had received another setback at the election, making it by far the smallest of the three major parties. As mentioned before, however, minority cabinets are not infrequent under P.R., and they may, under that system of voting, have advantages. Léon Blum was at least not plagued by continuous quarrels within his own cabinet; its homogeneity made it possible for him to make a new start both in economic and in foreign policy. He was in power for only thirty days, as he refused to carry on after the necessary steps had been taken to put the new constitution formally into operation. He had, however, managed to give to France's political institutions a slight boost in prestige, which they badly needed.

Léon Blum's successor was another Socialist, Paul Ramadier. Once again the deadlock between the two major parties, the Communists and the M.R.P., led to the choice of a Socialist. Similarly, the President of the Republic, Vincent Auriol, had been taken from Socialist ranks. The cabinet of Ramadier was at first based on a coalition of the three major parties. We have discussed above the circumstances under which, in May, 1947, the Communists were eliminated from the government. Throughout the entire period of three-party government (not only for the duration of the Ramadier cabinet), there applies what Gordon Wright, who then, as a member of the American Embassy in Paris, observed developments in detail, described in these words:

". . . France had long known coalition cabinets, but it had never before seen such flagrant civil war within a government. . . . France was treated to an example of coalition government at its worst. The opposition, instead of attacking the cabinet from the outside, was within the cabinet itself. Collaboration gave way to cohabitation; instability was replaced by near-paralysis. . . .

"The 1946 laboratory experiment in government left an offensive odor in the nostrils of many truly democratic Frenchmen." [25]

After the elimination of the Communists, Ramadier carried on with a combination of Socialists, M.R.P., and smaller groups. Although his cabinet was no longer as heterogeneous as before, there remained a great deal of friction among the partners of the coalition. It must be borne in mind that the Socialists desired a centrally-directed planned economy, whereas the Radicals and the other groups of the Right and Center, whose votes became more and more important, insisted upon a free economy. Similarly, the coalition included the

Christian Democrats as the leaders of French anti-clericalism. Thus, there was always friction and suspicion.

When, in October, 1947, General De Gaulle's Rally of the French People (R.P.F.) scored its great victory, the heterogeneous coalition found itself surrounded by a heterogeneous opposition. There were the Communists at the Left who grew more and more radical, and the DeGaullists at the Right. The number of the DeGaullists in the National Assembly remained small, as no new elections had taken place for this body. Yet, there was a new center of attraction at the Right, and while some deputies definitely joined the DeGaullist camp, others occupied an intermediate position, following DeGaullist leadership at first, and being willing, a year or so later, to support the Republican government if its policies seemed acceptable.

Ramadier's cabinet, as well as those of his successors, were comparable to Dr. Bruening's "coalition of all reasonable men." The Republicans in the Center found themselves encircled. They had a monopoly of the responsibility, and their opponents a monopoly of opposition. Léon Blum tried to bolster the morale of the government parties by coining the term "Third Force," which soon gained general circulation. The term was of some help, and so was the President of the Republic, who did his best to support a cabinet when it existed, and to find a new one when the old one had resigned. Yet, the heterogeneity of these coalitions was a never-ending source of trouble. Their prestige was low, because everybody knew that, in case of new elections held under the existing system of voting, the Third Force would lose its parliamentary majority. As in Germany, where, in the elections of 1932, the Communists and the National Socialists together obtained a majority, the Communists and DeGaullists would have secured a combined majority in France. The DeGaullists were, of course, not to be compared with the National Socialists, and it is not inconceivable that a compromise could have been arranged between them and the Third Force. Yet, the only development certain to come was a defeat of the Third Force, and the justification of the claims of the DeGaullists that the cabinets governing the country did not represent the electorate.

There is no reason to discuss the following cabinets in detail. The two marathon crises of summer and fall, 1948, and of October, 1949, have been amply reported by the newspapers of the entire world. The first practically extended from the resignation of the government headed by Robert Schuman, on July 19, to the appointment of the cabinet Queuille on September 11. The intermediate government of André Marie was hardly in office long enough to begin serious work. The second crisis lasted officially from October 7, 1949, when Queuille resigned, to October 27, when the designation of Bidault as Prime Minister was approved by the National Assembly. Unofficially, it lasted about a week longer because the cabinet of Henri Queuille was unable to function after the final attempt to settle the difference between the Socialists and the other coalition parties had failed.

These two crises exceeded everything which had occurred during the Third Republic, when the formation of a new cabinet usually was a matter of days and never took more than a week. One must read French newspapers for this period in order to realize the full depth of the confusion then existing. Furthermore, after the government of Bidault had been formed, a minor crisis was created almost immediately by the resignation of two ministers, and a major one a few months later by the withdrawal of the Socialists from the cabinet. The latter then became "a tolerated minority." Bidault was saved by the unprecedented vehemence of the Communist attacks, which were directed indiscriminately against all parties, including the Socialists, and were accompanied by extensive physical violence. These attacks antagonized the Socialists so strongly that they gave Bidault their votes simply in order to frustrate the designs of the Communists.[25(a)]

France's political difficulties have been exaggerated by sensational reporting which disregarded the attempt, partly successful, of the permanent civil service in the ministries to fill the gaps caused by cabinet instability. There remains, however, enough even if we make allowances for sensationalism. Suffice it to quote two observers who both are active supporters of the Third Force and opponents of DeGaulle. Thus, in December 1948, Professor Maurice Duverger, the well-known political scientist, wrote: "How could, from this juxtaposition of the lack of particular wills, there develop a common will? How could one define an over-all policy of the majority if each one of the parties constituting it is unable to define its own policy? One no longer acts; one is satisfied to last. There still are ministers who attempt to solve current problems as they arise; but there is no longer a government." [26]

During the crisis of October, 1947, Duverger wrote an article, under the heading *Le Cloaque* — "The Sewer." Bitterly, he spoke of "the impotence of ministries when they live," and of "the difficulty to replace them when they die." He mentioned the possibility that a reform of the electoral system might bring about a measure of improvement, and added, "but the risks are great, and those who ought to run them are pusillanimous." He continued: "The most probable development is that each day we shall bore ourselves a little more deeply into the sewer. At the end there stands Caesar (meaning a dictator) and the terrible feeling of relief with which we ought to welcome him on the day when his shield alone will separate us from Soviet terror." [27]

Let us add a comment by Rémy Roure, who is as competent and moderate an observer as Duverger. He concluded an article in October 1949 with the remark: "The government is in a stage of decomposition; it is impotent to propose a policy to a parliament which can no longer fulfill its function of control, because one does not control the void. Really, it is the crisis of the regime which we witness." [28]

Experiments With Majority Voting

The question arises whether the possibility of a way out of the permanent crisis in which France finds herself can be viewed a little more optimistically than was done by Maurice Duverger. Three elections were held in which the majority system was applied, and the results demonstrate that the majority system is an integrating force, even when it is combined with the second ballot. The first experiment took place in the municipal elections of October, 1947. The Ramadier cabinet had initially introduced a bill which admitted P.R. only in municipalities with more than 50,000 inhabitants. Communists and M.R.P. insisted that P.R. be used also in smaller communities. Finally, Ramadier made the concession that P.R. was to be used in all communities with 9,000 or more inhabitants, with the majority system being applied in the others. He forced passage of this bill by asking the question of confidence.

The municipal election of 1947 saw DeGaulle's R.P.F. for the first time as an open competitor. The statistical picture is complicated by the fact that in many cases DeGaulle's supporters concluded coalitions with other groups, on this occasion with the smaller Rightist parties, and with some of the Radicals. In the cities with more than 9,000 inhabitants the R.P.F. secured 28.1 per cent of the votes, and coalition lists formed under R.P.F. leadership 10.6 per cent. The Communists had 28.9 per cent.[29] This means that in the cities where P.R. was applied, the extreme Left and the extreme Right, taken together, had a majority, and a two-thirds majority if we include the coalition lists formed under DeGaullist leadership.

The Ministry of the Interior did not publish official figures for the smaller constituencies where the majority system applied. A private estimate[30] reached the result that the Communists received 20 per cent of the votes in these municipalities in comparison with 28.6 per cent in the election to the National Assembly. This means a loss in voting strength of a good fourth, for which there was to be, for a long period, no parallel in elections held under P.R.

So far as seats in the municipal councils are concerned, the different size of the communities involved makes over-all figures meaningless. Yet, there is agreement to the effct that in the small municipalities the Communists fared badly. Subsequently, their spokesman, Dumusois, said in the National Assembly in the course of a speech in which he opposed majority elections: "It happened (as a result of the majority system) that in a very large number of municipalities ... the Communist party saw itself excluded from the municipal council, although its candidates had secured forty-five per cent, forty-seven per cent, and even forty-nine per cent of the votes." [31] For the second ballot, if not for the first, a coalition of almost all parties was formed against the Communists, against which the latter could not prevail even with a very high percentage of the votes, as long as they did not have an over-all majority.

The Socialists did comparatively well in these elections, and the Radicals even better. Next to the Communists the M.R.P. was the great loser, as more than one-half of its supporters had deserted it in favor of the R.P.F. It must, of course, be borne in mind that in 1945 and in 1946 the M.R.P. had openly campaigned as "the party of fidelity," meaning fidelity to General DeGaulle. Thus, it was inevitable for it to lose a large percentage of its supporters as soon as DeGaulle presented candidates of his own.

The tendencies revealed by the municipal elections became clearer in the election to the Council of the Republic. In November and December, 1946, this body had first been elected in two stages, both of which applied the principle of P.R. The distribution of seats was similar to that in the National Assembly, with the Communists as the strongest party, followed in this order by the M.R.P. and the Socialists. The elections of October and November, 1948, took place under a new law,[32] the principal characteristic of which was that in the seventy-nine *départements* which elected less than four members of the Council, the majority system was used. The remaining eleven *départements* used P.R. Election was again in two stages. First, the 100,011 electors were determined. The deputies to the National Assembly and certain groups of municipal councilors were electors by right, and they were supplemented by candidates chosen by municipal councils. The designation of the electors took place on October 17, the election of the members of the Council of the Republic on November 7.

For the final elections in the *départements* with majority system, there were formed on the Left coalitions of Radicals, Socialists and small groups, whereas at the Right the R.P.F. represented the point of attraction. The Communists proved unable to form any coalition. As a result, the newspaper, *Le Monde,* was able to predict that in these *départements* not a single Communist would be elected.[33] The *départements* with P.R. gave the Communists sixteen seats, half of which came from Paris. The continued strength of the Communists and their allies increased, on the basis of subsequent elections in the Colonies, to twenty-four. In the new Council of the Republic, they occupied fifth place, whereas in its predecessor they had been leading with eighty-eight seats.

For subsequent developments in regard to P.R. it was of decisive importance that next to the Communists the M.R.P. was the principal sufferer of the return to the majority system. Its group in the Council of the Republic declined from seventy-five to twenty-one members. The M.R.P. was not included in the coalitions of the Left on account of the anti-clericalism which continued to exist in that quarter. On the Right the M.R.P. had to reckon with the enmity of the R.P.F. It must be borne in mind that in some cases in the *départements* using the majority system, that system of voting, with the formation of coalitions accompanying it, was applied twice in succession, first for the election of the electors, and second for the final determination of the councilors, with the M.R.P. being in an uncomfortable position on both occasions.

The R.P.F. gained considerably from the election, but its parliamentary group, called Democratic Action, was joined by only fifty-eight members. The total number of those who, according to the secretariat of the R.P.F., had received its electoral support, is 120. The councilors — soon to be called senators again — who had been supported by the R.P.F. but did not join its parliamentary group, followed their own views in casting their votes in the Council.

If the expectations of the DeGaullists were not quite realized, the Radicals, relegated to the position of a minor party in the National Assembly, did very well. Their group in the new Council counted eighty-five members, and occupied the top position. It is, of course, a characteristic result of the majority system that a party with a strictly centrist position should gain so strongly. The Socialists, with sixty-two seats, came second; they too fared much better than they could have done if P.R. had been applied in all *départements*. The DeGaullists occupied third place, followed by five smaller groups, including the Communists and the M.R.P.

The details concerning the composition of the new Council of the Republic must not be allowed to overshadow the over-all result. This consists in the fact that, at a time when nation-wide elections under P.R. would still have led to a majority of Communists and R.P.F., the Council of the Republic showed a majority for the parties of the Third Force. This majority, to be sure, was more conservative than were the representatives of the Third Force in the National Assembly, but even most Socialists preferred it to the kind of heterogeneous majority which P.R. was likely to produce.

The trend which began with the municipal elections of October, 1947, continued in the provincial elections (*élections cantonales*) of March 20 and 27, 1949. These elections covered one-half of the total membership of the provincial parliaments; they took place in single-member constituencies, the so-called *cantons*. When evaluating the results, it must be borne in mind that no elections took place in the *Département* Seine, which includes Paris.

The Communists were the chief losers. Their total popular vote declined to 23.5 per cent, as compared with 28.6 per cent in the elections to the National Assembly of November 10, 1946. It must be remembered that they presented candidates in every *canton*, and also that in elections held under P.R. during the same period (such as in the city of Grenoble and in the Paris suburb, Issy-les Moulyneux) they increased their share of the total popular vote. Inasmuch as the provincial elections were the only ones which up to that time show a drop in the Communist vote, this drop must be ascribed to the effects of the majority system. Communist leaders had, to be sure, issued orders to their followers that their candidates were to be supported even in constituencies where they had no chance. The voters apparently judged the matter differently, and cast their ballots in a number of cases for the candidates presented by other left-wing parties who had a better chance to be elected.

The Communists obtained a total of thirty-seven out of a possible 1508 seats, a little more than two per cent. They were, of course, aware of the reason for this discrepancy between votes and seats, and their party stated, the day after the second ballot: "If the election vote had been just and democratic (in other words, if there had been P.R.) the Communist party would have obtained 350 seats." [34] We might add that this is one of the few cases where Communists were guilty of an under-statement, as the calculation was based only on the percentage of votes obtained under the majority system, disregarding the fact that a higher percentage could have been expected under P.R. It is also interesting to note the relative deterioration of the Communist position since 1945, when they had obtained 184 seats. Immediately after the Liberation they were still able to form campaign alliances in many constituencies. In 1949, the Communists could not form such alliances, but they might still have benefited from the confusion created by the competition among the much divided non-Communist parties, since in the second ballot a simple plurality sufficed. The newspaper, *Le Figaro*, commenting on this situation, adds: "Wherever the splitting up of the national-minded people created an opportunity for the Communists, the voters themselves spontaneously gave their votes to that non-Communist candidate — whatever his label—who seemed to have the best chance to bar the road to the man of Moscow." [35]

On this occasion the M.R.P. did not suffer losses comparable to those of the Communists. It was able to win one more seat than in

1945. With eight per cent of the popular vote it obtained somewhat more than seven per cent of the seats. This means that the M.R.P. secured practically as large a number of seats as it could have expected under an "integral" system of P.R. Under the P.R. system used for the elections of the National Assembly, it might have done worse.

The R.P.F. was certain to be the big winner in the cantonal elections, since it had not participated in the elections of 1945, and disposed of a sizable bloc of votes. Yet, neither in regard to the popular vote nor in regard to the seats did it fare as well as in October 1947. According to the statistics of the Ministry of the Interior, the R.P.F. candidates obtained 25.34 per cent of the votes cast in the first ballot;[36] they obtained 380 of the 1508 seats, about the same percentage of the total. This is a far cry from the thirty-eight per cent of the votes (and seats) which the R.P.F. and its allies had obtained in the municipal elections of 1947.

When the provincial elections were over, the government claimed a decisive victory. The then Prime Minister Queuille said: "The majority had accepted the challenge of the opposition; it has won." [37] From the point of view of the seats obtained by the Third Force, this was true, as the parties constituting it won 910 of them. It was less convincing when Jules Moch, the Minister of the Interior, claimed that 51.12 per cent of the popular votes had been cast for the parties standing in between the Communists and the R.P.F. The De Gaullists denied the validity of this calculation. It certainly has the defect of failing to take into account that there had been no voting in the *Département* Seine. The correspondent of *The Manchester Guardian*[38] assumed that the two extremist parties were about as strong in that *département* as in the neighboring *département*, Seine-et-Oise, where each obtained thirty-three per cent of the votes. Assuming a like percentage for them in the *Département* Seine the share in the popular vote of the government parties would definitely fall below the half-way mark. Since the two extremist parties would, under P.R., have been likely to obtain more popular votes, the victory of the Third Force in the provincial elections was clearly due to the effects of the majority system.

The Opposition to P.R.

The result of the provincial elections strengthened the position of those who had long since demanded the abolition of P.R. In September, 1948, the parliamentary group of the Radical party had introduced a bill in the National Assembly providing for a return to the majority system with the second ballot.[39] The only proposed change was the limitation of the candidates allowed to run in the second ballot to those who had participated in the first.

General De Gaulle had come out in favor of the plurality system in 1947. According to a poll undertaken by the French Institute of Public Opinion, at that time a majority of those voters in France who had an opinion on systems of voting was in favor of a return to the majority system. In fact, a majority of the voters of all parties, except the Communists, expressed themselves as opposed to P.R.[40] If we eliminate the Communist vote in favor of P.R., the popular majority against it becomes overwhelming.

The parties lagged far behind the people in their opposition to P.R. Yet, much progress was made as a result of a series of articles which Léon Blum published, in June, 1949, in the Socialist daily, *Le Populaire*.[41] Blum reversed a lifelong stand by rejecting P.R., and advocating a modified majority system. He began by asking the question whether the necessary "return of the forces of health" could be brought about solely through "moral" factors, or whether it did not require the assistance of institutional reform. He said that after long reflection he had found the solution in the return to the *scrutin d'arrondissement*, i.e., the majority system in single-member constituencies. The criticism that such a solution sounded too simple he answered by saying: "The great remedies which one must apply to political crises are always very simple and very commonplace."

Blum further emphasized that P.R. had disappointed the expectations of Jaurès, as well as his own. Both had hoped that there would develop under P.R. a clear struggle between political ideas (he terms them "doctrines")," but that facile slogans had taken the place of serious ideological discussions. In addition, the party bureaucracy had been strengthened, and this rigidity had served as a bar to rejuvenation. In Blum's words:

"In this manner, if I can judge things correctly, the tremendous and fortunate possibility of rejuvenation which the Resistance movement offered to all political parties has been destroyed. One was not able to introduce into the political personnel more than the minimum doses of new blood. Who would deny that in the single-member constituency the operation would have been more comprehensive and more life-giving? Yet, the single-member constituencies would have done better."

Visible emotion characterizes his concluding remarks on this point: "Yes, it (P.R.) is a system of passion, a system of lottery, a system unsuited to the propaganda of doctrines and to the debating of doctrines, a system unsuited for giving a faithful, serious and 'just' picture of the political structure of a country."

The Socialist leader did not propose an unqualified return to the majority system. He suggested that three-quarters of the deputies, about 450 of a total of 600, be elected in single-member constituencies with second ballot. One hundred and fifty were to be elected under P.R. on a national list, on which the seats were to be divided on the basis of the votes obtained by the parties in the first ballot. The meaning of this proposal depends upon details.[41(a)] If, as is probably the case, Blum intended the seats on the national lists to be divided among the parties without deducting seats obtained by the parties already in the single-member constituencies, he would arrive at a comparatively minor modification of the majority system, although any attenuation of this system will be regarded critically since the English elections of February, 1950, have shown that, even under a plurality system, a near stalemate is not impossible.

The result would be entirely different if, as is the case in Western Germany, the seats obtained by a party in single-member constituencies were to be deducted from those which it could claim on the national list, which then would become a monopoly of the small parties. This would interfere seriously with the formation of majorities. However, it is interesting that the concession to P.R. contained in Léon Blum's proposal was generally rejected in the French press; most newspapers expressed themselves in favor of the majority system without modifications.

Another question discussed vigorously in France is whether the majority system should be introduced in single-member constituencies or in multiple-member constituencies within the *département*. It has been mentioned above that Michel Debré demanded the latter solution in order to eliminate subservience to local interests. A similar position was taken by François Goguel, one of the keenest observers of the French political scene, who wrote in regard to the single-member constituency: "It is very favorable to individualism; it creates the danger that the part played by political parties is reduced to very little, and even if this part is at present too great, parties are nonetheless necessary." 42

So far as the M.R.P. is concerned, Goguel drew attention to the fact that the French version of P.R. could inflict great damage on comparatively small parties, to which category the M.R.P. has belonged since the formation of the R.P.F. Goguel adds:

"But it seems that P.R. has its most fervent supporters, in particular among the leaders of the M.R.P. — among those who are certain to be at the head of the party lists — as well as among certain members of the braintrust of the party. The deputies with places farther below on the list are much more inclined to hesitate, and some of them do not conceal their preference for the majority system; they complain that the issue has never been discussed freely within the party."

Goguel felt that some of these deputies might support the proponents of the majority system even if this should be proposed in the form of the single-member constituency, which might be less favorable to the M.R.P. than multiple-member constituencies within the framework of the *département*.

Articles like those by Blum and Goguel presuppose a high degree of independent thinking and of political courage on the part of their authors. In the case of Goguel, it might be held that, in the long run, the plurality system in single-member constituencies would suffice to give France strong political parties, always assuming a workable right of dissolution. On the other hand, it is unlikely that the proposed plan would seriously endanger the advantages of the majority system; if practical experience should suggest a return to the single-member constituency, it would not be too difficult to bring it about.

Before resuming the discussion of the prospects of electoral reform in France, let us briefly discuss a question which in French discussions is invariably raised in this connection. It is contended that a French two-party system would, like a possible duel between the Communists and the M.R.P., or between the Communists and the DeGaullists, divide the country into two. Those who raise this argument transfer essential characteristics of P.R. elections to those held under the majority system. The elections to the provincial parliaments of March, 1949, have demonstrated how the majority system deals with political extremists such as the Communists. It might perhaps be held that this result is possible only in case of a second ballot, and that under a plurality system greater successes of the Communists could be expected. However, as it has been put often, the abolition of the second ballot would in reality mean the abolition of the first. During the Third Republic the first ballot was a kind of test match, with the real decision being taken in the second. If the results of the first ballot are final, the laws of concentration and of moderation would go into effect immediately. French voters are discerning enough to realize that an extremist candidate, even with a large number of votes behind him, has little chance to secure the support of the marginal voter in the center. Therefore, the plurality system would force political moderation on large French parties as it forces moderation on English and American parties.

As mentioned above, DeGaulle's supporters had never succeeded in recapturing, under the majority system, the percentage of the total votes which, in October, 1947, they had obtained in the cities using P.R. That thereupon many of the supporters of the General cooled off considerably in their enthusiasm for the majority system only goes to prove that, for political leaders, in such matters the immediate advantage is everything and long-run considerations nothing or next to nothing.

The effect of a "political bomb" was, however, produced when the daily, *L'Epoque*,[44] asserted that there was a secret protocol of a conversation between DeGaulle and the M.R.P. leader, Georges Bidault, who at that time was attempting to form his cabinet. Bidault was said to have promised that, as Prime Minister, he would ask the question of confidence as often as serious difficulties should develop in the National Assembly. Two rejections of such a request by the assembly within an 18-month period, or votes of censure under the same conditions, would provide the constitutional requirements for a dissolution of the assembly. It must be borne in mind, of course, that during the first 18 months of a particular assembly, no dissolution is permitted. A dissolution and new elections would fulfill a demand made by General DeGaulle ever since the election of October, 1947.

General DeGaulle's counter concession was to be his agreement with, or toleration of, continued support of P.R. by the M.R.P. The latter was to work for "integral P.R.," meaning a system with extensive utilization of surpluses, which alone could preserve the M.R.P. from the fate suffered by the Radicals in 1945 and 1946, who then saw a large part of their votes unutilized. *L'Epoque* adds: "Since this system fulfills the wishes of the Communist party, it would receive a large majority in the National Assembly."[45]

General DeGaulle vigorously denied the existence of such a protocol, but when, in a press conference, he was asked about the system of voting, he ridiculed, according to the reporter of *Le Monde*,[46] the proponents of a return to *scrutin d'arrondissement,* the old single-member constituency with the second ballot. He added that the system of voting should, if possible, assume the form of majority elections in multiple-member constituencies, but if that could not be accomplished, P.R. would have to be accepted. The reporter of *Le Monde* adds that such an effort to secure a compromise between the R.P.F. and Republican groups resulted naturally from the political situation, since the R.P.F. had been compelled to abandon the hope of winning a majority of its own. No secret protocol was necessary to prove a political necessity.

A brief examination of the bills providing for electoral reform introduced in the National Assembly may help to clarify the various contemplated solutions. First there was a bill introduced by the deputies, René Coty, Roclore and Lalle,[47] who are independents and "Liberals" of the Right. They proposed multiple-member constituencies, with the *départements* as the normal units, the larger *départements* being subdivided. Those candidates would be declared elected who received an absolute majority in the first ballot. If necessary, a second ballot takes place in which again the deputies with an absolute majority are elected. If there is no such majority, the seats are divided according to P.R. A French observer suggested to this writer that perhaps the latter feature in this bill was the reason why the DeGaullists might accept it, as it assured them of the benefits of P.R. in the larger *départements.*

It is worth mentioning that in the "exposition of motives" preceding this bill it was emphasized that the capital error of the Third Republic consisted in permitting the right of dissolution to become obsolete; regret is expressed that the Fourth Republic has practically abolished this right by surrounding it with too many restrictions.

A similar bill was introduced in July 1949 by the deputy, Barrachin,[48] a member of the DeGaullist group. It differs from the Coty proposal primarily by refusing to make any concession to P.R. If there is no majority in the first ballot, a plurality suffices in the second. While, however, under the Coty plan candidates would be voted upon as individuals (their grouping on lists becoming relevant only for the seats which might have to be distributed under P.R. following the second ballot), Barrachin would have the votes counted only for lists.

Reference has been made above to a bill introduced in September, 1948, by a number of Radical deputies, which was apparently approved by the entire Radical group in the assembly, and which provided for the return to the single-member constituency with two ballots. It may be added that, while the "exposition of motives" which accompanies the bill criticizes the obvious defects of P.R., it does not mention a workable right of dissolution as a companion feature of the return to the majority system.

The Radicals were aware of the difficulties which any attempt to secure the passage of this law would encounter. The chairman of the Radical group in the assembly, François Delcos,[49] presented an interesting report on the "General Policy" of his party to the party congress of Toulouse (November, 1949), in the course of which he outlined the Radical stand on the election system. As he said in regard to the existing law, "All parties have condemned this system except the Communists and the M.R.P. who are its beneficiaries." He mentioned that he and his friends in the Assembly concentrated upon winning individual deputies to the cause of the majority system which, in his opinion, had created a "favorable climate" in which perhaps a measure of transition would be possible. He expressed willingness to accept a system of multiple-member constituencies in the framework of the *département,* which would "leave to the absolute majority a large place." He ended, however: "In case of despair, integral P.R. might receive our votes." As mentioned above, such a system would, from the point of view of the Radicals, have the advantage of freeing them from the drawbacks of the "bastard system" applied in 1945 and 1946.

Since the M.R.P. occupies the key position in the Assembly, it is interesting that two of its deputies, M. Roques and M. Taillade,[50] introduced, in October, 1949, a bill which makes certain concessions to the majority principle, which are real even if in the "exposition of motives" the principle of P.R. is defended in the same harsh language to which Léon Blum found it necessary to take exception in one of his articles. Two provisions of this bill are of major importance. First, different lists within the same constituency may be "linked" by a declaration to this effect, signed by all the candidates involved. "Linked" lists form a unit so far as the assignment of seats is concerned. Second, any list, or a group of "linked" lists, which obtains fifty-five per cent of the votes, gets all of the seats. It is mentioned that this percentage represents a somewhat arbitrary choice, and that it is guided only by the consideration that very weak majorities should not take all seats. The seats won by "linked" lists, either under P.R. or under the — qualified — majority principle, will be divided among them according to P.R.

Under this system, there would be a strong tendency to form campaign coalitions, and it is hoped that they would lay the basis for cooperation in the forming of governments. The Communists would hardly find any partners for such coalitions; it is possible that coalitions securing fifty-five per cent of the votes would be formed in most of the rural *départements,* from which in that case the Communists could not elect a single deputy. Such coalitions would, however, not necessitate the degree of assimilation required under the majority system, where the voters belonging to the allied parties must vote for the lists presented by their own parties, the coalition process largely consisting in an adding up of the final figures. Even so, there would be a significant departure from the present law.

It might be mentioned in passing that the proposal also provides that the voter can change the order of the candidates on his list by giving a preferential vote to one of them in the smaller, and to two of them in the larger constituencies. In other words, what in Germany was called "the free list" would be instituted, assuming that the provision proves to be effective, which would not necessarily be the case. A "free list" can have the result of a *bellum omnium contra omnes* — "war of all against all"— among groups within the party's membership. The only alternative in multiple-member constituencies is, of course, determination of the position of the candidates by the party leaders, which is largely tantamount to appointment.

These are the major types of reform plans submitted: we disregard those which aim at minor modifications of P.R. The final question concerning the chances for reform is difficult to answer. In such a case, reason has always to battle the vested interests, so powerful in this case because the strongest voting bloc in the Assembly — the Communists — will never support a move to abolish P.R. There are also the vested interests within other parties. When, in 1944, this writer was asked his opinion on P.R. for a discussion of "The Fundamentals of French Democracy" he concluded: "One thing should be clear. If elections for the French National Assembly are held under P.R., no one will be able to abolish it, no matter what happens afterward." [51] This pessimism may prove to have been premature; yet, it is a necessary starting point for any realistic discussion of the subject.

If, on the other hand, anything will bring about a return to the majority system, it is the pressure of events. Shortly after the Socialists had left his cabinet, Georges Bidault made a speech, part of which *The New York Times* summarized as follows:

"The Premier went on to show that the French internal struggles and the scandals in French politics were affecting the standing of the country and showed the danger the nation would incur by ministerial crises that leave the country for long intervals without a responsible government.

" 'Our present peril,' M. Bidault said, 'forbids another vacation period of official authority.' " [52]

It goes without saying that if Bidault is an opponent of a return to the majority system, his warning belongs in the category of what theologians call "counsels of perfection." Still, there are an increasing number of observers in France who realize, as Alexander Hamilton did when he warned the people of his country against "reliance on mere patriotism," that the essential requirements of stability must be secured by institutional arrangements, among which the system of voting holds first place. The fact that in France the Communists are the principal beneficiaries of P.R., helps to underline this realization; there are few who would hope to impress them with appeals to their patriotism. In particular, the large-scale violence to which Communists resorted in the National Assembly, in March, 1950, created sympathies for the abolition of P.R. in quarters where they had not existed before.

A mere abolition of P.R. would not, however, be enough, in particular if the second ballot were retained. France needs a workable right of parliamentary dissolution if she is not to fall again into the crises typical of the Third Republic, even if these went less deep — and were more likely to lead to a wholesome reaction — than those of the Fourth. In this regard the question is whether French Republicans will turn away sufficiently from the modes of thought characteristic of "frightened democracy," whether they will consider calmly the right of dissolution and realize that it is a democratic as well as an effective means of restoring government authority. On this point we come up against certain obstacles which caused some French observers to use vigorous language after the failure of Doumergue, in 1934, and which induced *The New York Times* to remark more recently: "The French politicians are far too fond of riding the political merrygoround, which gives everybody a chance to be premier, to abandon that game before they have to." [53] That was as true in 1950 as it was in 1934.

Problems to be solved before a constructive reform is possible arise among the ranks of the DeGaullist camp as well as from among their opponents. So far, the General has not stated his constitutional views in a manner which would leave absolutely no doubt that he is interested in institutional reform alone, and not in "personal power." His denunciation of political parties is too general to be reassuring: nor were his opponents entirely wrong in claiming a certain affinity between the "corporative" façade of Italian fascism and the ideas on the reordering of the relations between capital and labor which the General proposed in his speech at St. Etienne.[54] Finally there exists the possibility that the R.P.F. might become a mere party among parties, and that as such it would judge everything from the point of view of its immediate interests as an organization, rather than of the purposes which it was founded to accomplish.

The way for General DeGaulle to place his republicanism beyond doubt would be acceptance of the proposals made by his own constitutional experts, if possible with the simplification which has been outlined above, i.e., concentration upon the majority system and a workable right of dissolution, allowing all other adjustments to work themselves out in practice.

Republican opponents of DeGaulle, on the other hand, need not make a fetish of their mistakes; reform is no less urgent because DeGaulle has been its earliest and most persistent advocate. There does exist the basis for a constructive compromise between them and the DeGaullists, which in fact would not require any real concession on the part of either side, and would give to both what serves their long-run interests. Action along such lines would be greatly assisted by clarity in the discussion of the problems involved; so far, a comprehensive and dispassionate analysis has not been provided. There is as yet too much partisanship and too little political common sense.

Prime Minister Pleven, as a former DeGaullist, was ideally prepared for the task of attempting a synthesis between DeGaullism and traditional republicanism. He sketched his ideas in a speech made on September 11,[55] in which he enumerated minor reforms to be made in the constitution, and emphasized the need for electoral reform. In regard to the latter, *Time* magazine later reported: "In place of proportional representation, a clumsy failure because it encourages multiple-party paralysis, the Premier proposed a *'système majoritaire,'* which would build up a few strong parties at the expense of the weakest. Pleven determined to fight for this program, even if it meant his downfall." [56] The seriousness of the risks which he had to take became evident when, in November, a Communist proposition to impeach the Socialist Minister of Defense Jules Moch obtained a vote of 235 for to 203 against, not sufficient under the constitution but damaging. This majority became possible only because a number of M.R.P. deputies, apparently anxious to force new elections before the electoral law could be changed, made common cause with the Communists.[57] Christian-Democratic-Communist cooperation, otherwise relegated to such freaks as the vote against Coca Cola, is of long duration so far as the defense of P.R. is concerned; it only goes to show that parties can succumb to the temptation of mere partisanship no matter how strongly they proclaim their devotion to the general welfare. The new French crisis coincided with the Chinese invasion of Korea; the President of the Republic refused Pleven's offer to resign, and the latter managed to obtain a vote of confidence from the National Assembly, which was meant to annul the political effects of the vote against Moch. It could not obscure the fact that the vested interests connected with P.R. represent powerful obstacles to any serious policy of electoral and constitutional reform.

Chapter 8. P.R. in Post-War Italy

P.R. Discussions

At the end of the Second World War, Italy returned to P.R. without the intensive discussion of the subject which one might have expected after the events of 1919 to 1922. The political leaders who were familiar with the effects of P.R. during that period were too old to initiate a vigorous discussion; during twenty years of fascism there was no opportunity to train younger men to see those requirements of democratic government which their own painful experience had made clear to them.

In addition, the controversy, monarchy versus republic, absorbed almost all energies which the Italians were willing to devote to constitutional problems. An observer as circumspect as Prime Minister De Gasperi warned that a republic would not automatically mean freedom. Instead it presupposed a sense of responsibility. He repeated the words of Victor Hugo: "Let us, if possible, have a public matter (he was alluding to the literal meaning of the Latin term, *res publica*) before we have a republic." [1] The Italian republicans disregarded the warning. The word republic had a magic sound, which sufficed to give to its proponents, after they had won, a sense of triumph and of final success.

The decision in favor of a return to P.R. was brought about by the so-called mass parties, the Communists, the Socialists, and the Christian Democrats. The Italian Communists favored P.R. for the same reasons for which Communists the world over favor it. The Socialists in Italy, like the Socialists in the other countries of Continental Europe, could not detach themselves from the tradition of the Second International, and demanded P.R. The Christian Democrats still felt that under a majority system they would be confined to certain parts of the country, whereas P.R. would make success easy for them everywhere.

Attention must also be given, without exaggerating its influence, to what in Greece later came to be called "the Allied factor." The political advisers accompanying the victorious Anglo-American armies had not been systematically acquainted with the pros and cons of various systems of voting. In the absence of such knowledge they were bound to follow the path of least resistance, which led to P.R. This was the case not only because the "mass parties" in general insisted upon that system of voting, but also because the Communists in particular, then already very active, would not have been prepared to accept the majority system.

Where there was a systematic approach to the subject it came from the proponents of P.R. A Canadian supporter[2] of that system of voting had, in 1943, published a pamphlet in which he proposed to force P.R. on the vanquished as part of the peace treaty. The British and American P.R. organizations could not officially go that far, but did all they could in other ways to assure the same result. Their literature was immediately made available to anyone in Italy who was interested in the subject. An American major organized, in the south Italian city of Atri, elections under the Hare system of P.R. on his own initiative; he received favorable publicity from the British and American P.R. organizations.[3] In Italy a fair degree of attention was apparently given to a letter to the editor of *The Times* (London) by a Mr. T. E. Harvey, a translation of which was published in the *Bulletin* of the Ministry for the Constituent Assembly;[4] the letter was reported in many newspapers. The author wrote in regard to the elections to be held in the countries under Russian occupation, and argued that they could not be fair except under P.R. (They were, of course, held under P.R., without any detriment to Communist control.) An Italian observer stated in a memorandum prepared for this writer: "This news item (concerning Mr. Harvey's letter) had its importance, for the readoption of P.R. took place while Italy was under Allied control." [5]

Still, there was criticism of P.R. in Italy, and it naturally originated with those who, while in leading positions, had witnessed the collapse of the pre-Fascist P.R. parliament. Thus, on October 17, 1945, a manifesto[6] was published which was signed, among others, by the future President of Italy, Luigi Einaudi, by the Independent leader, Arturo Labriola, the philosopher, Benedetto Croce, and the former prime ministers, Ivanoe Bonomi, V. E. Orlando, and Francesco Nitti. This manifesto opposed P.R. because it took away from the voters their true freedom and placed decisive power in the hands of the respective party bureaucracy. The manifesto continued:

"The only system, which under present conditions creates a representation effectively designated by the electors — and which can reeducate the Italians for the exercise of freedom — is the majority system in single-member constituencies, as it existed before 1919, with such modifications and adjustments as might prove opportune in the course of time."

It was added that no decisions in questions relating to the electoral system could be made by a government which lacked investiture by the people, and that the issue must be submitted to the judgment of the country by means of referendum.

This letter, due to the prestige of its signatories, found a certain amount of respectful attention, but it did not affect the result. It contained, however, two arguments of general significance. First and above all we must bear in mind that no government derived from parties as shaped by P.R. can be an impartial judge in such a matter. It will automatically readopt P.R. as the only means of perpetuating the power relations prevailing among the partners to the coalition. If a truly democratic verdict is desired a direct decision by the people is needed.

Similar general significance attaches to the argument concerning P.R. and political reeducation. Political education is inseparable from political responsibility, and such responsibility in its turn presupposes power. Since small minorities do not have the power to ally themselves, they can always shift responsibility to someone else. Countries under the majority system, on the other hand, develop parties which, alone or in cooperation with related parties, can assume clear responsibility. Such parties can be held to account, and through them the people themselves can acquire a feeling of responsibility.

So far as subsequent discussions are concerned, reference may be made first to an article by the historian, Professor Gaetano Salvemini, which was published in the November, 1945, issue of the Florentine monthly, *Il Ponte*.[7] Salvemini stated that a system of voting must fulfill two requirements: give the country a majority, and give expression to all political views in the country. Analyzing the effects of the majority system in single-member constituencies, he said: "The so-called 'two-party system' does not arise from any congenital idiosyncrasy in the Anglo-Saxon political spirits, but is made necessary by the single-member constituency." Salvemini did not, however, expect the single member constituency to lead to a two-party system in Italy where, in fact, it would be likely to promote the success of local cliques without much interest in national affairs.

Criticizing P.R., Professor Salvemini pointed out its share in producing parliamentary paralysis in pre-war Italy. He emphasized that it was only a share. Other factors were involved, such as the extremism of the Socialists, although that extremism would to some of us seem to be a logical consequence of a P.R. feature which Salvemini himself characterized as its "essential defect:" it "obligates each party to present itself to the electorate with a flag of absolute intransigence, accentuating what divides and not what could associate it with other parties." Later Salvemini says: "To sum up, P.R., where more than two parties exist with forces which more or less balance each other, makes impossible the formation of a homogeneous parliamentary majority, and also makes those coalitions which, if a government has to be formed, are necessary in the absence of a homogeneous majority, extremely unmanageable."

As a remedy Professor Salvemini proposed constituencies with about five seats, three of which were to go to the party, or parties, with the largest number of votes, and two to the minority. He expected two major party coalitions to be formed, of which one would have a parliamentary majority. Seats within the majority and minority coalitions (or parties) would be distributed according to voters' preferences.

If Salvemini wanted to make concessions to P.R., this does not apply to the internationally known economist, Luigi Einaudi, who subsequently became the first President of the Republic of Italy under the new constitution. He made a brilliant speech on the subject in the Consultative Assembly (an appointive parliament) on February 11, 1946.[8] Einaudi started from the assumption that he was fighting for a lost cause; the powers that be had decided in favor of P.R., although he had been surprised by the opposition to that system expressed by so many. He rejected the argument that P.R., even if otherwise objectionable, was needed for a constituent assembly, since that also would have to support, or replace, governments, and since it needed a majority for the adoption of a constitution. Like Salvemini, he explained the British two-party system on the basis of the plurality system; and he added that, if the British Liberal party had to disappear, it would be because both large parties were "profoundly permeated with Liberal sentiments."

Einaudi's further arguments refer to the frustration of government under P. R., which facilitated the rule of minorities, both in pre-Fascist Italy and in other countries. He emphasized the great value of the safety valve which the swing of the pendulum has for democratic government; he demanded a democratic opposition as well as a democratic government. Taking up the objections to the majority system in single-member constituencies one by one, he showed that all of them refer to what in reality constitutes an advantage; thus, large losses by a particular party in an election provide an opportunity for a renovation of the political élite, a task in the performance of which the single-member constituency was unexcelled.

Other arguments of Einaudi could be taken up; the speech is, in its author's knowledge of the subject and the self-assurance of his presentation, comparable to the classical statement of the case against P.R. in Walter Bagehot's *English Constitution*. The concluding sentence was: "P.R. creates a machine where we need, in particular in the present tragic moment, free men, apt to persuade and willing to be persuaded." The speaker must have felt himself reminded of this prediction when, in the years that followed, he viewed the actions of the Communists and the Nenni Socialists in Italian parliaments.

The First Elections

Actually, the elections to the Italian Constituent Assembly of June 2, 1946, took place under a list system of P.R. The voter could express from two to three preferential votes, but little use was made of this possibility. The constituencies returned (if we disregard the single-member constituency of Valle d'Aosta) from five to thirty-three deputies; thus they were comparatively large. Any seats assigned to these constituencies which, under the prescribed rules, were not filled, were shifted to the national list. The following table[9] gives the result of the elections:

P.R. IN POST-WAR ITALY

PARTIES	VOTES	PERCENTAGE OF VOTES	SEATS	PERCENTAGE OF SEATS
Christian Democrats	8,080,664	35.2	207	37.3
Socialists	4,758,129	20.7	115	20.7
Communists	4,356,686	19.0	104	18.7
Nat'l Democratic Union (Liberal and Democratic Labor Party)	1,560,638	6.8	41	7.4
Qualunquists	1,211,956	5.3	30	5.4
Republicans	1,003,007	4.4	23	4.1
Nat'l Freedom bloc (Democratic party and Monarchists)	637,328	2.8	16	2.9
Action party	334,748	1.4	7	1.3
Democratic-Republican Concentration	97,690	0.4	2	0.4
Italian Unity Movement	71,021	0.3	1	0.2
Christian-Social party	51,088	0.2	1	0.2
Local parties (4)	292,781	1.7	8	1.4
Lists receiving no seats (60)	412,550	1.8	..	..
Totals	22,968.286	100.0	555	100.0

The outstanding characteristic of the results is the strength of the Christian Democrats, who were much stronger than Don Sturzo's Popular party was after the First World War. In this case a number of "material" factors united in order to neutralize to some extent the effects of the "formal" factor of P.R. The Vatican showed nothing but feelings of friendship for the Christian Democrats, while it had been less favorable to the Popular party. This was significant because the Church, and in particular Pope Pius XII personally, were most popular. It was known that the preservation of Rome from aerial bombardment was due to the efforts of the Pope, who also in the following years expended every effort to secure adequate food supplies for Italy. In addition, we must take into account the general strengthening of religious feeling, which developed in Italy as it did in France. Last but not least there was the general fear of communism. To many non-Catholic voters it seemed that the Christian Democratic party offered the only true safeguard against "the Red danger," and therefore they voted for it without accepting its principles.

Formation of Governments

The formation of governments was, in Italy as in France, at first characterized by the need of cooperating with the Communists. There had been two ministries under Badoglio, followed by two ministries of Bonomi, and one ministry of Parri. De Gasperi formed his first cabinet in December, 1945. His appointment meant that the leader of the strongest party was officially entrusted with the leadership of the government. This is always desirable under the parliamentary system, and in this case it had the advantage of forestalling the quarrels concerning the person of the prime minister, which were characteristic of the pre-Fascist coalitions between the followers of Giolitti and the Popular party, and prevented, after Giolitti's fall, any strong candidate nominated by either side from having a chance.

Besides, De Gasperi enjoyed extraordinary personal prestige. Italians often called him *Un partito per conto suo,* — "a party by himself," a saying by which they meant to express not only his personal strength, but also his position above the din of party strife.

De Gasperi had his share of troubles, however, during the period of Communist cooperation. He managed to get rid of them in May, 1947. At that time an Italian journalist wrote: "In the government they (the Communists) did everything to prevent it from governing." He added that in the country they attacked their coalition partners with great violence, and concluded: "The Communists were in the government as a chain, and in the opposition as a whip." [10]

Polarization

During the period of the coalition with all major parties, including the Communists, the position of the Christian Democrats was endangered from both sides. At the Right there were the neo-Fascists (L' Uomo Qualunque[11(a)] was at that time the strongest group of this kind), and the Monarchists. Their attacks on the Center were hardly less violent than those which came from the Communists and Nenni's Socialists. Two elections demonstrated a serious danger of polarization. This was clearest in the municipal elections held in the city of Rome, November 10, 1946.[11] The percentage of the votes obtained by the Christian Democrats fell from 29.5, in the elections to the National Assembly, to 20.3; the number of popular votes which they had received declined, on account of a weaker popular participation in these elections, from 218,383 to 104,627. The so-called People's bloc (Communists, Socialists, and other small Leftist groups) came at the top with 190,038 votes, followed by the Qualunquists with 106,780. The Christian Democrats were a strong third, but a third all the same, and the danger of polarization was clear for everyone to see. The Socialist leader, Nenni, coined the slogan: *In mezzo non si sta* — "One does not stand in the middle." In other words, the political future lies with one of the extremes, and all the people can do is to enter their option for one or the other.

If we divide the seats obtained by the People's bloc among its participants, a total of eleven parties shared in the eighty seats of the Municipal Council of Rome. Every attempt was made to form a majority,[12] but in the end it was necessary to admit failure. A government commissar was appointed, and the Municipal Council was dissolved.

The Christian Democrats fared a little better in the elections to the parliament of the region of Sicily, held April 20, 1947. Even so the result was a typical P.R. parliament: People's bloc 29 seats (22 of them went to the Communists), Christian Democrats 19, Qualunquists 15, Monarchists 9, Separatists 8, Republicans 4, Moderate Socialists (Saragat) 4, Democratic Union of Messina 2. It was inevitable that a government coalition of Rightist tendencies was formed, but, of course, it constituted a political burden for the Christian Democrats.

When at last the Communists were eliminated from the government of De Gasperi the position of the Christian Democrats was made easier. From then on they were able to speak frankly in regard to their former coalition partners at the extreme Left. Also, the voters believed them when they emphasized the vital differences which separated them from the Communists. The result was a considerable increase in strength which expressed itself in the new election to the Municipal Council of Rome of October, 1947. The Christian Democrats were able to almost double the number of votes received, and secured 32.8 per cent of the popular vote, in comparison to 20.3 per cent in the preceding year. Those who in 1946 had, for the most part, abstained from voting, supported the Christian Democrats in the main, who also received the votes lost by the smaller Rightist parties. With twenty-seven of a total of eighty municipal councilors, the Christian Democrats remained, however, dependent upon the support of Rightist groups, if the appointment of another government commissar was to be prevented.

Prime Minister De Gasperi found himself in the same situation as his friends in the Roman municipal administration. The Christian Democrats had 207 of a total of 556 seats. If the government was to have a majority, at least 72 additional votes had to be found either at the Right or at the Left. The Prime Minister succeeded in maintaining himself, even if at times the support of the Moderate Left consisted in their abstaining from voting. Nothing would be more wrong, however, than to forget the problems by which De Gasperi was confronted. They are typical of the situation created by P.R., and the subsequent consolidation represents the exception. During the time in question, as judicious an observer as Anne O'Hare McCormick compared the Italian situation unfavorably with the French, and commented that in Italy "anything may happen any time, but holding it (the political structure) together is a job for a contortionist or a conjuror." [13]

Some of the characteristics of the Italian situation before the elections of 1948 remain. Thus, conditions were similar to those in France, so far as the origin and the outcome of cabinet crises was concerned. Constitutional theory in both countries expected a crisis to originate in parliament, after an open debate of the issues involved, with the government resigning if it failed to obtain a majority. Actually, everything depended upon the political parties which were partners to the coalition. Mr. Arnaldo Cortesi reported to *The New York Times* of May 18, 1947, under the headline, "Italian Instability Has Deep Roots":

"The present crisis, like the one before it, in January of this year, is noteworthy because it was not caused by an adverse vote of the legislative body. Indeed, Premier Alcide De Gasperi had received a vote of confidence from the Constituent Assembly not long before he resigned. It was caused rather by disruptive forces within the cabinet itself."

The same report continued that the Socialist leader, Saragat, had reproached the Prime Minister for violating the constitution, since he had resigned without presenting himself to parliament and explaining his motives. De Gasperi, of course, acted in the same manner, and for the same reasons as Prime Minister Queuille, when he resigned in France in 1948, and rejected the request, made in this case by the President of the Republic, that he present himself to the National Assembly and make his decision dependent upon a formal vote. There was, to be sure, in this case in Italy the difference that the occasion for the crisis was De Gasperi's decision to do without the Communists; the initiative in this inescapable move lay with himself. Yet, any study of contemporary reports will give ample details which prove that the general condition of Italian government at that time was similar to the French.

The nature of Italian parties was likewise identical with that of their French counterpart. After the new municipal elections, held in Rome in October, 1947, a Liberal newspaper commented:

"P.R. — with the result of the formation of large constituencies — compels the creation of large parties, with large financial resources, with a gigantic bureaucracy and a rigid discipline. . . . Parliament is no longer the seat of fruitful and unprejudiced debate between free and responsible men, but a tribune of rhetorical gymnastics between rigid groups, whose votes are inflexibly directed by the party secretariats." [14]

The "shift in the constitutional order," which Professor Smend described a generation earlier as an inescapable consequence of P.R., thus clearly developed in Italy after the Second World War.

A further characteristic feature is the deterioration in the quality of Italy's political élite. It must, of course, be borne in mind that in a parliament we want a ball team rather than a collection of prima-donnas. The mass parties which rose in post-war Italy responded to a deep political need. It was vital that the party system should be stronger at its base, and that a measure of discipline be enforced at the top. Yet, as the English example shows, there is a tremendous difference between this development under the majority system, where it strengthened and harmonized the political parties without interfering with the need of providing sound and intelligent leadership on the top, and developments under P.R. where the principal beneficiary was the party bureaucracy, with the tendency of making the deputies into mere ciphers. So far as the quality of the new deputies is concerned, let us only recall that the English Labour party, when making its successful bid for an over-all majority in 1945, made a very careful effort to select competent candidates. It went systematically beyond the ranks of the trade union bureaucracy, and succeeded in finding a number of candidates whose qualifications the constituencies were willing to accept, and whose subsequent political performance was good. So far as Italy is concerned, Professor Bellavista[15] speaks of "that scarcity of prime material which everyone sees through so much impressive silence (i.e., on the part of a large number of deputies), which at last the diligence of some functionaries of the Montecitorio (the name of the palace in which the Italian Chamber meets) has translated into precise, if discouraging statistics, or, worse, through interruptions and interventions of people who do not know either to keep silent or to speak." The place of deputies with real qualities has, according to the same observer, been taken by the *partitocrazia*, the substitution of party rule for democracy, which "finishes democracy." The parties, new style, have, in Italian political life, "assumed rigid, military, disciplined and oligarchic" shape. He concludes: "The partitocracy inherent in P.R. kills Parliament."

It took all the political mastery of which De Gasperi was capable to pilot the Italian ship of state past the cliffs which threatened it in the fall and winter of 1947-48. Communist propaganda continued to be active and successful. The left-wing Socialists persisted in placing everything on the card of cooperation with the Communists, come what may. De Gasperi reacted to this tactical weakness by adopting the only sensible course: he postponed the elections. Matters could not get worse than they were, and there was a chance for them to get better. Thus new elections — the elections to the first Chamber of Deputies of the new Italian Republic — were fixed for April 28. The system of voting remained substantially the same as in 1946.[16]

Panic and Victory

The turn of fortune, for which De Gasperi had hoped, came to pass. American Marshall Plan assistance helped to promote economic recovery. Two last-minute events dramatized the danger threatening from the extreme Left. In Czechoslovakia the Communists, afraid of facing new elections in which they were certain to lose, assumed absolute control. The suicide of Jan Masaryk followed, and gave to the Christian Democrats the opportunity of depicting on their campaign posters the fate awaiting Nenni, if he should be too successful with his pro-Communist policy. The other event which helped to turn the tide in favor of the Christian Democrats was the increase in the Leftist vote in the municipal elections in the city of Pescara on February 15. The Communist-Socialist bloc managed to poll 48.6 per cent of the popular vote; Socialists and Communists presenting different lists had secured together only 39.8 per cent in the previous municipal elections of April 7, 1946. Arnaldo Cortesi concluded his report to *The New York Times*[17] with these sentences: "The election result was received with elation in Leftist and with gloom in Rightist circles. It confirms the opinion that the left-wing parties have a good chance of winning the general election scheduled for April." Actually, the Pescara election galvanized the opponents of the Communists into doubling their activities, and into driving home to the supporters of the smaller parties that they would accomplish little unless they united their votes on the largest anti-Communist group, the Christian Democrats.

Finally attention must turn to the civic committees which the physician, Professor Luigi Gedda, founded among members of Catholic Action. The work of these committees was non-partisan; they confined themselves to clarifying the consequences of a Communist victory. An editorial published in *Life* magazine commented: "In ways the professional party workers could not match, the Pope's legions carried the battle deep into the slums, the farms and the fishing villages. They reached voters at a level which only the concentrating and hardworking Communists had reached before." [18] The Pope himself addressed a crowd at St. Peter's square, which was estimated to number 300,000 people. His remarks avoided partisan politics, but contained an effective warning on what was at stake in the elections for Italy and for Christian civilization as a whole.

During the final weeks before the elections the atmosphere changed completely. Even definitely anti-clerical Liberals and Monarchists were ready to support the Christian Democrats with their votes, and at times with substantial financial assistance. These Rightists had not changed their political views, but saw themselves confronted by a danger on the part of the Communists and their allies, which they wanted to ward off at any cost.

Thus the outstanding result of the election[19] was an unprecedented victory of the Christian Democrats. With 48.5 per cent of the votes they received 53.5 per cent of the seats, a clear parliamentary majority. The discrepancy between the Christian Democratic percentage of votes and seats is mainly due to the fact that, according to the election law, only those parties could secure seats from the national lists which had received at least one seat in a regional constituency. Altogether the smaller parties (meaning all parties with the exception of the Christian Democrats, the People's Bloc, and Saragat's Socialist Unity party) secured 13.4 per cent of the vote and 9.0 per cent of the seats. Even Saragat's group suffered, receiving 7.1 per cent of the vote and but 5.7 per cent of the seats. The leftist People's Bloc did secure 31.0 per cent of the votes and 31.9 per cent of the seats, and was the only group, outside of the Christian Democrats, which derived an advantage from the absence of complete proportionality between votes cast and seats obtained. The Christian Democrats, however, were the principal ones to gain, securing ten per cent more than their proportionate share in the way of seats. The small premium for large parties which the Italian system of voting contained, changed a minority into a majority.

The victory of the Christian Democrats was almost entirely the result of the decline in the voting strength of the smaller rightist parties. The losses of the groups participating in the People's bloc are infinitesimal. If we take into account the number of votes obtained by Saragat's Socialists, we find that the vote of the Communists and Socialists taken together declined by one percentage point; it would have been necessary for the People's bloc to have secured thirty-two per cent instead of thirty-one per cent in order to maintain the same strength as the Left held in June, 1946. The Christian Democrats, in addition to assistance from many who had previously voted for the smaller parties, were supported by the bulk of those who had heretofore not voted at all.

Nothing should induce us to minimize De Gasperi's victory. With one stroke the political atmosphere in Italy had changed. The defeatism rampant up to that time disappeared overnight, and the people again faced the future with confidence. Everyone knew that a good half of the battle for Italy's reconstruction had been won, and that economic consolidation could henceforth proceed without being upset by too much political turmoil. Financial policy, which had been shaped soundly by Luigi Einaudi, had already solved its essential task, and economic life had secured enough of a stable currency to have a reliable basis for future advance.

Prospects of "Normalcy"

And yet there is a reverse side to the picture. It is no argument in favor of a lottery if one wins. Elections under P.R. are such a lottery. De Gasperi's victory is entirely due to exceptional circumstances, which no one expects to repeat themselves in the foreseeable future. According to Anne O'Hare McCormick,[20] De Gasperi himself felt that in the case of the new election his party would not again secure a majority. One of the reasons for this assumption is the very fact that the danger of a Communist victory had receded somewhat. It took a definite "Red scare" to drive so many previous non-voters and convinced Rightists into the arms of the Christian Democrats. In the future other questions will occupy the front of the political stage; they are unlikely to create a clear front such as existed between Communists and Christian Democrats in 1948. The strength of the latter rested, however, on this clear-cut opposition.

De Gasperi drew the conclusion that his party should not govern alone, but in coalition with all parties willing to cooperate. Thus he wanted to make sure that there was a popular majority behind the government's parliamentary majority. The Prime Minister was greatly preoccupied with certain projects, such as agrarian reform; he welcomed the opportunity of opposing on this and other questions the pressure of moderate Socialists within the coalition to the conservative tendencies of the right wing of his own Christian Democrats.

These tactics are easily understandable, and for the time being they corresponded to a political necessity. Yet, they had the essential drawback so clearly predicted by Luigi Einaudi in 1946; there was no opposition capable of forming an alternative government. Let us repeat that a democracy is in danger unless those whom responsibility has overburdened can change sides with a responsible opposition. De Gasperi's cabinet had too much the character of a "government of all reasonable men" to do justice to the irrational factor in politics. Saragat's Socialists were, in 1948, the only visible point of crystallization for a constructive opposition. Keith Wheeler reported: "Many Italians who dislike the Christian Democrats almost as heartily as they dread the Communists, now pray for the survival of Saragat's liberal Socialist union. They hope he will provide a haven for dissidents from both directions and five years from now will achieve a much more dominant place in the political heavens." [21] The presence of this group in the government had the inevitable consequence of weakening them, and of contributing to the tendency of some of their number to join groups such as the one subsequently founded by Romita. So far Saragat's group has been losing rather than gaining ground.

How would the majority system have affected the Italian opposition in April, 1948? Igor Thomas summarizes a significant part of the answer in the sentence: "The Front (the Communist-Socialist bloc) has undoubtedly suffered a major reverse, which only proportional representation saved from being a rout." [22] It suffices to recall the experience of the French Communists in the provincial elections of March, 1949, in order to realize that the diagnosis of Thomas is correct. The French Communists, to be sure, obtained only about twenty-two per cent of the popular vote on that occasion, whereas the Togliatti-Nenni bloc had thirty-one per cent. Yet extremists secure more votes under P.R. than under the majority system. Under the latter, in the numerous constituencies where the candidates of the Togliatti-Nenni bloc stood no chance of winning, many leftist voters would rather have voted for the followers of Saragat than throw their votes away.

Actually, the situation would have been different long before the elections. Under a majority system Nenni was bound to suffer within his own party from the fundamental weakness that he was farther removed from the marginal voter than his competitors for the party's leadership. His slogan, *In mezzo non si sta*[23]—"One does not stand in the middle," sounded fine under P.R.; under the majority system it would have appeared, to his own followers, as a signpost on the road to ruin. By way of contrast, let us recall the very great care with which the two major parties in England appealed to the marginal voter before the elections of February, 1950. Groups unable to follow such a procedure, such as the Communists and Independent Socialists, the latter constituting Nenni's counterpart, suffered utter defeat. The dynamics of the majority system are an open book, and the Italian Socialists are not too illiterate to read it. More moderate leaders, such as Saragat and Romita, stood to gain, with Nenni (unless he, too, should have been willing to heed his lesson), being relegated to the political fringe of those regarded, perhaps, as idealistic, but certainly impractical.

Turning to subsequent developments, it was soon demonstrated that the Christian Democratic majority in the Chamber was a crisis majority. On May 8, 1949, the elections to the Sardinian parliament took place.[24] The Christian Democratic share of the popular vote declined from the 51.5 per cent, obtained in the Chamber elections of April, 1948, to 34.1 per cent. The strength of the Leftist bloc rose from 20.3 to 25.4 per cent. The Monarchists followed with 11.6 per cent of the votes, and secured almost seven times as many votes in April, 1948. The neo-Fascist MSI (Italian Social Movement), also gained, securing 6.2 per cent of the popular vote. Saragat's right-wing Socialists declined from 3.7 to 2.9 per cent. The third coalition partner, the Liberals, lost about three-fourths of the votes which they had received in 1948.

The losses of the Christian Democrats benefited rightist parties whose members, once the atmosphere of crisis had passed, returned to their old political allegiance, with the modification that participation in the government coalition proved to be a burden for all concerned. Even in definitely Catholic areas heavy losses of the Christian Democrats occurred, in the main to the advantage of the Monarchists. The latter were on the way toward establishing themselves throughout the country as the leading party of the Right. According to an English report,[25] they are not disinclined to engage in a certain cooperation with the Communists. In addition, the MSI was advancing, which drew its votes in particular from the young generation.

Some observers were inclined to reduce the tendencies which manifested themselves in the Sardinian elections to the simple formula: *Si ritorna alla normalità* [26] —"return to normalcy." Normalcy is, however, always relative. In this case it relates to the tendencies characteristic of P.R., under which such a splitting up of parties is in fact "Normal." What such a normalcy signifies becomes evident from the distribution of seats in the Sardinian parliament.

PARTIES	SEATS
Christian Democrats	22
Communists	13
Monarchists	7
Sardinian Democrats	7
Sardinian Autonomists	3
MSI	3

The question who was to form the government under such conditions was answered by Franco Porru in typical fashion: "That is a problem which only the labors of the lobbies (meaning discussions among parties and party leaders) will be able to solve." [27] Besides, the Sardinian elections also indicate that the trend toward polarization, which appeared in the Roman municipal elections of November, 1946, could be resumed.

The problems besetting Italian politics manifested themselves clearly in the crisis, which began October 31, 1949, with the resignation of the three cabinet members belonging to Saragat's right-wing Socialist party. Saragat and his two political associates left the cabinet, not because of a disagreement with its policies, but because they wanted to secure themselves a free hand for the impending congress of their party, as well as for negotiations with other Socialist groups. De Gasperi at first declined to take the crisis seriously; he called it a *crisetta* — "little crisis." The cabinet did not resign, and the ministries of the Socialists were temporarily entrusted to the administration of other cabinet members.

It soon resulted, however, that the resignation of the right-wing Socialists brought all the old frictions between the coalition partners to light, thereby aggravating them. The Liberal ministers found it necessary to make their stay in the coalition dependent upon their party directory — an extra-parliamentary body, which, at long last, and for the time being, permitted them, with a vote of eleven to nine, to remain in the cabinet. The next step was taken in the Chamber, where these events gave to the extreme Left the welcome opportunity to shed crocodile tears over the pretended unconstitutionality of the procedure employed by De Gasperi.

At last the party congress of the right-wing Socialists met and permitted, after long discussions, the members of its parliamentary group to resume their participation in the government. Simultaneously, however, a number of deputies and senators left Saragat, and joined the new Socialist group established by Romita. On January 12, De Gasperi submitted to the President of the Republic the resignation of his cabinet, in the expectation of being able to reconstitute it without delay. Yet, the ensuing negotiations among parties lasted two weeks, and De Gasperi experienced difficulties within his own party, whose left wing could not be satisfied, and refused further cabinet participation. Finally, it proved impossible to keep the Liberals in the cabinet, and De Gasperi's sixth cabinet, appointed on January 27, 1950, consisted only of Christian Democrats, Republicans, and right-wing Socialists.

The *crisetta* shed interesting light on the attitude of the various parties toward P.R. The Christian Democrats had begun to revise their attitude; after the elections of 1948 they developed certain sympathies for the majority system. The party was ready to accept compromises for municipal and regional elections, but emphasized, as was done in particular by De Gasperi, that considerable difficulties had developed in the municipalities with P.R. (the cities with more than 30,000 inhabitants), in which often there was no possibility of "a stable and effective administration . . . whereas there was no such inconvenience to be lamented in municipalities with majority system." [28] De Gasperi rejected the thought of using pure P.R. for such elections.

The strongest objection to the majority system came, paradoxically enough, from the Liberals, who had almost unanimously opposed P.R. in the first years after the Liberation. This time the left wing of the Liberal party insisted on P.R., maintaining that without it the party would disappear from municipal, provincial and regional parliaments.[29] The Liberal party executives approached the Republican and right-wing Socialist parties in order to bring about a united front of the smaller parties within the coalition in favor of P.R.

The Liberal assumption that, under a majority system, their party would be eliminated from all parliaments shows how much continued application of P.R. blurs political vision. Quantities are decisive under P.R. rather than under the majority system. Under the latter, much depends upon personalities, and in this respect parties like the Italian Liberals (comparable on this score to the French Radicals, although the Liberals are much weaker) are always relatively strong. In Italy, to be sure, the Christian Democrats drew the right conclusion from their electoral success in 1948; they made every effort to bring good candidates into their party. If such a process is carried far enough it means that such a party loses whatever narrow denominational characteristics it may have had, and that it becomes one of the points of crystallization for a two-party system. Still, in Italy, the physician, the lawyer, and the apothecary, who are more likely to belong to the small non-Socialist parties than to the Christian Democrats, have no less influence than the pastor on whom the Christian Democrats can generally but not always rely. This local élite is, under a majority system, a definite asset for parties like the Liberals, the Republicans, and the right-wing Socialists. They are one reason why such parties do comparatively well under the majority system. The other reason is the ready availability of these parties for campaign alliances, as well as for support by independent voters. All of them could attract support at their Right as well as at their Left.

The Italian situation was complicated by the Christian Democratic preference for the limited vote. The latter can produce excellent results in countries with a two-party system, where it merely assures an adequate opposition. With a multiple-party system the two largest parties (in Italy Christian Democrats and Communist-Socialists) are certain to qualify for either the majority or for the minority seats, leaving nothing to the smaller parties. This would be different under a majority system with single-member constituencies, where the smaller Italian parties would stand to benefit substantially from the losses of the Communist-Socialists and the neo-Fascists.

Toward the end of 1950 the Christian Democrats and their allies agreed (for the municipal elections) upon a limited vote with proportional distribution of the majority seats among a group of "linked" party lists.[29(a)] It was not the worst solution. Still, one asks why there was no serious attempt to return to the majority system. A complete answer would be complex, but one cannot help thinking of the special position of the party leaders, to whom P.R. gives power, as well as a feeling of security. If their party is strong, they control it. If it becomes as weak as did the German Democratic party in the 1930's, when it was said that their entire parliamentary group could ride to the Reichstag in a taxicab, the party leaders are at least certain that they will constitute the small band of the lucky ones. While the majority system holds out the prospect of growth, it entails risks, and as was pointed out by the then Social Democratic Premier of Schleswig-Holstein, Hermann Luedermann,[30] party leaders prefer a policy of "safety first."

The Republic and the Future

The old and new proponents of P.R. in Italy rarely ask themselves the question where their *res publica* will be a few years from now. At the moment, there is a majority, and a chance to assert the country's general welfare against centrifugal tendencies. A preview, however, of what may be expected to happen if and when new elections destroy the present majority was given by the extremists early in 1950. The Communist-Socialist bloc did everything in its power to obstruct the work of the government in all fields, in particular in that of agrarian reform. There the difficulties are immense; Italy pays the price of a neglect which goes back a full 2000 years, having begun in Roman times. A simple redistribution of agricultural property, such as took place in eastern and southeastern Europe after 1919 (which worked well enough after the initial setback to agricultural production had been overcome) will not do. Uncultivated lands have to be irrigated, and to be provided with roads and buildings before the new owners can expect to harvest anything but disillusionment. Yet, political reasons impel reform even where economic considerations stand in the way. As one observer said: "Italy cannot afford agricultural reform, and she cannot afford not to have agricultural reform."

The government of De Gasperi tries hard to get measures adopted which will make a bad situation better rather than worse. Even so, as Professor Mario Einaudi has pointed out in his careful analysis of the subject,[31] one of the measures under consideration, the so-called

Segni bill, is more likely to go too far than not far enough. Wherever the government submits a plan, the Communist-Socialist bloc responds by simply doubling the carefully considered official promises, certain to benefit if these demands are not adopted, and equally certain to gain if they are, as they would involve the government in failure. Their guiding motive is that the King's (or rather, the Republic's) government must be destroyed.

Lack of inhibitions is characteristic of the extreme Left, in the industrial as well as in the agricultural field. Aggressive demonstrations of workers are organized which, as long as De Gasperi and his Minister of the Interior, Scelba, do not want to reenact the part of Facta, must be resisted by force of arms, and are bound to lead to clashes with the police. Such clashes serve the purposes of the extremist opposition well, particularly if they produce the propaganda corpses which form an integral part of Communist (as of Fascist and Nazi) agitation. In their exploitation the large Communist-Socialist delegation in the Italian Chamber and Senate is most useful. Deputies and senators can attack the government without any restraint, protected by parliamentary immunity. Scores of them can be mobilized, as was done after the killing of six workers in Modena, in order to lend dignity to a monster demonstration of mourning, in which people devoted to the smashing of the constitutional order will shed copious tears over the "unconstitutional" behavior of the government. No discriminating political observer can fail to see through such tactics, but then the masses of voters are simple-minded folk who see the dead and sympathize with their fate. Nor should we forget that foreign correspondents, constantly under pressure to send "lively copy," find it easier to cable stories excoriating "police brutality" than to explain Communist conspirational policies.

The acts of wholesale violence committed by the Communists in the Italian, as well as in the French, parliaments only serve to discredit democracy which, as professor Guiseppe Ferri [32] remarked some time ago, is already less than respected among the younger generation. So far as violence in the country is concerned, the neo-Fascist MSI does its part according to its — at present somewhat limited — abilities, providing welcome pretexts for the extreme Left to retaliate. The word *basta*—"enough!" which helped prepare the road for fascism, enjoys again a measure of popularity. To Leon Dennen it seemed, after a study of conditions on the spot, that Italy was threatened by a crisis comparable to the one preceding the rise of Mussolini.[33]

We must, of course, not forget that men like Prime Minister De Gasperi, Minister of the Interior Scelba, and Minister of Defense Pacciardi, will defend their country's institutions to the best of their ability, ready to pay the price of unpopularity. All that is needed to undermine their position, however, is that "return to normalcy" which new Chamber elections are likely to produce under the present election law. New elections must be held no later than in the spring of 1953. What is not done before that time to assure the country's political stability will hardly be done afterwards. Italy may, of course, again try to get along with that type of crippled democracy from which other P.R. countries have suffered for decades. But Latin passions are not likely to tolerate for long (as Signor Alessio pointed out in his warning against P.R. in 1919) conditions which the Belgians have tolerated for more than a generation. "Normalcy" would again make Italy a country "where anything may happen any time."

CHAPTER 9. GERMANY

The Chance for a Two-Party System

The attempt to rebuild German democracy after the Nazi collapse in May, 1945, was beset with many obstacles. It did, however, start with one asset which even the greatest optimists had not expected. A report to *The New York Times,* dealing with some of the first elections held in Germany, began with these words: "A two-party system in the American zone of Germany, comprising the Christian Social Union and the Social Democratic party, appeared today to be a logical and eventual consequence of yesterday's municipal elections combined with the April county elections and the January elections in the smaller communities." [1] Testimony by others could be quoted to the same effect. The American Association for a Democratic Germany, for example, stated in a report: "In all three Western zones, something very close to a two-party system has emerged. Christian Democrats and Social Dmocrats together account for seventy to eighty per cent of the total vote." [2]

This degree of concentration developed in elections held under P.R., in which every dissident group of more than minimum size had a chance to elect its own candidates. By way of comparison let it be mentioned that the Liberals secured 29.7 per cent of the vote in the British elections of 1923; under the plurality system, this marked the beginning of an irresistible decline. Before the elections of February, 1950, according to the British Institute of Public Opinion (the British Gallup poll) "thirty-eight per cent of the voters questioned said they would vote Liberal if they thought the Liberals had a chance of winning." [3] This may well be an over-statement of the potential "Liberal vote;" yet, the distance between 38 per cent and 9.1 per cent (the percentage actually obtained by the Liberals) is so great that the effect of the plurality system is obvious. In the German case, the minor parties were, under a plurality system, certain, to all practical intents and purposes, to disappear from all parliamentary bodies. They were so disunited among themselves that they could not have agreed on common candidates, and they had nothing comparable to the proud political tradition which has sustained the morale of the British Liberals in the face of repeated defeats. Most of the German minor party voters were not likely to resist their absorption and assimilation by the two major parties. Under P.R., the small number of candidates elected by several minor groups operated, as it was called in the Belgian P.R. debate in the 1890's, like a "center of infection," certain to spread the disease.

Paradoxically, actions of Hitler and of Stalin were responsible for the high degree of democratic consolidation in the early days of postwar Germany. Hitler, instead of following Machiavelli's advice to "divide and rule," persecuted the German Catholics and Protestants with impartial severity. Within a few years he succeeded in breaking down barriers which, in the land of Luther, had existed for four hundred years. When a Protestant minister was arrested, a Catholic priest might preach in his congregation; when the Catholics could not use their church, the Protestants might make theirs available to them. After the war, those who were the political leaders of what constituted the great majority of the churchgoing members of both groups, founded the "Christian Democratic Union." (CDU; called Christian Social Union — CSU — in Bavaria.) The left-wing American Association for a Democratic Germany says, in reference to the first elections held in the British zone: "These elections were the first test as to whether the Christian Democrats would succeed in overcoming the traditional cleavage between Catholics and Protestants. They passed this test with flying colors." [4]

Stalin did for the German Left what Hitler had done for the Right and the Center. First, he ordered the annexation of large areas in Eastern Germany, which had been settled by Germans since before the first white man set his foot on what now is the United States. Then came the brutal expulsion from these provinces, as well as from the satellite states of eastern and southeastern Europe, of fifteen million people, in the course of which hundreds of thousands vanished and the rest were reduced to beggary. He retained the German prisoners of war long after the Western Allies had returned them, and once again hundreds of thousands were unaccounted for when the operation was declared to be ended. Meanwhile, the Communist terror in Eastern Germany continues. All of these factors have united to reduce the strength of the German Communist party to a level not only smaller than it had been during the depression, when the Communist vote rose for the same reason as the Nazi vote, but even below that of the 1920's. The Communist party has ceased to be a major party; under a plurality system, it would have found itself excluded or nearly excluded from practically all German parliaments.

Thus, the Social Democratic party seemed destined to be the one large party of the Left. At first it appeared to be willing to grasp its opportunity; even Dr. Kurt Schumacher, shortly after his liberation from a concentration camp, made conciliatory statements on the basis of which his party would have been in a fair position to make a bid for a majority. If matters changed subsequently, we must bear in mind not only the element of personal tragedy which they contained on the part of Dr. Schumacher, whom a serious illness continued to hold in its grip, but also the fact that only under P.R. was the Social Democratic party in a position to disregard the marginal voter in the center, without paying the severe penalty which the plurality system would have exacted for this cardinal political offense. The Social Democrats lost ground, but their strength remained close to that of the Christian Democratic Union which, to the satisfaction of their leading opponents, was suffering more from the disintegrating effects of P.R. than their rivals at the Left.

There was in Germany, when the first elections were held in 1946 and 1947, substantial agreement on the fact that a majority system, and in particular a plurality system, would mean a two-party system. More sincere proponents of P.R. opposed the majority system openly because of its tendency to create a two-party system.[5]

The question arises as to what attitude was taken by the Allies in regard to P.R. in Germany. They were unanimous in proclaiming the "democratization" of Germany as their goal. As to the relation between P.R. and democracy, let us only quote what Professor Hearnshaw wrote during the war in his widely read book, *Germany the Aggressor Throughout the Ages*:

"Early in 1919 a National Assembly was summoned to Weimar to frame a constitution. The scheme which ultimately emerged was a thoroughly bad one, eloquent of the political incapacity of the German people. It was doctrinaire, ultra-democratic, complicated, replete with paralysing checks and balances, and, above all, cursed by the principle of 'proportional representation,' which is the devil's own device for rendering democracy unworkable. The net result was that the electorate was split up, not into compact and clear-cut parties, but into a crowd of wrangling groups, not one of which had any chance of obtaining a clear majority in the Reichstag. The result was administrative chaos." [6]

The Allies were in a position to prevent the repetition of Weimar's worst errors. We must, of course, bear in mind that they had no common concept of democracy. The Russians spoke of "people's democracy"— a pleonastic term at best, since democracy means "people's rule" in Greek; if it is the intention to carry out a stated conviction, it suffices to say so once. Still, the term "people's democracy" entrenched itself, and the demand for P.R. became an integral part of what it meant at least in the initial "Trojan horse" phase of Communist seizure of power, as is shown by all Communist constitutional drafts, from the French down to the so-called "Volksrat Constitution" proposed for Germany, where this provision is listed in Article 51.

Russian foreign policy did not hesitate to associate itself with the Communist demands. When, on March 22, 1947, Molotov submitted his plans for German political reconstruction to the Moscow conference, they contained this sentence: "The Parliament and the *Lantags* of the *Lands* will be elected on the basis of a universal, equal and direct electoral law, with secret voting *and the proportional system*" [7] (Italics supplied). P.R., then, was to be required by the peace treaty, not only for the German federal parliament, but also for the parliaments of the *Laender*.

Molotov was consistent, but one wonders why the Western Allies failed to realize where their interests lay. As Dorothy Thompson wrote on a later occasion:

"The great danger to the concept of coalition governments and to all governments constituted by proportional representation is that they give aspirants for total (and permanent) power access to key ministries which they could never invest by straight majority rule.
Experience of this is so overwhelming that I have never understood why — in the German case, for instance — the Western Allies did not insist on the principle of majority rule being clearly written into the Western German constitution, or why we still look with indulgence on the multiple-party system. The fractionalizing of political life is the first condition for the realization of totalitarian ambitions." [8]

The only public reference to early American attitudes in this field is to be found in the Hearings on the *Third Supplemental Appropriation Bill for 1948,* held before the Subcommittee of the Committee on Appropriations of the House of Representatives. Congressman Francis Case, who had been in Germany during the summer of 1947 as the head of a subcommittee of the Herter committee, said, in the course of an informal discussion:

"The War Department sets up military government. Military government acquiesced in the decision, if it did not encourage — and I am inclined to think that they encouraged it — that they should use proportional representation in electing members of the *Landtag* and setting up the ministries in the various *Laender,* which certainly means that you will have Communists in government, if they get a minimum percentage of the votes of the entire whole." [9]

In the following discussion Army Secretary Royall expressed his own bewilderment on learning of the presence of three Nazis in the Danish parliament before, during and after the German invasion, as a result of P.R., but concluded:

"That is a very broad question. I suppose it is a matter of policy. You have got to take into account a great many factors. I do not defend proportional representation, and certainly I am not in favor of it in this country. But I am sure that in some of these countries we must make some practical concessions to the customs of the country and the customs of the surrounding countries. Possibly we have made too much; I do not know. But I think it is a factor we cannot entirely disregard." [10]

In commenting upon these views we must, in order to avoid misunderstandings, first of all, emphasize that those American officials who favored, or acquiesced in, P.R. in Germany were not pro-Communists. The opposite view is known to have been held by those concerned in these decisions. Second, the Communists were not the only beneficiaries of P.R. As Congressman Case expressed it on a later occasion, that system of voting "would . . . at the same time encourage the development of splinter parties which would create governments characterized by the indecision so often associated with governments where there is no direct majority party." [11] Among these splinter parties were parties of a nationalist, and neo-Nazi, character, which held out the prospect of being in the long run as dangerous, if not more dangerous, than the Communists, who, in Europe, at least, are unlikely to obtain power except where Russian troops are either present, or waiting at the border.

GERMANY

The third factor to be considered was expressed as follows in a letter to the editor of the *Neue Zeitung*, written in December, 1945, by a Dr. Harries:

"But I do not agree . . . that the decision between the two-party system and the multiple-party mess (*Vielparteienwirtschaft*) will be taken only in the forthcoming elections. That decision will be made earlier: the multiple-party mess is a necessary consequence of the proportional electoral system, as the Weimar constitution presented it to us; the two-party system is likewise a necessary consequence of the system of voting customary and proven in England and in the U.S.A. . . . The question whether we are politically mature or immature will, therefore, already be answered by the shape of the electoral law of tomorrow, and these considerations should be accorded the same attention as the question who can and who cannot vote." [12]

Dr. Harries, apparently, meant to imply that a P.R. system, once adopted, created enough vested interests to make its later abolition, if not impossible, at any rate what medieval theologians termed a "work of supererogation." In such a case, the scales are weighted so heavily in its favor that its supporters have little cause for concern. This fact had escaped the notice of American policy-makers even at a later date. C. L. Sulzberger, reporting to *The New York Times* on the Moscow conference, under the date of March 19, 1947, wrote:

"The elections would be held in all *Laender,* under the American plan. As the Allied Control Commission report demonstrates, the United States would be willing, for the initial elections, to accept the formula of proportional representation, although basically the Americans oppose this method and would demand that the Germans have the right to select their own electoral method later." [13]

The right of a people to decide against P.R. is largely hypothetical, if this decision is entrusted to a parliament elected under P.R. Professor Loewenstein had political logic on his side when he reversed the process and said:

"It is suggested . . . that for elections to a national assembly the majority system should be universally applied. If subsequently the assembly decides, in any country, in favor of proportional representation for future elections, it may do so. The British people were able to retain the beneficial two-party system . . . only because they obstinately refused to be lured into the political quagmire of proportional representation. What is good enough for the British, may be good enough for other peoples." [14]

If the Germans were to be given a chance to decide on the system of voting by a method which did not in itself prejudice the result, a plebiscite provided the only solution. Such a solution had, as mentioned above, been demanded in 1945 by the Italian opponents of P.R.; it was also demanded by a group of prominent scholars and writers in Heidelberg, who, in November, 1946, made an appeal to the governments of the American zone, demanding that the P.R. provisions of the respective constitutions be submitted separately to the popular vote on the constitution. They included the well-known economist and sociologist, Professor Alfred Weber, the commentator of the Weimar constitution, Professor Gerhard Anschuetz, the former president of the state of Baden, Dr. Willy Hellpach, and the editor of the monthly, *Die Wandlung,* Dr. Dolf Sternberger. These Germans naturally addressed themselves to the German governments. The American Military Government should not, however, have failed to pay attention to the request, since General Clay had set a precedent by causing the provision of the constitution of Hesse, which governs the socialization of basic industries, to be voted upon as a separate question in the plebiscite on the constitution of that state.

It might be mentioned in passing that wherever an attempt was made to ascertain how the people at large felt on the question of P.R., the result was overwhelming opposition to that system of voting. The Heidelberg monthly, *Die Wandlung,*[15] the Berlin newspaper, *Der Tagesspiegel,*[16] and the Wuerzburg newspaper, *Die Mainpost,*[17] requested their readers to express their views for or against P.R. Ninety-five per cent of the answers rejected P.R. The results were, of course, not entirely typical. *Die Wandlung* had published articles opposing P.R. by a number of distinguished writers, including its editor, Dr. Dolf Sternberger; *Die Mainpost* had run forceful articles by the jurist, Dr. Guenther Willms, and *Der Tagesspiegel* had published articles critical of P.R. by Dr. Johannes Leo and others. Besides, only those interested in the subject took the trouble to answer; the others are likely to be influenced by whatever party orders they receive. Yet, these experiments are in accord with other manifestations of the same sentiment, such as letters to radio stations, and, taken together, they create a strong enough presumption that a majority of the German voters opposed P.R. The German party organization, of course, decided differently; they only followed the example of their French counterparts. The explanation lies in what Professor Goetz Briefs has called, *Das organisierte Verbandsinteresse,* the fact that organizations tend to develop interests which are those of the organization itself rather than of its members.

So far as the French zone is concerned, the author lacks the information upon which any judgment would have to be based; it is, in any case, the least important. The British zone is the only one in which the competent officials, including the top officials, reached a negative verdict on P.R. as soon as they went into the subject. Subsequently, they never failed to emphasize that, as it was put in a letter to this writer, "The electoral system is the foundation stone of any constitution. It is, therefore a matter of grave concern to us that present-day political leaders fail to realize the significance of P.R. and that, despite their good intentions, they are building a democratic structure on the same unsound foundations that caused the collapse of the Weimar Republic." [18] These views were expressed to German political leaders, although quiet persuasion was the only means at the disposal of the officials in question. To this writer it has always been a matter of regret that some of the excellent briefs which they wrote on this topic, and which could find a place in any anthology on constitutional government, were not made public. Thus the average German in the British zone might learn that the British opposed P.R., but he could not inform himself about the reasons. He was inclined to shrug it all off as another interference of an occupation power with his domestic affairs.

For the sake of completeness it might be mentioned that before the British opposition to P.R. crystallized, Mr. John Fitzgerald, the successor to the late Mr. John H. Humphreys as the Secretary of the Proportional Representation Society, was sent to Germany, in March, 1946, in order to explain a compromise between the majority system and P.R., which had been adopted for German municipal elections. This selection was simply due to the fact that the officers of the P.R. society came first to mind when the London authorities looked for experts on electoral systems. Naturally, Mr. Fitzgerald used this opportunity to defend P.R. in general, and the single transferable vote (Hare system) in particular. He later reported to have met five thousand German officials.[19] At that time, there were as yet no postal communications with Germany, and opponents of P.R. outside Germany were unable to write to interested people in that country to make material available to them.

German opponents of P.R. also complained that when the British appointed provincial and *Land* councils, they, without reflection, did so on the basis of proportional representation of the recognized parties, making their estimates as accurate as they could. A prominent member of the Diet of North-Rhine Westphalia said in a meeting held in June, 1948, in the city of Muenster in Westphalia, which this writer attended: "The occupying power selected the members of the *Land* council on the basis of P.R. That body thus naturally proposed a P.R. law for the Diet elections. The Diet, elected under P.R., will continue P.R." The speaker apparently had the fact in mind that if Diet elections in North-Rhine Westphalia had been held under the plurality system, the Christian Democratic Union would have secured an overall majority. It would have used it to make the plurality system a part of the *Land* constitution, in the hope of setting a precedent which other *Laender* and the Federation would follow. British officials were, of course, right when they pointed out that it would have been difficult for them to constitute the *Land* council differently from the way they did and that, in order to defeat P.R. it would have sufficed to win over the Social Democrats, who had as much reason to take this stand as had the British Labour party.

The question arises why the Germans themselves did not oppose P.R. with more force, and why, in fact, a majority of the leaders of the newly-licensed parties demanded it. Part of the answer lies in the absence of leadership. Death had made gaps in the ranks of the opponents of P.R. which could not be filled in time. This applies in particular to the Social Democratic party, upon which the decision depended. The most brilliant among its younger leaders was, in pre-Hitler days, Dr. Carlo Mierendorff. He is best known as the founder of the "Iron Front," the one anti-Nazi organization which succeeded in infusing a measure of vitality into the Republican fight against the Nazis. Mierendorff had taken exception to P.R. in dozens of articles;[20] he used every conceivable opportunity to press his point, ever willing to brave the ridicule of dogmatic Marxists, for whom systems of voting could not really be relevant, with the result that they dispensed themselves from studying the issue. Dr. Mierendorff, a survivor of several years in a Nazi concentration camp, was killed during an air-raid on Leipzig.

Among other Social Democratic opponents of P.R. we must mention first Dr. Julius Leber,[21] who was hanged for his participation in the anti-Hitler plot of July 20, 1944. Albert Grzesinski,[22] former Prussian Minister of the Interior, died shortly before he was to have returned from New York to Germany to lead the fight against P.R. in his party. Dr. Rudolf Hilferding,[23] the former Reich Minister of Finance, had also expressed himself in opposition to P.R.

Several Social Democrats took up the struggle against P.R. in Germany soon after the revival of their party; the names of men such as Herrmann Luedemann,[24] for a while Social Democratic Prime Minister of Schleswig-Holstein, and Gustav Dahrendorf,[25] were, however, not well enough known to give them the authority to challenge Dr. Schumacher effectively on a major question.

The Free Democratic party was, in postwar Germany, as much responsible for the reintroduction of P.R. as was the Social Democratic party. Dr. Erich Koch-Weser[26] had for years been the chairman of the parliamentary group of its predecessor, the German Democratic party, in the Reichstag. In a book published in 1945 he had said, in relation to the claim that P.R. was needed as "a mirror of public opinion" that "actually it shattered that mirror into splinters." Koch-Weser died shortly after he finished his book; he might have offered a powerful challenge to his colleague, Dr. Theodor Heuss,[27] subsequently the President of the "Federal Republic of Germany," who, in particular in his excellent biography of his teacher, Friedrich Naumann, had expressed himself critically of P.R., but became its defender when he was heading a party too small to expect great success under the plurality system. In this connection it might be mentioned that there was another outstanding case of change from opposition to P.R. to its advocacy. Dr. Karl Spiecker had, in a book published in England during the war,[28] expressed himself in more forceful and more moving terms on the havoc wrought by P.R. than were used by anyone else. After the war, he was the founder and first president of the very small Center party which, it was quite evident, owed to P.R. its chances of survival. He later made an agreement to merge his party with the CDU, but had to discover that it is easier to start than to stop the process of disintegration characteristic of P.R.

This discussion would not be complete without a reference to the physical misery, and the intellectual isolation,[29] existing in Germany immediately after the war, and lasting well into the summer of 1948. One must have seen the gaunt look of people leading in the political life of their country in order to realize that there were physical limits to the energy which they could devote to even the most deserving cause. They had to face the difficulties of transportation, of communication (the mails were slow, and long-distance telephoning abominable), of securing paper, typewriters, office or meeting space, and the like, not to mention licensing requirements of the various military governments. Under such conditions, it is natural if many take the path of least resistance which, in this case, led to P.R. on the Weimar model.

Turning Away From the Two-Party System

Once P.R. became again a part of the pattern of German politics, its dynamics were bound to assert themselves. Centrifugal forces edged their way forward against the centripetal forces, although at first the two major parties held more ground than they yielded. In the United States zone, for example, elections for constituent assemblies were held in June, 1946, and elections to the first diets in November.[30] The percentage of the CDU in the popular vote declined from 48.7 per cent to 43.5 per cent; that of the SPD declined from 33.9 per cent to 33.0 per cent. This means that the percentage of the minor parties grew from 17.4 per cent to 23.5 per cent in the space of six months.

It might be mentioned that certain provisions kept down the share of minor parties in the seats. In Hesse and Wuerttemberg-Baden a party had to obtain five per cent of the votes cast in the *Land* before it could obtain seats in the Diet; in Bavaria it needed ten per cent in one of the five administrative districts (*Regierungsbezirke*) into which the *Land* was divided. Thus, in Bavaria, the Communist party with 5.3 per cent of the votes cast in June, and 6.4 per cent of those cast in December did not obtain any seats in the Diet. As long as P.R. is used, such provisions seem artificial; the Bavarian Communists, for example, sent, after the second election, an open letter to ten Diet members asking them to resign because they owed their seats to votes cast for the Communist lists, and should be replaced by an equal number of Communists.[31] It did not occur to the British Communists to make a similar appeal to, let us say four, members of the House of Commons after the plurality elections of 1950!

The most interesting election results developed, however, in the British zone. The critical attitude of the British authorities toward P.R. had the result that each of the three *Laender* was divided into a number of single-member constituencies, in which the candidate was declared elected who received a plurality.[32] In addition, there was a "reserve list," for which the *Land* as a whole formed a unit; this introduced the principle of proportionality. In North-Rhine Westphalia and in Lower-Saxony a party which had obtained a number of seats proportionate to its share of the popular vote, received no seats from the reserve list, and the result was P.R. with minor modifications. This was even more the case in Lower-Saxony than in North-Rhine Westphalia, because the number of seats on the reserve list could be increased (by nine at the most) in order to establish proportionality.

While the election laws of these two *Laender* came fairly close to pure P.R., the Schleswig-Holstein law introduced a genuine compromise between P.R. and the majority system. It provided that the seats available on the reserve list were to be distributed according to (a) the number of votes obtained by a party in constituencies where its candidates had failed to secure a plurality, and (b) the difference between the number of votes obtained by the victorious (plurality) candidate and his nearest competitor. The result was that the Social Democratic party, with 43.8 per cent of the votes, obtained 61.4 per cent of the seats.

The following table[33] gives the results for the three *Laender* of the British zone:

BETWEEN DEMOCRACY AND ANARCHY

DISTRIBUTION OF SEATS ACCORDING TO PARTIES

| | | | | Percentage of Seats Obtained by Parties ||
Parties	In Single-member Constituencies	Reserve List	Total	In Single-member Constituencies	Reserve List
IN SCHLESWIG-HOLSTEIN					
Social Dem.	34	9	43	79.1	20.9
Christian Dem.	6	15	21	28.6	71.4
SSV*	2	4	6	33.3	66.7
	42	28	70	60.0	40.0
IN LOWER SAXONY					
Social Dem.	58	7	65	89.2	10.8
Christian Dem.	14	16	30	46.7	53.3
Free Dem.	2	11	13	15.4	84.6
Center Party	1	5	6	16.7	83.3
German party**	20	7	27	74.1	25.9
Communists	..	8	8	..	100.0
	95	54	149	63.8	36.2
IN NORTH-RHINE WESTPHALIA					
Social Dem.	53	11	64	82.8	17.2
Christian Dem.	92	..	92	100.0	..
Free Dem.	..	12	12	..	100.0
Center party	2	18	20	10.0	90.0
Communists	3	25	28	10.7	89.3
	150	66	216	69.4	30.6

* SSV stands for South Schleswig Association, and is the designation of the party which favors annexation to Denmark.

** The official name of the German party was, at the time of the election, still "Lower-Saxony State party."

GERMANY

In North-Rhine Westphalia the Christian Democrats obtained 92 of the 150 seats in single-member constituencies. This was a clear majority, which was transformed into a minority by the distribution of the seats from the reserve lists, the Christian Democrats retaining their 92 seats won in the single-member constituencies, as compared with a total Diet membership of 216. It might be added that they still obtained 42.6 per cent of the seats with 37.57 per cent of the votes. In Lower-Saxony the Social Democrats obtained 58 of the 95 seats in the single-member constituencies. After the reserve seats had been distributed, they had 65 out of 149 seats. With 43.4 per cent of the votes they obtained 43.6 per cent of the seats, demonstrating that the election law used in Lower-Saxony in 1947 came closer than that of North-Rhine Westphalia to being pure P.R.

Thus, in the two most populous *Laender* of the British zone, the leading party obtained a majority of the seats in the single-member constituencies, only to be reduced to a minority in the respective Diets after the distribution of the seats from the reserve lists had taken place. In the case of plurality elections the distribution of votes would, of course, have been different; parties would have been reluctant to present candidates in constituencies where they had no chance. The expense of the operation would, however, in most cases, have been borne by the minor parties; the lead of the major parties might have been increased over what it was in the single-member constituencies.

We can, therefore, only conclude that under a plurality system the situation would, in all *Laender* of the British zone, have been the same as in Schleswig-Holstein, where the leading party was able to form, without delay, a government on the British model. Under the P.R. laws used in the other two *Laender,* the situation was different. Edward R. Murrow reported to *The New York Times* that according to British political observers, "it will be interesting to watch the gymnastics which will be necessary in setting up coalition governments for the two more important states." [34]

Developments in North-Rhine Westphalia were subsequently discussed by Professor Ottmar Buehler, who stated:

"What we actually had to live through with the formation of a government in North-Rhine Westphalia, exceeded everything which we had seen in the Reichstag (of the Weimar period) in this regard. The formation of a government required fifty-seven days, and the coalition finally established had to be so broad (it included the Christian Democrats, Social Democrats, Center party and Communists) that the result is an obvious lack of homogeneity and a disastrous weakening of the freedom of action of this government — all of which happened at a time of the greatest need." [35]

Dr. Buehler was referring to the fact that while the negotiations for the formation of the government dragged on, there occurred what perhaps was Germany's greatest food crisis, doubly severe in North-Rhine Westphalia, which includes the Ruhr district. The actual negotiations for the formation of a government took, to be sure, less than fifty-seven days, but this did not shorten the period of uncertainty by one day, whereas, under a plurality system the nature of the new government would have been known the evening of election day.

The problems of the coalition in North-Rhine Westphalia were subsequently simplified when the Communists were eliminated. Yet, there remained the basic conflict between the Social Democrats and the Christian Democrats. The small, but not insignificant, Center party (engaged in bitter warfare, in particular on the local level, with the CDU) sided with the Social Democrats on issues of economic, and with the Christian Democrats on issues of religious (in particular educational) policy. It also formed part of the coalition. The great asset of the government was Prime Minister Arnold, a leader of the left wing of the CDU, who enjoyed the respect even of those who disagreed with him. The fundamental heterogeneity of the coalition remained, however, and exacted its toll of indecision, procrastination, and confusion.

Let us give only two illustrations. The first concerns the "State Commissariat to Fight Corruption and Mismanagement." The major reason for its establishment was the demoralization of the civil service arising from the fact that, before the currency reform of June, 1948, the salaries of the government employees were paid in all but worthless papermarks; they were tempted to augment their income by accepting gratuities. A contributing factor was the absence of a real opposition. The Free Democratic party, to be sure, stood outside the coalition, and so did the Communists eventually, but neither could provide the type of challenge which, for example, a Social Democratic opposition would have offered to a Christian Democratic government.

The commissariat had been established by government decree

rather than by law. The CDU proposed to abolish it as a measure of economy; this was after the currency reform, when such a move seemed advisable. The Social Democrats favored a law which was to give the commissariat the proper legal foundation. The *Rhein-Ruhr-Zeitung,* a newspaper published by leading members of the Center party and, therefore, vigorously opposed to the majority system, commented:

"The debates concerning the arguments for and against the proposed economy, which, in view of the peculiar majority conditions of the House are often difficult to follow, required three hours on the first day of the session. . . . The CDU proposal, to abolish the commissariat, was rejected by a small majority. Likewise, on the occasion of the third reading of the law which was to give a firm legal foundation to the commissariat, no majority could be found. . . . Thus the State Commissariat, which is now functioning for nine months, continues to exist for the time being, but the legal foundation continues to be denied it." [36]

The "peculiar" majority conditions which produced this confusion are, of course, a result of P.R.; the plurality system would have resulted in a clear majority, and in clear responsibilities.

The second example concerns the constitution for North-Rhine Westphalia, which this assembly was elected to tackle as its primary task. Serious consideration of the issue did not begin in the Constitutional Committee until January, 1950, almost three years after the Diet had been elected. The government proposal submitted to it was a curious document, as it contained different proposals by the majority and minority within the government, printed side by side. The CDU was responsible, in the main, for the majority proposals, and the SPD for the others. The Minister of the Interior, Dr. Menzel, whose task it was to introduce the draft, was a Social Democrat, so he defended the minority plans! A member of the Diet wrote to the author:

"It is the draft of a coalition government which could not agree upon a unified draft, and therefore introduced two drafts, which are being submitted to the Diet on an equal footing. Here, once again, the absurdity of P.R. is demonstrated. One sees clearly that there are, in one cabinet, two governments which suspect each other, spy on each other, paralyze each other, and take care that no real government activity can develop. An impossible situation. Here, instead of a two-party system, there comes into the open a two-government system within one cabinet."

The only reason why this condition could continue for the first years — although even then it was responsible for many omissions, including the failure to provide adequately for the expellees — was the continued supervision by the Military Government, with which many important decisions lay. The same applies to the government of Lower-Saxony, which also had to be formed on a basis of a coalition which included Social Democrats and Christian Democrats. At one time a government crisis in that *Land* lasted three months; it ended without reestablishment of a formal coalition. The ministers entered the new cabinet on their personal responsibility rather than as representatives of their parties.

This is not the place to discuss the governments of the other *Laender*, except in order to mention that, with the exception of Bavaria and Wuerttemberg-Hohenzollern (if we may disregard Hamburg and Bremen) none of them had a one-party majority, whereas under a plurality system, practically all would have had one. The general picture is one of heterogeneous coalitions, producing the customary crop of crises; some of the small-town cabinet members are said to feel very important when a cabinet crisis occurs.

It is too often overlooked that comprehensive coalitions exclude the possibility of a serious opposition, and thus there is no watchdog able to sniff persistently enough and to bark loudly enough when symptoms of collusion and corruption appear. In Wuerttemberg-Baden the police developed unusual perseverance in the face of official discouragement when they unearthed the trail of scandal which involved a high official of the Ministry of Denazification. The government, formed by a coalition of the Social Democratic, Free Democratic and Christian Democratic parties (and until January, 1950, willing to permit a Communist the supervision of a camp in which expellees, and refugees from the East, were received) was inclined to hush matters up. The favorite instrument for this process were parliamentary committees of investigation, which the weekly, *Rheinischer Merkur*, termed "chambers of obscuration." [37] On this occasion, the facts could not be hidden. High Commissioner McCloy had, in addition to others, taken an interest in the matter. We should not conclude, as most American newspaper correspondents do, that these developments were simply a result of German unwillingness to deal with corruption — as if investigating committees in the United States relied upon the government party to unearth secrets which the administration hopes to hide! The trouble in Stuttgart was of a constitutional order, as was emphasized again in the *Rheinischer Merkur,* which has frequently pointed out the results of extending the principle of proportional representation to governments, and thereby excluding any chance for a serious opposition. Similar incidents could be reported from other P.R. countries. Let us add that all-inclusive coalitions are suspect to the people; even if there is no concrete evidence of scandal it is widely believed that the purpose of these coalitions is that the parties concerned intend to divide the spoils without fighting over them.

P.R. and the Federal Constitution

The initial discussions of a Western German government began in the summer of 1948. At first, there was reason for hope. The Conference of Prime Ministers for the Western Zones appointed a committee of experts, one from each *Land,* who were sent, together with fourteen other experts, to Herrenchiemsee in Bavaria in order to prepare, in non-public deliberations, the ground for a constituent assembly. The majority of the men selected were of a high caliber, and they took advantage of their freedom from partisan ties. The report which they submitted is a useful piece of work, and was helpful in the crystallization of views and issues.[38]

Several members of this constitutional conclave did their best to provide their associates with information on electoral systems; their difficulty consisted in the fact that whereas there is, on account of the existence of the English and American P.R. societies, never lack of material favoring P.R., there was, at that time, hardly any material available which presented the other side. Even so the report leaves little doubt as to how a majority of the members felt on the subject of P.R. The report says:

"In its work, the constitutional conclave came again and again upon the extraordinary importance of the electoral law. It did, however, not consider itself competent to undertake a systematic investigation of this subject, since, apparently, not even the basic features of the election law are to be included in the constitution." [39]

The latter sentence may refer to the specific tasks set to the conclave; it may also imply that the authors did not feel free to challenge the traditional view which sees in voting systems something "technical" and, therefore, by definition minor.

In the main body of the report, the experts consider "the danger of a parliament which is unable to work." Among possible remedies, the majority system is listed in first place. As the report states:

"Electoral reform must bring a principal guarantee. The Committee did not want to anticipate the decision in favor of the majority system, but the latter is prepared by the fact that the election of deputies is firmly defined. Also, the election law can provide that parties which receive less than five per cent of the votes are not to obtain any seats, and that a party may not receive more seats for the sum of its surpluses than it has secured in the constituencies." [40]

The meaning of this paragraph is not quite clear. If, in the last sentence the word "constituencies" means single-member constituencies of the type instituted in the British zone, it suffices to look at the table on page 202 to see that such a provision would have all but eliminated the minor parties.

A decision as to procedure was to anticipate the result of this and all subsequent criticism of P.R. The new constitution was to be drafted by what came to be known as the Parliamentary Council, which met in Bonn on September 1. The members of this body were selected according to P.R. by the state legislatures, which in their turn had been elected under various P.R. laws. It was agreed that Social Democrats and Christian Democrats were to have an equal number of the members; consequently, the representatives of the minor parties — all of which had a vital interest in the preservation of P.R. — turned the scales. It is characteristic that a member of the Free Democratic party was the chairman of the committee on the electoral law, as well as its reporter to the full council. Before this committee the leading members of the "German Voters' Society" presented an imposing array of facts to demonstrate the implications of P.R.; they were supported by a forceful talk given by the former Chancellor, Dr. Luther, who told the members how his own experience under P.R. in Weimar Germany compared with the subsequent observations and studies of the plurality system in the United States and England.[41]

It goes without saying that none of these arguments had the

slightest effect on the votes cast either in committee or in the full meeting of the Parliamentary Council where, among others, the Bavarian deputy, Dr. Kroll, ably presented the arguments for the plurality system. The minor parties were for P.R., even if many of their members were against it. The Social Democrats sided with them. Their immediate motive was that, as long as the areas with a large bloc of Socialist voters, in particular Berlin and Saxony, were not able to vote in the election to the new federal parliament, the majority system would give a majority to their Christian Democratic opponents. This result Dr. Schumacher was determined to prevent, regardless of the consequences. As mentioned above, several leading Social Democrats held a different opinion as to the long-run interests of their party, and the needs of German democracy, but the centralizing influence of P.R. upon the structure of their party had already been so great that the opinion held at headquarters was the only one that counted.

The "German Voters' Society" made a final attempt to have the issue submitted to the people themselves. A proposal drafted by Dr. Gerhard Schroeder would have combined the elections to the first Bundestag with a plebiscite on the voting system. Western Germany was to be divided into a number of single-member districts. The Schroeder plan provided that if the voters decided in favor of the plurality system, the election would end with the victory of the candidates with the highest vote; otherwise, the provisions concerning the reserve lists would be applied. Naturally, the P.R. majority of the council turned this plan down without serious consideration.

Elections were held on August 14, 1949, with a system similar to that of Lower-Saxony. The parliamentary Council had at first decided in favor of a plan under which only fifty per cent of the members of the Bundesrat were to be elected in the single-member constituencies, and the remainder from reserve lists. The military governors asked the German prime ministers to suggest any improvements which they cared to make. They proposed that the percentage of the deputies to be elected in single-member constituencies be raised to sixty and that lists which either failed to secure five per cent of the votes in the respective *Laender*, or did not elect at least one candidate in a single-member constituency, were not to get seats from the reserve list. The military governors decided in favor of these suggestions, which thereupon became part of the election law.[42] American cooperation in this procedure may or may not indicate that the opinion of those American officials who were critical of P.R. had by this time prevailed.

The First Bundestag

It must not be assumed that the concessions to the majority principle contained in the election law were substantial. The votes cast for the various parties in a particular *Land* were added up, and the number of seats to be attributed to each was determined in proportion to the votes, applying the system devised by the Belgian mathematician, d'Hondt. A party kept the seats obtained by pluralities in the single-member constituencies. If the number of seats won by a party in these constituencies exceeded the number due it under the d'Hondt calculation, the total number of seats in that particular *Land* was to be increased so as to offset this fact. There was enough of the principle of P.R. in these provisions to make the emergence of a majority impossible, and the further splitting up of parties inevitable.

The following table[43] gives the number of seats obtained by the respective parties, together with the number of seats which would have been won in the case of strict proportionality between votes cast and seats received:

PARTY	SEATS RECEIVED	SEATS UNDER P.R.	VOTES PER SEAT RECEIVED
Christian Dem.	139	125	52,932
Social Dem.	131	117	52,918
Free Dem.	52	48	54,382
Bavarian party	17	17	58,036
German party	17	16	55,299
Communists	15	23	90,667
Econ. Recon. party	12	12	56,832
Center party	10	12	54,382
German Rightists	5	7	85,790
Independents	2	15	422,315
South Schleswig Assn.	1	1	75,387
Refugees	1	5	318,418
Other	--	4	-----
Total	402	402	59,711[1]

[1] Average number of valid votes for each seat.

GERMANY

It will be seen that the advantage received by the larger parties was slight, although it is interesting to note that the Social Democratic party, which protested the small concession to the majority system made by the prime ministers and the military governors, benefited as much as the Christian Democrats. These gains were made possible by the losses of "Independents" and "Refugees." The law provided that only licensed parties could participate in the distribution of seats from the reserve lists; others might present independent candidates, who were elected if they secured a plurality in their constituency, but whose votes were lost if they did not. Without this provision — which, since licensing has been abolished, will not apply in the future — proportionality was almost complete, the only further interference with it being caused by the requirement that a party had, in a particular *Land*, to obtain either five per cent of the total vote, or secure a plurality for at least one of its candidates. Failure to do this in some cases is the reason why the smaller parties, in particular the Communists, did less well than they would have under P.R.

On the other hand, the question arises what the result would have been under a majority system. An article by a State Department official contains these sentences:

"A stable majority-party government can pursue a policy without constant concern over precarious coalition arrangements. But the single member district would by no means guarantee a two-party system in Germany. The minor parties are primarily regional with their strength concentrated in certain areas of the Laender. The Economic Reconstruction Party and the Bavarian Party in Bavaria, the Center Party in the Ruhr region of North Rhine-Westphalia, and the Germany Party in Lower Saxony are examples of these. The number of seats the minor parties received in the recent elections would not be appreciably reduced under a single member district system." [44]

The author would never have made such statements had he taken the simple precaution of presenting the election results for the single-member constituencies and comparing them with the over-all results. It is the one good feature of the current law that it does divide Western Germany into comparatively small districts, which provide a clear indication as to whether a party has the local strongholds needed under the majority system or not. The details follow: [45]

PARTIES	SEATS THROUGH PLURALITIES	SEATS FROM RESERVE LISTS	TOTAL
Christian Democrats	115	24	139
Social Democrats	96	35	131
Free Democrats	12	40	52
Communists	..	15	15
Bavarian party	11	6	17
German party	5	12	17
German Right party	..	5	5
Economic Reconstruction party	..	12	12
Center party	..	10	10
Independents	3	..	3
South Schleswig Association	..	1	1
	242	160	402

It will be seen that the Communists, the Economic Reconstruction party, the Center party, the German Right party, and the South Schleswig Association did not receive a plurality in a single constituency. Had the plurality system obtained, and the distribution of the votes been the same as it was on August 14, no candidate of these parties would have been elected. Had the plurality system actually been in force, the distribution of the votes would have been different, but that difference usually turns out to the disadvantage of the smaller parties. These parties then are, at any rate so far as their parliamentary representation is concerned, children of P.R.

Considerations of space make it impossible to reproduce the exact distribution of the votes in the constituencies where these parties reached their highest vote; a glance at the detailed statistics published by the various *Laender* confirms the impression created by the above table — that the parties in question had hardly a leg to stand on under the plurality system. They could, in some instances, turn the scales between the major parties, and the redistribution of the votes given them might have affected the balance of power within the parties to which their supporters turned, causing, for example, within the Christian Democratic Union a shift to the Left (or, in the Social Democratic party, a shift to the Right). Occasionally one of their members might even have attracted enough support from other parties to be elected, but experience under the majority system indicates that success on such a limited scale is not enough to keep a party alive. Certainly, then, these parties owe their existence to P.R. It must be added that, if we look at the results closely, not even the Bavarian party, which had a plurality in eleven constituencies, did well. Its margin of success was generally small; it did not poll forty per cent of the total vote in any constituency, and, as an extremist party, it would have found it difficult to attract needed support from other parties.

It is interesting to note that the P.R. proteges include the extreme Left (the Communists) as well as the extreme Right (German Right party). The other rightist party is the German party, which secured five deputies through pluralities, and ten through the reserve lists. This party arose out of two entirely different elements. The nucleus came from the "Guelphs," the party favoring the independence of the former kingdom of Hanover from Prussia. The Guelphs were, in the pre-1918 Reichstag, associated with the parliamentary group of the Center party, which means that they were definitely opposed to nationalism; Bismarck included these groups among the *Reichsfeinde* — "enemies of the Reich." The five seats of the German party were won by pluralities from the Hanoverian strongholds of the old Guelph party. Most of the remaining ten seats, picked up by way of the reserve list, came from Rightists with a nationalist tinge. The former Guelphs were tempted by the fact that, after the formation of the Chrisian Democratic Union, there was no Rightist party, and they tried to fill this "gap," without realizing that they would have to abandon their old traditions if the combination were to last. The majority system would have guarded them effectively against the temptation to expand by an appeal to nationalism.

P.R. promoted German nationalism in other ways. The Economic Reconstruction party has strong nationalistic tendencies; its success was due to the support of the expellees, whose political creed is a nationalism of despair. All of its seats were won from the Bavarian reserve list; under a plurality system, the party would have stood no chance whatsoever.

To complete the picture, we must mention the fact that the Free Democratic party did not develop into the Liberal party which some of its outstanding members, such as Professor Heuss, wanted it to be.

As time progressed, it tended to place itself to the Right of the Christian Democratic Union; in Hesse it allied itself with the definitely nationalistic National Democratic party, which was not licensed for the elections of August, 1949. That the Free Democratic party secured forty of its fifty seats on reserve lists shows that, under a plurality system, it would have been that much weaker.

By calling the roster of the nationalistic elements in German politics, we see, therefore, that their success is almost entirely due to P.R. In speaking of nationalism we must, however, guard against using the term loosely. A person is not a nationalist just because he defends the legitimate rights of his country. As long as he is aware that others, too, have their rights we should call him a patriot. Nationalism begins where men elevate the rights of their own nation above all others. The Germans were, after the Nazi collapse, at first passive. It was to be expected, however, that once they awoke from their post-war stupor, they would reassert their rights. Still, there is a difference between the attitude of a man like Dr. Adenauer, who watches carefully for a constructive solution for old conflicts (and who, for that reason, has been the subject of vilification by the true nationalists of his country), and those gathered in the smaller Rightist groups (such as the German Right party), who do not care where their highly emotional propaganda — at times consisting of sheer demagoguery — will lead. An Adenauer may, and will, be wrong on occasion but, as his attitude towards Germany's entry into the Council of Europe, and towards the pooling of the French and German heavy industries shows, he is willing to come to terms, and to assume domestic risks in the interest of international understanding. If he, too, sounds different in an election campaign, this is to some extent due to the time-honored habit of the politician to pay his tribute to the demands of campaign oratory; it is, in this case, also a result of the competition offered by truly nationalist small parties, which were a real political threat in most of Germany in the elections of 1949, thanks to P.R.

The latter consideration demonstrates, once again, **the value of the** majority system as an agency of social control. We cannot engage in "thought control," and, speaking of Western Germany, we cannot remake the minds of fifty million people. We can, however, place bars in the way of the extremists, and, on the other hand, make matters easier for the moderates. By giving institutions a chance to promote the success of our friends and drive our enemies to failure and frustration, we can accomplish more than by praising here and scolding there, or, for that matter, by preaching political sermons everywhere.

The Election and the Prospects for a Two-Party System

At the same time that the elections to Western Germany's first Federal Diet gave aid and comfort to nationalist elements, they prevented the rise of a homogeneous government majority. The Christian Democrats won 115 of the 242 seats in single-member constituencies. Under a plurality system, a party which enjoys such a strong lead is likely to gain added support, and the Christian Democratic Union was in a favorable position because it could attract votes from the smaller rightist as well as the centrist groups. It is not impossible that, even after four years of P.R.-promoted political disruption, the reintroduction of the plurality system on the eve of these elections would have led to an over-all majority of the Christian Democrats.

On the other hand, the Christian Democrats, with 115 pluralities, and the Free Democrats with 12, were certain to win a combined majority. They were united on the major campaign issue, as both endorsed the economic policy of Professor Erhard. Under a plurality system, their own supporters would have forced them to sponsor joint candidates in all constituencies where a split would have endangered the success of their policy. Under such conditions, the combination stood to gain even more seats than the number of its pluralities indicates. The political effect of such a combination is illustrated by the joint victory of the Liberal and Country parties in Australia in 1949; the result differed only in minor respects from the victory of a single party. Such cooperation can, in the long run, lead to fusion and, under a plurality system (which Australia does not have) it is almost certain to do so.

Christian Democratic gains did not have to be won at the expense of the Social Democrats, as is assumed by the authors of the analysis of these elections in the State Department *Bulletin,* who say that the plurality system "would probably have resulted in a straight CDU-FDP majority *and a correspondingly weaker SPD*" [47] (italics supplied). The ones certain to lose were the minor parties. The Social Democrats were likely to gain some of the Communist vote, regardless of instructions by Communist party leaders. They also stood to gain expellee votes, most of which went, under P.R., to the Economic Reconstruction party and the rightist parties. Furthermore, the SPD might have gained some of the votes of the Center party, whose leaders have often stated that, if they had to choose between CDU and SPD, they would support the latter. Lastly, it could expect support from those Free Democrats who placed their "cultural liberalism" (opposition to denominational schools and the like) above the issues of economic policy. The extent of these gains depended primarily on the attitude of the Socialist leadership. Moderation was as certain to make friends as radicalism was to make enemies.

The basic solidarity of the two major parties also results from the losses inflicted equally upon both by the disintegrating effects of P.R. In comparison to the latest Diet elections the Christian Democratic Union's percentage of the total vote declined from 37.7 to 31.0, and that of the Social Democratic party from 35.0 to 29.2.[48] The combined total of the two declined from 72.7 per cent to 60.2 per cent. This decline took place in from two to three years. One commentator wrote: "The decision of August 14 has finally destroyed the dream of a two-party system for Germany." [49] The statement was premature; the flame of the two-party system burned low in August, 1949, but it was burning, and could have been rekindled. If, on the other hand, the trends revealed up to that time should continue a few more years, the above statement will constitute a correct appraisal of the facts.

If we want to see how far fragmentation can go under P.R., the best example is Bavaria. The following table[50] gives the percentages of the total vote obtained by the various political parties in the Bavarian Diet elections of December 1, 1946, and the results in the Bundestag elections:

PARTY	DIET ELECTIONS	BUNDESTAG ELECTIONS
Christian Democrats	52.3	29.2
Social Democrats	28.3	22.8
Communists	6.4	4.1
Liberal Democrats	5.6	8.5
Economic Reconstruction party	7.4	14.4
Bavarian party	..	20.9

The losses of the Christian Democrats (called Christian Social Union in Bavaria) were catastrophic, even though they remained the strongest party. The greatest gainer was the Bavarian party, which was federalist to the point of being separatist and was supported, in particular, by those who resented the expellees. It was followed by the Economic Reconstruction party of the eccentric Mr. Loritz, who had the foresight to place his chauffeur on his list of candidates so that he, as a member of the Bundestag, would not need a salary. Mr. Loritz appealed, as mentioned above, primarily to the expellees. It is significant that the two parties taking the extreme view on this thorny question should make the most substantial gains.

Few stopped to ponder the implications of the election results for the future of self-government in Bavaria. Fragmentation on the Weimar model had taken the place of the over-all majority of the Christian Social Union. The claim was made immediately that the CSU government, by staying on, was "offending the voters." One commentator added: "That remains true even if, on the basis of the latest election results, an alternate government majority in Bavaria appears problematic." [51] While such a conclusion constitutes a logical deduction from the premises of P.R., it is hardly encouraging from the democratic point of view.

Bonn and Weimar

The election results seemed, however, fairly favorable for Western Germany as a whole. The formation of a government was expected to take place without difficulty. Most observers agreed that a coalition of Christian Democrats and Social Democrats was undesirable, since it would have excluded the possibility of a strong democratic opposition. Besides, Dr. Schumacher insisted that any coalition would have to accept the economic policy of his party, which the electorate had just rejected. The position of chancellor in the new government was to go to Dr. Konrad Adenauer, the leader of the Christian Democrats, whose reputation had been enhanced by the manner in which he had presided over the Parliamentary Council.

Before the new cabinet could be formed, however, P.R. arithmetic asserted its rights. There was no particular difficulty in securing the cooperation of the Christian Democratic Union and the Free Democratic party. In a parliament consisting only of the 242 deputies elected in single-member constituencies, the two parties had 127 seats, a majority which — since German standards are not as exacting as English standards — would have appeared ideal. In the full P.R. parliament, however, the 139 Christian Democrats and the 52 Free Democrats added up to only 191 out of 402 deputies. In the search for a majority there was little use turning to the seventeen members of the Bavarian party, or the twelve deputies of the Economic Reconstruction party, or the ten of Center party. These P.R.-produced parties were satisfied, each in its own way, to express a resentment rather than to make a policy. There remained then the German party with seventeen members, which, together with the Christian Democrats and the Free Democrats made a combined total of 208, still not a strong majority but the best that could be hoped for. Difficulties followed from the heterogeneity of the German party; while cooperation with the old Guelphs was easy, the nationalist elements in the party presented their problems, one of the deputies in question soon becoming involved in a sensational case necessitating his expulsion from the party.

The German party was determined to exact its price for government participation, and received in the end two cabinet positions. Since the Free Democrats with a strength of fifty-two deputies had to be satisfied with three cabinet posts, the German party with its seventeen fared well by comparison. The apportionment of party strength within the cabinet was, in fact, not successful until two new positions had been created; a Free Democrat became "Minister for ERP Affairs," and a member of the German party "Minister for *Bundesrat* Affairs." (The *Bundesrat* consists of delegates of the *Laender* governments.) The new jobs were, as the opposition did not fail to point out, "tailor made" to suit coalition requirements.

The final success of the negotiations was preceded by other troubles. For a few days there was talk of discarding Dr. Adenauer and establishing a coalition on a basis different from the one which he was contemplating. Trouble came also from the left-wing of the CDU; as a result, Mr. Arnold, the Prime Minister of North-Rhine Westphalia, rather than Mr. Ehard, the Prime Minister of Bavaria, was elected President of the *Bundesrat*. It seemed necessary to compensate the Bavarian Christian Democrats (CSU) by offering the ministry of finance to one of their members, which previously had been reserved for Dr. Bluecher of the FDP. The change led to a rift between the newly-elected Federal President, Dr. Heuss, and Dr. Adenauer. In the words of Jack Raymond:

"As not expected . . . this nomination (of Dr. Adenauer for the chancellorship) took place only after sudden strong dispute between Dr. Heuss who was leader of the Free Democrats, and the Chancellor designate. Dr. Heuss apparently insisted that he was not a mere figurehead and intended to exercise fully whatever authority he could eke out of his position under the Constitution, including even veto rights over Dr. Adenauer's proposed ministerial nominations." [52]

The wording of the Bonn Constitution leaves no doubt that its authors intended to entrust the composition of the cabinet to the chancellor, once he had been elected by the Bundestag, natural as it was for Dr. Heuss, before his election to the presidency a Free Democrat, to resent the shelving of one of his friends, whose competence for the job was uncontested.

The constitution required — in the best manner of frightened democracy, French style — that the chancellor, after having been designated by the president, be supported by a majority of the total Bundestag membership. Dr. Adenauer received 202 votes, including his own; since the Diet had 402 members, there was no vote to spare. The Chancellor-designate had failed to get the support of several members of the government parties, a fact which did not augur well for the future. *The New York Times* reported:

"The vote ended two weeks of government organization in the West German state, marked by continuous political battling between parties and within parties. An experienced Western official summed up the feelings of the Allies and the Germans alike when he commented: 'The new government is off to a shaky start.'" [53]

For the time being it seemed, however, that, once in office, it would be all but impossible to dislodge Dr. Adenauer. The French daily, *Le Monde*, entitled a report by its special correspondent, Alain Clément, "Mr. Adenauer Gets Ready to Exercise a Veritable Regency Over Germany," and the report stated: "The time of parliamentary horse-trading is over, as Mr. Adenauer thinks; there will be an Adenauer policy or anarchy. There will be a Germany founded by Adenauer, or there will be no Germany." [54]

The constitutional basis for this self-confidence of the chancellor was Article 67, according to which the Bundestag can vote the censure of the government only by first electing a new chancellor, with an absolute majority of its members. Similarly, Article 68 provides that if a request by the chancellor for a vote of confidence is not granted by a majority of the members of the Bundestag, the president can, within twenty-one days, dissolve the Bundestag at the request of the chancellor. Such provisions can do no harm, and they may do some good from the psychological point of view, but they fail to meet the basic issue. In Germany as in France, there is little use in protecting a cabinet from the threat of parliamentary assassination if the real trouble comes from the coalition cancer within. It is difficult to imagine Dr. Adenauer's staying in office if one of the coalition parties, even though it were the comparatively small German party, left his cabinet. He would then, as long as the Bundestag could not replace him, hold responsibility without power, for which few men care, Dr. Adenauer least of all. Article 68 of the Bonn Constitution, to be sure, has real value insofar as it makes possible the dissolution of a parliament unwilling to support a cabinet and unable to replace it.

Still, two questions arise: First, whether any constitutional limitation of the right of dissolution is commendable. Constitutional authorities in Britain or the Commonwealth countries, old-fashioned enough to be unaffected by the notions of frightened democracy, would answer this question in the negative. They would insist that a prime minister, when supported by the head of the state (whose support can be taken for granted, except in unusual circumstances), should always be able to dissolve the popular branch of parliament. And the second question is, of course, whether any dissolution in Germany, coupled with elections under the law of 1949, would not, as all Weimar dissolutions did, at best leave matters fundamentally unchanged, and at the worst intensify the evils of a heterogeneous opposition. There is reason to expect that party fragmentation will, in future elections, increase beyond the level reached in August, 1949. After the lifting of licensing restrictions, the extreme Right will assert itself more vigorously, thereby facilitating the work, and the arguments, of the extreme Left.

As could have been expected, Dr. Adenauer did not have smooth sailing with the Bundestag. The government parties constitute, in the words of *The Manchester Guardian,* an "unruly and often tactless" [55] combination, and there have also been charges that the chancellor is rather autocratic in his decisions, seeking to impose common policies rather than to have them emerge from common counsel. The government failed repeatedly of support by the Bundestag, the outstanding example occurring during the debate on the government plan to combat unemployment. On that occasion, the government's floor leader, Dr. von Brentano, ordered abstention by his followers when he realized the imminence of defeat because many coalition members were absent. The cabinet is, of course, free to ignore such defeats, but the heterogeneity of its following places it in a position which compares to its disadvantage with that of the Attlee government after the elections of February 23, 1950.

Adenauer's opposition is more heterogeneous than his following. It is difficult to find a possible alternative government in the 1949 Diet, except a "Great Coalition" including both Christian Democrats and Social Democrats. That would mean the end of the democratic opposition, and make certain the rise of a new Hugenberg at the Right (if not a new Hitler), as well as a strengthening of the Communists at the Left.

It contributes to the trouble that a P.R. parliament is always tempted to remove any "impurities" in the election law. An article in the — usually well-informed — *Deutsche Kommentare*, reports rumors according to which the Adenauer government was to be unseated by means of a coalition extending from the Left to the extreme Right. It is said that:

"The promoters of this plan hope to get the support of the smaller parties through a promise of revising the electoral law. One has in mind the old Weimar electoral law with pure P.R., which the SPD had already advocated, unsuccessfully, in the Parliamentary Council, and one calculates on paper that this would give the smaller parties a larger number of seats." [56]

If such rumors are not true, they are, according to an Italian saying, "well invented." The mere fact of their spreading weakens the government. Such developments lend support to what the correspondent of *The New York Times* had to say on the establishment of the Adenauer cabinet. Under the headline, "Old Weimar Troubles Cropping Up at Bonn; Splinter Parties and Nazi Intrigues Threaten Stability of German State," the dispatch begins with this paragraph:

"One of the precepts of post-war Allied policy and wise German leadership has been that political instability of the Weimar Republic was caused by a multiplicity of parties. Now many observers here feel that a similar, and possibly explosive, situation is being generated in the new German Federal Republic. Several indicators in that direction were uncovered during the past historic week." [57]

The paper provisions of the Bonn Constitution will not prevent another collapse of democracy on the Weimar model. Attention must be paid to manifestations of an extreme nationalism, as well as of neo-nazism, although in order to avoid misunderstandings, it has to be emphasized that nothing is gained by retaliating measures which, as our own leading officials in Germany know only too well, would accomplish the opposite of their stated purposes. The American reader may want to recall that the temptation for journalists to report from a foreign country in terms of popular stereotypes[58] and sensational events is nowhere greater, or less resisted by the home office (which, in fact, has been said to demand it), than in the case of Germany. If, for example, Dr. Adenauer terminates a speech in Western Berlin with the third verse of *Deutschland ueber alles,* our newspaper readers will not be told that when only this third verse is sung, it implies a definite rejection of what interpretation has, rightly or wrongly, been read into the first two verses. Nor will the reader be given an inkling of what the third verse does demand: "unity and justice and freedom for the German fatherland"— which, in the German original, sounds so clearly democratic that true German nationalists sing the first two verses and shun the third.

The outstanding case of neo-nazism was a speech by the deputy, Hedler, of the German party, who was reported to have said that Germany lost the war on account of the treachery and sabotage of the anti-Nazi Resistance. People, he was said to have continued, made too much fuss over Hitler's alleged barbarism against the Jews; one might differ as to whether they should have been gassed, because other means might have been used to get rid of them.[59]

Hedler was indicted; he denied having made the most incriminating part of the statements attributed to him. The court found that not everything charged against him had been proven, and that the remainder belonged in the category of matters which a member of the Bundestag might discuss at his own discretion and responsibility.

By that time, Hedler had been expelled by the German party. Much indignation at the acquittal was expressed in the German press, in particular in the opposition press. When Hedler returned to the Bundestag, he was beaten by the Social Democrats.

In Hedler's case we must remember that he was elected on the reserve list of the German party, which means that we are confronted with another P.R. product. Why give to such people the prestige, the remuneration, and the indemnity of a deputy?

A similar case occurred in Bavaria, where the deputy Meissner, who belonged to the "German Bloc"— a splinter from Loritz' Economic Reconstruction party — had ridiculed democracy "with its thousand parties" and demanded its destruction. According to some reports, several Socialist deputies grabbed him, kicked him, and dragged him down a staircase. The federal deputy, Willy Brandt, wrote in an official Social Democratic publication that his friends were prepared "to repeat this drastic process, if necessary." [60] The indignation of the Social Democrats against people who use the facilities of democracy in order to destroy it can be understood. Yet, are such methods compatible with the democratic process? Meissner, like Hedler, owed his seat to P.R. The people, if equipped with the majority system, would have kept him from entering the Bavarian Diet, saving his fellow deputies the trouble of ejecting him.

Finally, there are two more P.R. products, the Communist deputy, Reimann, and the German party deputy, Ewers, who brought the Bundestag into an uproar in the same session.[61] Ewers referred to the black-red-and gold flag of the Republic as "black-red-and yellow," a favorite insult of the Rightists during the Weimar period. Reimann called the Oder-Neisse line a "border of peace," and said that if the Polish government were Catholic, Dr. Adenauer would hardly oppose that borderline. The Bundestag reacted to the two remarks impartially with a fine show of disorder. Frankness compels us to add that an American parliament might, under similar circumstances, have reacted similarly. Still, in this country we prefer to use the plurality system of voting, and find this sufficient to bar men of the Reimann and Ewers type. Reimann was elected through the reserve list as were all other Communist deputies; Ewers, like Hedler, was a member of the German party who entered the Bundestag through the same back door.

Subsequently, the Social Democrats introduced in the Bundestag a "bill against the enemies of democracy," [62] designed to reenact the legislation contained in the Weimar Republic's "Law for the Protection of the Republic." If adopted, the bill will protect the Republic no more than its predecessor did. The technical difficulties of enforcing such a law defeat its purpose. Besides, the defense of the Republic belongs in the hands of the republican voters; we might recall that the Third Republic in France, which governed itself so badly, "defended itself well," despite the defects of the second ballot.

P.R. and Future Allied Policy

Much work remains to be done before Germany becomes safely democratic. What has been said above is not meant to dispute what Anne O'Hare McCormick expressed in these words: "It is foolish to forget that Hitler rose from the depths in a time of mass unemployment and that by hook or by crook he did fulfill his promise of providing 'full employment.'" [63] That remains true even if we must emphasize that economic conditions never occupy the stage of history alone, and that political factors require attention. Let us quote a part of a report from Frankfurt by Joseph E. Ridder:

"We noted the destructive effects of proportional representation, which has been written into all the German constitutions. It is difficult to place responsibility for this piece of political folly. In any event we cannot understand how anyone familiar with the futility and eventual collapse of the Weimar Republic could permit the Germans to sow the seeds of destruction with proportional representation which must lead to fragmentation, irresponsibility and the eventual loss of the kind of democracy we cherish.

"The Germans should be urged to eliminate proportional representation, adopt a two-party system and follow the lead of the two great democracies, the United States and England." [64]

Our comment can be limited to repeating that the decision in favor of P.R. was not made by the people of Germany; it was made by leaders of the P.R. parties, who have rejected all requests to submit the matter to the people themselves by way of a referendum. The demand was made with particular insistence in a meeting held in historic Paul's Church in Frankfurt, which was addressed by Professor Karl Geiler of Heidelburg University, the Social Democratic leader,

Gustav Dahrendorff, by the Christian Social deputy, Dr. Gerhard Kroll, the former Chancellor, Dr. Hans Luther, the Free Democratic Bremen Senator, Dr. Erhardt Heldmann, and by Dr. Dolf Sternberger, the President of the German Voters' Society. A resolution demanding a plebiscite on the system of voting was accepted by all but five of those present, which numbered about a thousand (a capacity meeting for the Paul's Church).[65]

One provision in the Occupation Statute should be of interest to the Western Allies in this connection. Article 2 reserves the power of the Governments of France, the United States, and the United Kingdom, to watch for the "Respect for the Basic Law and the Land Constitutions." Article 38, paragraph 1, of the Bonn Constitution reads:

"The deputies of the German Bundestag shall be elected by the people in universal, free, equal, *direct* and secret elections. *They shall be representatives of the whole people, not bound to orders and instructions and subject only to their conscience.*" (Italics supplied)

It hardly needs mentioning that the deputies "elected" on the reserve list are not directly elected. The fifteen Communists in the Bundestag, for example, all of whom owe their entry into the Bundestag to the reserve list, were practically appointed by their party bosses. As long as the "Basic Law" is to be "respected," reserve lists are incompatible with the requirements of "direct" election.

The same applies to the requirement that deputies should be "representatives of the whole people." P.R. deputies do not represent "the whole people"; they represent fragments, for which their separate interests are clear and real, and the interests of the whole people nebulous and remote. An excessive version of party discipline, *Fraktionszwang*, is, as Professor Ernst W. Meyer has pointed out, natural under such a system of voting, which is "mathematically excellent and practically catastrophic."[66]

The Occupation Statute provides further, in article 3:

"The Occupation Authorities . . . reserve the right, acting under instructions of their governments, to resume, in whole or in part, the exercise of full authority if they consider that to do so is essential to security or *to preserve democratic government in Germany* . . ."

Reference to this provision would hardly be necessary if the implications of Article 2, paragraph f, are borne in mind. Arguments like those contained in *The New York Times* editorial of November 11, 1948, entitled "A Warning to Germany," [67] which is reprinted in the Appendix, might, however, be used to advantage.

Allied, and in particular American, statements on systems of voting, have so far done nothing to discourage the German proponents of P.R. General Clay, who during his stay in Germany did excellent work, for which he never received full recognition on the part of a public unaware of his difficulties, was asked in an interview given before he left Germany, what he thought of a parliament elected under P.R. He answered, according to the daily published by the American Military Government, the *Neue Zeitung*:

"I do not love that system, but it exists in many democratic countries. Personally, I am inclined to disapprove of it (*Ich habe eine Abneigung dagegen*), but much depends upon how it is applied and who applies it. I believe it is being applied to a large extent by nations which are members of the British Commonwealth, and that it has appealed in a manner satisfactory to them; but these countries have a long democratic tradition. My objection to P.R. is that it makes the citizen vote for a party rather than a person. Many countries, however, have applied P.R. for years without it leading to a dictatorship. Therefore, one cannot say that it is undemocratic in itself." [68]

General Clay was in error. The only member of the Commonwealth to use P.R. in national elections was Ireland, which is now outside the Commonwealth. Use of P.R. in parts of a country, such as the Australian state, Tasmania, cannot be compared with its use in national elections; for the Australian Senate (which again is not comparable) P.R. was used for the first time in the election following General Clay's interview. General Clay's most important statement was that P.R. was not undemocratic in itself; contrary to his intentions, this went far toward providing the German proponents of P.R. with ammunition. The General might also have qualified his reference to use of P.R. in countries where no dictatorship developed by mentioning the weakening of the democratic process which took place in every instance.

In a vein similar to that of General Clay, Mr. Bolton, in the above-mentioned article, says that "MG could hardly have vetoed proportional representation when it was being successfully employed by a

GERMANY

number of democracies throughout the world. . . . (German) party preferences indicate that the majority still favor some form of proportional representation." [69] Mr. Bolton served with the Civil Affairs Division of the Military Government for three years and was at one time the Executive Officer of the Political Activities Branch. Statements like the one that P.R. was "successfully applied in a number of countries throughout the world" is all the supporters of P.R. need to make their case. Besides, the German opponents of P.R., such as the *Waehlergesellschaft* did not ask that P.R. be vetoed; they did demand that the people themselves be allowed to decide the issue, knowing that under P.R. parties, "party preferences" are one thing, and the will of the people something else again.

The above quotations would seem to indicate that, if American authorities are aware of the importance of electoral systems for the future of German democracy, the task of making this known has yet to be solved.

CHAPTER 10. RECENT DEVELOPMENTS IN AUSTRIA, ISRAEL,

JAPAN, INDIA AND TURKEY

Austria

Austrian democracy made a new start soon after Russian troops entered Vienna. Dr. Karl Renner, the leader of the right-wing Socialists, contacted the Russian commander, who accepted his suggestion to reestablish an Austrian government. The Western Allies showed, at first, some hesitation in admitting Dr. Renner's authority in their zones of occupation; they were not certain that, operating from Russian-occupied Vienna, the Chancellor and his colleagues would be free agents which, however, they soon proved to be. Thus, Austria was spared the experiment of a Military Government on the German model, with four occupying powers attempting to mold their respective zones according to four different patterns. Also, the independent Austrian government kept the friction between Russia and the Western powers to a level somewhat below that reached so soon in Germany.

The Austrian parties which formed the new coalition were different from those existing before 1933. The various rightist groups were not allowed to reorganize. Communists, Socialists, and Catholics (who changed their name from Christian Social party to Austrian People's party) were, until the summer of 1949, to be the "monopoly parties" from among whom the voter had to choose. The Socialists dropped the distinctive features of "Austro-Marxism," and turned to the path of political moderation. They came, even in regard to educational and related policies, closer to the middle of the road than before, although most of the effective difference between them and the new People's party lay in that field. The People's party was, in its turn, aware of the mistakes made by its Christian Social predecessor in the 1930's. It was determined to find common ground with the Socialists if at all possible. There was neither a leftist nor a rightist private army to poison the country's political life anew.

The constitution under which the post-Anschluss Austria was to operate was that of 1929,[1] which differed from that of 1920 by giving the president the right to appoint and dismiss cabinets, to dissolve the lower house of parliament (the so-called National Council), to issue emergency decrees within carefully defined limits. At the same time, this constitution provided for the president's election by popular vote, an objectionable feature which was, however, applied neither before nor, as yet, after the war. The Socialists, who had merely submitted to this constitution in 1929, now willingly and wisely accepted it. Belatedly, the Communists protested; they would have preferred a constitution on the French model, with the executive weakened as much as possible. The Allied Council, apparently under Russian pressure, at first attempted to induce the Austrians to accept such modifications, but the Austrian government and parliament successfully refused to do so.

The first elections took place on November 25, 1945, under the old election law, and yielded the following result: [2]

PARTY	PERCENTAGE OF VOTES	NUMBER OF SEATS	SEATS UNDER FULL P.R.
Austrian People's party	49.8	85	82
Socialist party	44.6	76	74
Communists	5.4	4	9

It will be seen that the People's party, which had benefited greatly from the ban on the former rightist parties, secured, with a little less than a majority of the votes, 85 out of 165 seats, an absolute majority. This is due to the election law, which makes it difficult for small parties to make full use, or sometimes any use, of their votes; according to the percentage of the popular vote, the Communists should have elected twice as many deputies as they did. Unless a party receives a so-called "basic mandate" in a compartively small constituency, it cannot utilize any surpluses, and this utilization is limited to the respective association of constituencies. The Communist vote proved unexpectedly small; the polling was as free in the Russian as in the other zones, and the Austrian government could exercise its authority in all zones.

After the election, Dr. Renner was elected President; he appointed Dr. Leipold Figl, the leader of the People's party, Federal Chancellor. The latter formed a coalition cabinet with the Socialists, which operated with compartive ease. It governed, of course, according to the P.R. pattern; each minister pursued his own policy, or rather his party's policy, in his particular department. In view of the Russian occupation there were, however, reasons for the coalition; cooperation between the two major parties was also desirable until such time as the bitter memories of an unhappy past had been lived down.

Serious problems arose in the spring and summer of 1949, when a typical pre-election atmosphere settled over the country. The principal bone of contention was the licensing of parties. The ban on the rightist parties had led to a result which bore some similarity to what might have been expected under a majority system, with the exception, of course, that four Communists were elected. Also, the structure of the major parties showed all the effects of P.R., making them top-heavy with bureaucracy and, in the case of the People's party, reducing the party itself to a holding company for the interest groups of the peasants, the middle classes, merchants and businessmen, and the workers. The fact that the People's party majority in the National Council was due to the ban on the rightist parties did not lead to any aggravation of partisan differences. The American officials, in particular General Keys, were inclined to credit the country's political stability to this over-all majority of the leading party. The People's party was more than ready to divide the government responsibility with the Socialists; that it did not *have* to do so kept the Socialists from putting their price too high.

The new elections were complicated by the fact that 450,000 former Nazis, who were not allowed to vote in 1945, could do so in 1949; in addition, about 100,000 expellees, who had been given Austrian citizenship, could vote. The question was where these voters would turn. The Socialists assumed that the People's party would be their only beneficiary. They drew the conclusion that maintenance of the ban on new parties would give their major opponent an unfair advantage. Had the assumption been correct — the election returns were to disprove it — admission of rightist parties would still have been a matter of doubtful wisdom. As long as former Nazis voted for the Austrian People's party they had to accept a democratic leadership, and there was a chance, at least, to neutralize and, perhaps, assimilate them politically.

The Austrian Minister of the Interior, a Socialist, made it clear

DEVELOPMENTS IN AUSTRIA, ISRAEL, JAPAN, INDIA, TURKEY

at an early stage that he would permit the "Independents" to participate in the elections unless prevented from doing so by the Allies. His connections with the British Labour party took care of possible difficulties from the British, and the decision hung with the Americans. As John McCormac reported to *The New York Times*: [3]

"It has not been a secret in Vienna that United States Army representatives had sympathized with this aspiration (of the People's party to retain its majority by way of a ban on the "Independents"), but have been over-ruled by a State Department decision in Washington. That decision was grounded on the fear that to permit the People's party to admit Nazis into its councils would endanger the coalition with the Socialists that has enabled Austria to stand firm against Communism even when the latter is backed by the Soviet Army."

One wonders whether the fear that the People's party would "admit Nazis into its councils" was based on any concrete information; it would have been rather damaging for the party to do so. As long as no party appealing primarily to former Nazis, such as the "Independents," was admitted, the voters in question would, basically, have been in the same position as under the majority system: they had only a choice between supporting one of the major parties, or throwing their votes away. The sole difference would have been that, as long as P.R. applied, a rightist party would have to be permitted some time or other; for this reason the bargaining power of the voters in question was a little greater than the majority system would have permitted it to be.

The actual results of the election were somewhat different from what the strategists of the Austrian Socialist party, and their friends outside Austria, had expected it to be.. They are summarized in the following table: [4]

PARTY	PERCENTAGE OF VOTES	SEATS	PERCENTAGE OF SEATS
Austrian People's party	44.1	77	47
Socialists	38.7	67	40
Communists	5.0	5	3
Union of Independents	11.7	11	10
Splinter groups	0.5	..	..

223

BETWEEN DEMOCRACY AND ANARCHY

The People's party did lose its over-all majority, although, with forty-four per cent of the votes it obtained forty-seven per cent of the seats. The hope of the Socialists that they would become the strongest party and, on that basis, be able to claim the position of the chancellor in the new cabinet, was disappointed. Their losses in terms of the percentage of the popular votes won, as well as of seats, were as large as those of the People's party; the "Independents" attracted, obviously, votes which would in their absence have gone to the Socialists as well as to the People's party. In the words of John McCormac: "The Socialists were, in a sense, hoisted by their own petard..." [5] The Communists gained one seat; they had been strengthened in areas where, under the Austrian election law, it was most useful, by the accession of a few left-wing Socialists, who were loath to abandon the pre-1933 version of "Austro-Marxism."

The Independents did somewhat better than expected and found themselves, for the time being, in the center of world-wide attention. Most of their candidates were former Nazis and, whatever their future policies would be, there was no doubt that they were not a party of democratic tendencies.[6] Their first appearance in the National Council demonstrated the benefits to Communist propaganda inherent in their presence. While the Communists had practically ignored the Independents during the election campaign — evidently glad to see them emerge — one of their deputies turned their fire on them in the National Council, calling them "worthy successors of Starhemberg." (Prince Starhemberg had been a prominent leader of the *Heimwehren*, the pre-1934 private army of the Right.) The Independent deputy, Steuber, a former Nazi, interrupted to compare camps in which he and other Nazis were interned in 1945 with Hitler's concentration camps. There followed an uproar, which the Speaker was unable to curb for a quarter of an hour. That scene had its parallels in other countries, but it did not help the prestige of democratic institutions in Austria.

The daily published by the "Austrian People's party" took, in a front page editorial in its October 16 [7] issue, vigorous exception to the fact that the Allies had permitted the Independents to participate in the elections. The editorial asserted that "in certain Allied countries" considerations of partisan politics were placed above the desire, loudly announced, to exterminate Nazi ideology. The British, it continued, left no doubt, from the first day of the controversy, that their Labour government would act as requested by the Austrian Socialists. American circles, it was charged, were not free from such partisan influences. That might be due to unjustified considerations of a denominational or cultural order, to the agitation of Socialist emigrés from Austria, or to the activities of the "so-called 'left-wingers' in the State Department." The Allies were advised that, if henceforth they should refuse to grant Austria a peace treaty, or threaten her with reprisals on account of neo-Nazi influences, they would be reminded that the neo-Nazi party was in the Austrian parliament by their admission.

The immediate result of the election outcome consisted in difficulties in renewing the government coalition. The cabinet had resigned as a matter of form; since both major parties had, before the elections, announced their willingness to continue the coalition, prompt success was expected. On November 4, however, the United Press reported a statement by Dr. Figl, the outgoing Chancellor, that his party and the Socialists were "dangerously deadlocked." [8] The Socialists demanded several new ministries in the cabinet; their losses had made them sensitive, and they wanted to reassert their power. Finally, on November 7, four weeks after the election, the new government was formed. The Socialists obtained the newly established Economic Ministry; it was to be in charge of all government-owned enterprises, which, on account of nationalizations, were numerous. They also obtained the Ministry of Justice which had been in the hands of a non-party man. *The New York Times* reported: "One remark tonight was 'the Socialists lost the election but won the government.'" [9]

It seems, then, that the coalition between the Austrian People's party and the Socialists was easier to establish when the latter had an absolute majority than when both partners had been exposed to severe losses at the hands of a group which admittedly drew the bulk of its strength from former Nazis. Once the coalition was formed anew matters more or less proceeded as previously, with each party running its own ministries according to its own political conceptions, and willing to let the others do the same. The Independents, after first making quite a splash, soon suffered from internal difficulties; it became obvious that their "leader," Kraus, had no effective control over their deputies. This fact is, however, unimportant. If the Independents should disintegrate, continued use of P.R. would mean a standing invitation, certain to be accepted sometime or other, for others to move in and absorb Austria's rightists.

The one objection which the Western Allies could make to the demands of the Austrian People's party to ban the Independents was that any restriction of the number of parties admitted to an election has the appearance of being undemocratic, even if a neo-Nazi party is involved. The appeal to democracy should, however, be consistent. That requires, in this connection, a system of voting which gives the people a chance to elect, *and defeat,* in every constituency whomsoever they want to elect or defeat. The people must have a chance to act as defenders of democracy, in particular if there is no other way of providing for this defense. Nor would it be a disadvantage if the Communists were defeated — as they would be — along with the neo-Nazis. That would free the Socialists from all fear of irresponsible opposition at their Left, and make it easier for them to continue the moderate and responsible policy which they have followed ever since 1945. As long as the Russians were willing to permit the Austrian voters to whittle the Communist party down to its present size, they would hardly be chagrined by its complete elimination from the Austrian parliament.

No one need fear that the effective two-party system which the majority system would be certain to establish in Austria would mean an intensification of existing differences. The British elections of February, 1950, have shown how strong the compulsion to moderation is on both sides. In Austria, a majority system would place before the Socialists the simple choice of adopting a policy acceptable to the marginal voter in the center, or of seeing their parliamentary strength reduced below present levels. Similarly, the People's party would have to extend its appeal from forty-four per cent to fifty-one per cent of the voters; its moderate wing would, in that case, be certain of a monopoly of power. A Socialist majority would become a possibility as soon as that party completes its present change by becoming the Austrian equivalent of the British Labour party. Both parties would become more democratic in their present structure; their deputies are practically nominated by the respective party committees in spite of the fact that the "rigid" list has now been somewhat modified in order to give the voter the appearance, at least, of an influence on the result.[10] The People's party would have less trouble with the economic interest groups as, in most constituencies, candidates would have to be elected who are not too closely identified with one interest to antagonize all others. Immediately following the election the disruptive influence of the organized interests on the party was stronger than ever.

The most important consideration is, however, the possibility of having a responsible opposition alongside a responsible government. The present coalition is both heterogeneous and irresponsible. As long as P.R. prevails, this will remain the case, unless either of the major parties should leave the government, a development which would immediately precipitate Austria back into the parliamentary troubles from which she suffered from 1920 to 1934. For the reasons mentioned above, a coalition of the two major parties remains desirable as long as the present international situation continues. It should, however, be the last, rather than the only, resort of Austrian democracy. The possibility of replacing one government by another is an essential requirement of true democracy.

Israel

Israel presents an unusual interplay of sociological and political factors. This is not the place to attempt an answer to all of the questions resulting from this fact; suffice it to refer to Professor Dunner's[11] comprehensive analysis of both the social and the political material. These brief remarks are only intended to emphasize some of the basic problems.

The most significant aspect of the social life of Israel is heterogeneity. The immigrants are coming in a rapid flow from all parts of the globe. Those from Eastern Europe, headed by Prime Minister Ben Gurion, form, at present, the core of the country's political organization; their coherence, resented by many as a form of clannishness, may in fact be the only power strong enough to hold the state together. The environment of the Jews coming from Eastern Europe differs strikingly from that of their fellow religionists coming from Western Europe, including Germany; the background of the latter was "Western" in the full sense of the term. Jews from the United

States are, a generation or two back, descendants of both groups and, therefore, form an intermediate element. The oriental Jews, who may be expected to constitute the largest percentage of the future immigrants, differ strongly from both European and American immigrants. Their social customs, including marriage — some of them accept polygamy — are largely those of the Mohammedan peoples among whom they have been living for centuries.

Ideological differences add their weight to those arising out of a different social environment. The orthodox Jews differ markedly from those who are unorthodox, or even anti-religious; they feel that religion made possible the survival of their people in the face of persistent adversity, and they cannot conceive of the land of the Bible without the religion of the Bible. Then there are the differences arising out of modern conflicts. Advocates of free enterprise find themselves face to face with advocates of socialism. Lastly, we have the political conflicts. The extremists on the Left and on the Right, who openly sponsor non-democratic policies, and are willing to practice non-democratic methods, are now not numerous. They are, however, flanked by larger groups, in whose case it is difficult to tell whether the magnet of moderation or the magnet of radicalism will, in the end, represent the stronger attraction.

If ever there was a need for the integrating effects of the majority system, it exists in a country characterized by so much heterogeneity. One is inclined to say that it constitutes the case of a society which has not yet become a state. Israel, during the time of mass immigration, must become a melting pot like the United States, not only in the sense of the eventual assimilation of groups coming from different environments by inter-marriage, but also in the more narrowly political sense. Some of the many groups now existing have to merge; the ideological parties of yesterday must become the functional parties of tomorrow, acting with the primary purpose of being instruments of government.

The only device which can induce the process of amalgamation is the single-member constituency. It has, to be sure, seemed strange to many to divide the territory of Israel into small geographic areas. In older countries, the inhabitants of a certain territory possess a spirit of community; in Israel, most people feel much more kinship with the ethnic groups of their origin, or the ideological groups of their choice, than with those whom mere accident has made their physical neighbors. Psychologically, their feelings are natural; politically, they may become fatal. Without the geographic constituency there is no catalytic agent to unite what is now divided — uniting it, not on the basis of force, but in a process of spontaneity which has caused us to say above that "government by majority is government by persuasion." Let us also repeat that in such a process there lies the best safeguard for minorities, as made clear in Thomas Woodlock's definition that "democracy is the protection of minorities by the rule of the majority," for the simple reason that it takes members of many a minority to make up a majority.

This applies even to the difficult relations between the Jews and the Arabs remaining in, or returning to, Israel. The Arab minority can become a center of unrest, always willing to side with the discontent in Israel and to look beyond her borders for help and final redemption. It can also become a bridge between the Jews and the Arab world, into the midst of which the Jews are placed like an island in the sea. We must recall that P.R. not only prevents a desirable merger between national majority and national minority; it has the further drawback of making it possible for the extremists within the ranks of both to get elected with the votes of their fellow extremists, instead of giving the level-headed ones within both groups an opportunity of exercising their influence in favor of a policy of "live and let live."

P.R. had been used in the election of the representative body of the Jews in Palestine before independence was won. Arthur Koestler reports a conversation with Dr. Abraham Weinshall, one of Israel's outstanding jurists, who drew attention to the fact that (in Koestler's formulation) there were, in the election of 1944 "round 250,000 votes cast and not less than 25 parties competing for them — including a list of 'The Young Men from Aden,' 'The Orthodox Female Workers,' and 'The Maccabi Sports Club.'" [12] Under these circumstances, we can understand when Anne O'Hare McCormick wrote: "She (Israel) has tried proportional representation and would prefer to start out with a system that encourages amalgamation rather than the splitting up of parties." [13] Previously she had reported that "It (Israel society) forms, in fact, an astonishingly divided society, and the divisions are unlikely to be lessened by proportional representation provided for by the new constitution under instruction of the United Nations." [14]

The elections to the Constituent Assembly took place under the list system of P.R., with the whole country forming one election district. The number of valid votes, 440,095, was divided by 121, the number of seats to be filled, plus one, resulting in a so-called "general quota" of about 3600. Each party was entitled to as many seats as it polled this quota,[15] additional provisions governing the distribution of the remaining seats. There were twenty-one lists, with a total of 1,228 candidates. The following table[16] gives the results:

PARTIES	NUMBER OF VOTES	NUMBER ELECTED
Mapai	155,274	46
United Religious Front	52,982	16
Jabotinsky's Movement (Revisionists)	2,892	..
Freedom party	49,782	14
Pro Jerusalem	842	..
Arab Labour bloc	3,214	..
List of Izhak Grunbaum	2,514	..
Democratic List of Nazareth and Surroundings	7,387	2
Fighters	5,363	1
Orthodox List	2,835	..
List of Traditional Jewry	239	..
Association of Yemenites in Israel	4,399	1
Mapam	64,018	19
Zionist Women's Organization—Association of Equality of Women's Rights	5,173	1
List of Union of Sephardic and Oriental Jews	15,287	4
Progressive party	17,786	5
Religious Women	2,796	..
General Zionists	22,661	7
Communist party	15,148	4
United List of Religious Labourers	1,280	..
Arab People's Front	2,812	..

The picture is typical of a P.R. election. Still, we must not overlook the relative strength of Mapai, the party of Prime Minister Ben Gurion, which polled about thirty-six per cent of the votes, and secured forty-six seats, placing it into a commanding lead in the Knesset (assembly). Mapai is comparable to the British Labour party (with variations due to the different environment), and the next group, Mapam, which obtained nineteen seats in the assembly, is comparable to the Zilliacus group in Britain. While we must not conclude that, under a majority system, Mapam would have suffered the fate of Independent Labour in February, 1950, it is obvious that a party so close to one extreme, and less than half as strong as its more moderate neighbor, would face great difficulties. These would be certain to whittle down its parliamentary strength, and make it likely for a large number of its followers to join Mapai, content to accept the indoctrination in the latter's more moderate views.

The third group is the "United Religious Bloc," with sixteen assembly seats. It constitutes "a cartel of four political parties which emphasize Jewish religious tradition . . ." [17] The existence of this group is as interesting as are the divisions within its ranks. The unifying element is the desire for a strong religious foundation to be given to the new state. This includes, as Hal Lehrman[18] has pointed out, emphasis on the strict observance by all, orthodox or not, of ritualistic prescriptions of the Mosaic law. While there is logic to the claims of the orthodox Jews, who cannot conceive of returning into the land of their ancestors without the religion of their ancestors, insufficient attention seems to be paid to the need of persuading their fellow citizens that their demands are just. As in other P.R. countries, a group is placed in a position where it can develop its own views without regard for what others may think, and then use its parliamentary bargaining power in order to force its demands on others. The majority system would cause the United Religious Bloc to turn to the voters themselves, and to share in a process of give and take. That might involve the abandonment, or mitigation, of certain aspects of the Mosaic religion which it is difficult not to qualify as external, but it might, by the same token, make it easier to secure general acceptance for its abiding spiritual values. As conditions are now, conflicts are at times so bitter that some speak of the possibility of a

"Kulturkampf" in Israel, an open conflict between church and state.

The next strongest group, Herut, or the Freedom party, an outgrowth of the terroristic Irgun Zvai Leumi, secured fourteen seats in the assembly. In view of its former radicalism, the question arises whether its conversion to the peaceful processes of democratic life is genuine. This is one more question which would lose much of its significance under a majority system. A party with about eleven per cent of the votes, and fairly evenly spread over the country, is less important than were the elder LaFollette's Progressives in 1924 with 16.3 per cent of the popular vote. Time would, of course, be required to convince its followers of the merits of moderation.

There is no need to discuss the smaller parties. Communists might, under a majority system, have a chance in concentrated Arab settlements, where in the minds of the voters, anyway, their communism would play second fiddle to their Arab nationalism. Otherwise, the Communists would elect no one, nor would the former Stern group which, with 1.2 per cent of the votes, just managed to provide its leader with a seat, parliamentary immunity, and release from jail, the election law containing the convenient provision that being in prison did not disqualify a candidate.

Israel, then, would have much to gain by accepting the majority system. In that case, a union of the Left, under the leadership of Ben Gurion and the Mapai, would seem inescapable, and also a union of the Right and Center. What form a merger of the several groups involved, including the United Religious Bloc, the General Zionists, and the Progressives, would take, it is impossible to foretell.

How much, on the other hand, does the young nation stand to lose under P.R.? At present, the government is composed of representatives of four parties, Mapai with seven seats, the United Religious Bloc with three, and the Progressive party, the Union of Shephardic Jews, and the Oriental Communities with one each.. The coalition parties hold 74 out of 120 seats in the assembly. For the time being, this is an adequate majority. Prime Minister Ben Gurion is personally very strong, and considered likely to weather any storm which might arise in the near future.

The basic situation is nonetheless that of a heterogeneous cabinet and a heterogeneous opposition. The United Religious Bloc is uneasy in the coalition with Mapai, whose background is socialist, secular and, in the eyes of many orthodox Jews, anti-religious. In February, 1950, the three ministers representing the United Religious Bloc absented themselves from cabinet sessions, and the Prime Minister threatened to regard continued absence as resignation. The crisis, arising out of a conflict as to the religious nature of schools for immigrant children, was adjusted, but it could develop again over a similar issue. Without the United Religious Bloc the coalition strength in the Knesset would be reduced to 58 seats out of 120. Minority governments are, of course, not unusual when party strength is distributed as it is in Israel, but we need not dwell upon their disadvantages.

The heterogeneous character of the coalition not only renders its work more difficult, but it places added burdens on the shoulders of the government parties. Each of the four parties has been able, during the election campaign, to develop its own views regardless of the others. The coalition requires cooperation with parties whose tenets have been attacked, and some voters are inclined to look upon such a process as a betrayal. To aggravate matters, there seems to be no alternative to the present government. The heterogeneous opposition has, in the Herut at the Right and the Mapam at the Left, two strong rallying points. Both have an unfair advantage over the government parties, which are saddled with a monopoly of responsibility. There exists, therefore, no equivalent of the safety valve which, under the plurality system, places a moderate majority and a moderate opposition side by side, making it possible for both to play their part according to the rules of the game, without having to fear that they could ever permanently lose their popularity. In Israel, it is quite possible that the centrist parties forming the present government will, some time, find themselves encircled by heterogeneous groups with a combined majority, as did happen in Germany in 1932, and as would have happened in France after the municipal elections of October, 1947, had new assembly elections been held under P.R.

Israel's political future depends, as long as P.R. is continued, on the interplay of two factors, neither of which the government can control. The positive factor is, paradoxically, the threat from abroad. As it was put in conversation with this writer: "The integrating power of the Arab League counterbalances the disintegrating effects of P.R." That, of course, is more true than desirable; threats from without do usually operate as an integrating factor within. Whether the same would be true in the case of a threat by Russia is something else again.

On the other hand, there is the problem of economic adjustment, the difficulties of which are slowly beginning to affect the political consciousness of the country. At present, the country lacks the productive resources needed to provide a living standard for the rapidly increasing population to which the majority have accustomed themselves. New industries and a new agriculture are needed; a number of developments are promising, but the scarcity of capital retards progress. Thus, the watchword "austerity" was adopted. While the economic problem of Britain is severe, a solution is by no means as difficult as it is in Israel — and even in England austerity did not win Labour any votes. We must bear in mind the harsh conditions in the immigrant camps in Israel, the high price of all essentials, and the dependence upon funds collected abroad, in particular the United States. At the moment of military victory, everything seemed tolerable in comparison to the dangers which had been averted; but people do not long allow the memories of military triumph to supersede their economic troubles. Everyday life and everyday needs and wishes reassert themselves. They press against the government, which, exposed to attacks from both sides, risks losses in both directions.

Lastly, Israel's internal party structure shows the typical effects of P.R. Arthur Koestler continues his above-mentioned account of his conversation with Dr. Weinshall in these words:

> The system of voting for party lists instead of individual candidates furthermore leads to the development of powerful Party Machines and Party Bureaucracies which play a decisive part in making or breaking the political and professional career of the Israeli citizen. The famous 'party key system' provides for a proportional distribution not only of the number of parliamentary seats, but also of the administrative jobs and the share in the budget allocated to each party. In fact, each political party in Israel is a kind of limited company, coterie, life insurance and masonic lodge, all in one." [19]

Party bureaucracy is strengthened by an extreme form of the list system; the country forms one constituency. This fact permits almost complete proportionality — the advantages conferred upon large parties by Articles 31 and 32 of the Election Law are all but insignificant — but it also lessens the contacts between deputies and voters.[20] Such conditions are hardly compatible with party vitality. Also, they are likely to weigh more heavily upon the parties saddled with government responsibility, and tempted by the rewards of government, than on the extremists. In this regard as in others,[21] there are too many features of the Weimar Republic in the state of Israel to warrant optimism in regard to its political future. What was won on the field of battle may yet be lost in the jungle of differences kept alive, or freshly created, by P.R.

Japan

The discussion of Israel already has ignored the geographic limitations of a study concerned primarily with the problems of Continental Europe. However, our basic problem is the prospects of democratic stability, insofar as they are affected by constitutional arrangements.

Japan might render to the cause of democracy in the Far East the same service that Israel might render in the Near East. This opportunity arises, first of all, from Japan's position as the one oriental power which carried through the process of modernization without Western assistance. This gives her a prestige in the Orient of which Westerners are not always aware; a successful Japanese self-government would do much to strengthen the cause of democracy in the Orient. The "social" conditions of democracy exist to a greater degree in Japan than among any of her neighbors. Literacy is high; competent leadership has developed in industry and in the military; there is no *a priori* reason why it should not develop in democratic politics.

Those who led Japan on the way to modernization had no intention of leading her on the path of democracy. A remarkable group of young men of the so-called "Western clans," comparable in their youth and energy to those who were responsible for the framing of the United States Constitution, set out to give their country the technical benefits of Western civilization without accepting its political institutions. The Constitution of 1889 was put into effect as a grant by the Emperor, rather than as a product of an assembly elected by the people. Like its models, the constitutions of Prussia and Austria, it left the control of the executive in the hands of the crown, and this meant that the Emperor, or rather the men behind him, held the political initiative. The Ministers of the Army and Navy had to be members of these two services; by withholding their consent from any general or admiral whom a prime minister wanted to appoint to his cabinet, the military could exercise a veto power over the composition, and the policies, of the cabinet. Finally, there remained the great social power of the amalgam between the old feudalistic and the modern industrial elements which played a decisive part in Japanese politics. For the details concerning the way in which its power was exercised, reference may be made to the literature on the subject, such as the volumes by Professors Vinacke and Quigley.[22]

When Japan participated in the First World War, she was exposed to strong democratic influences. A commoner was, for the first time, appointed prime minister, even though, comparable to a Giolitti, he was as much a political boss as a democratic leader.[23] While there was a lapse from party government between 1920 and 1924, it existed between that time and 1932, although the events accompanying the Manchuria invasion already showed the decisive influence of a younger, diplomatically less experienced, and morally less inhibited group of officers. Their rise to power had a great deal to do with the world economic crisis, which upset governments the world over and created an atmosphere in which adventurers thrived.

Before the war then, Japan's political developments were mainly influenced by extra-constitutional factors. Constitutional developments were not, for that reason, immaterial. Certainly, if parliamentary government was to develop, parties had to be strong, and in order to be strong they had to have a majority. In this connection, reference must be made to the election law of 1925.[24] It provided for constituencies electing from three to five deputies each. The voter was limited to one choice. There were two reasons for adopting this form of the limited vote. One of them was the desire to give "representation to minorities," which in other cases had led to the adoption of P.R., whereas the second was diametrically opposed to the first. Japanese parties had, like the parties of pre-1940 France and of pre-1919 Italy, often the character of personal cliques. It was believed that, by adopting multiple-member constituencies — they had previously been tried in combination with the majority system — purely local candidates would be sufficiently handicapped.

The political effects of the system were two-fold. On the one hand, a great deal of careful organizing had to be done. If, in a constituency electing five deputies a party was just strong enough to elect three, its vote had to be as equally divided among three as possible. The solution of this task required the gifts of the fortune-teller as well as those of the organizer. If a party guessed wrong as to how many men it would elect, it would elect fewer than it might have elected; even the strongest party in a district could fail to elect a single candidate if it spread its votes over too many candidates. After a good guess had been made, the next task was to divide the voters among party candidates, which was usually done by assigning to a candidate a part of the relatively large constituency. The need for careful organization was intended to provide a premium on party coherence, although an independent with a strong enough following could enter the contest without having to worry about how to distribute the vote; in his case it sufficed if his sympathizers all voted for him.

Effects which justify the description of the Japanese kind of limited voting as "an awkward kind of proportional representation favoring small groups" [25] follow from the fact that less than a majority, or a plurality, of the votes is needed. If, in a five-member constituency, a voter can vote for only one candidate, twenty per cent of the voters will always be certain to elect a deputy. In reality, the percentage will be smaller. It is impossible for parties to present just the right number of candidates; therefore, many candidates will either obtain more votes than they need, or less than is required to be elected. The five men with the highest votes will be the winners. This situation is ideal for a small party which has a chance to elect just one deputy in a large constituency. All it needs to do is to select the most popular candidate and concentrate all publicity on him.

Before the war four elections were held under the limited vote. In 1928 and 1936, no party secured a majority; there were clear majorities in 1930 and in 1932. Generally speaking, the experience under the limited vote was not as favorable as under the preceding forms of the majority system. The elections of 1928 constituted the second case in the history of the Diet that a government had failed to secure a majority. It need not be repeated, however, that while the limited vote, as used in Japan, would hardly commend itself, it cannot be related to the collapse of democracy in the same manner as, for example, P.R. in Italy and Germany. There was no "parliamentary paralysis" in Japan as there was in the above-mentioned countries before the rise of dictatorship.

After the Japanese surrender, much occurred to improve the outlook for democracy. Defeat is a forceful teacher; the Japanese militarists had demonstrated the dangers of accepting the industrial and military techniques of the West while ignoring its political processes. Furthermore, Allied policies removed many extra-constitutional obstacles to democracy. The Army and Navy were abolished; in the new constitution it was specifically provided that ministers must be civilians. An attempt was made to make civil liberties real, even if early pampering of the Communists allowed them to intimidate others where they could. Trade union and party organization were at last free, and the average Japanese could hardly fail to appreciate the absence of any further attempts at "thought control," nor to be glad he no longer had to wear a uniform and fight in foreign countries.

Political institutions became, under these conditions, more important than they had been previously. The new constitution did not, as did its French counterpart, stand in the way of an effective democracy. The right of dissolution remained intact; while the prime minister was to be elected by the Diet, including the House of Councillors, no specific majority was prescribed. The amending process, requiring a two-thirds majority in both houses of the Diet, and a referendum, were made difficult, but then, apart from the provisions renouncing the use of force, there was hardly anything in the constitution which would necessitate amendment.

The one point where SCAP (the name of the high command of the occupation authorities) worked in the wrong direction is the election law. It was natural that the Japanese government be asked to lower the voting age from twenty-five to twenty, and that women be enfranchised, but a request was also made to "liberalize" the voting system for the purpose of facilitating the success of smaller parties. Constituencies were enlarged so as to elect from four to fourteen instead of from three to five deputies; the voters were allowed to cast from two to three votes each rather than one. Members of SCAP, as well as left-wing Japanese, apparently felt that this system would help to end the power of the old bureaucracy; it was overlooked that if, for the sake of argument, we grant that it assisted in defeating the powers of pre-war days, it failed to strengthen any group which could

DEVELOPMENTS IN AUSTRIA, ISRAEL, JAPAN, INDIA, TURKEY

have taken its place. Danton, the French revolutionary, said: *On ne détruit que ce qu'on remplace* — "One does not destroy that which one cannot replace."

The first election results for the House of Representatives are summarized in the following table: [26]

1946

PARTY	PERCENT OF VOTE	NUMBER ELECTED	PERCENT ELECTED
Liberal	24.4	140	30.4
Progressive	18.7	94	20.2
Social Democrat	17.8	92	19.7
Cooperative Democrat	3.2	14	3.0
Communist	3.8	5	1.1
Minor Parties	11.7	38	8.2
Independents	20.4	81	17.4
Total	100.0	464	100.0

The results read like those of a typical P.R. election, except that the smallest parties secured substantially less in terms of seats than they secured in terms of votes. Even so, there were enough small- and medium-size parties to make the emergence of a majority impossible. Under a majority system, some of the smaller parties, including the Communists, would have received no seats; some of the larger ones would have been compelled to combine.

It took forty-one days before a government could be formed. Ultimately, success was achieved by Mr. Yoshida. The cabinet was based upon a coalition of the Liberals and the Progressives, who, together with minor elements, commanded a small majority. The coalition worked badly. The Progressives, having suffered what they considered a defeat, used every means to reassert themselves; the so-called Shakushi (schemers) had a field day. The cabinet was helpless in the face of mounting inflation, and of recurring labor offensives, staged frequently under Communist leadership. Labor unrest was, of course, largely a result of the inflation which, in its turn, was the consequence of an unbalanced budget. A government strong enough to put its finances in order was the prime need of the country. Yoshida did not head such a government; labor unrest spread, and when the Communists announced a general strike for February 1, 1947, General MacArthur banned it, and ordered new elections, which took place on April 20.

Before the elections were held, Yoshida had the election law changed, returning, in the main, to the law of 1925, with constituencies electing from three to five deputies and each voter limited to one vote. The opposition resorted to filibustering; according to Lindesay Parrot, "Several speakers are reported ready to talk for ten to twelve hours each in opposition to the bill." [27] The bill passed, but it is interesting to record the comment by T. A. Bisson, of whom the dustjacket on his book, *Prospects for Democracy in Japan*[28] says that "during 1946-47 he was an important member of the Government Section of General MacArthur's Headquarters in Tokyo." In Mr. Bisson's words:

"The Election Law discarded the large-constituency, plural-ballot system that had governed the election of April 10, 1946. Fifteen months earlier, liberal Japanese sentiment had cordially welcomed SCAP's initiative on behalf of this system, which was regarded as a preliminary step toward full proportional representation. Now the Liberal-Democratic majority in the Diet reversed the process by returning to the small-constituency, single-ballot system of the old regime."

This paragraph constitutes an unqualified admission that a part of SCAP at least regarded P.R. as the ideal election law for Japan.

The following table[29] gives the results of the April election:

1947

PARTY	PERCENT OF VOTE	NUMBER ELECTED	PERCENT ELECTED
Liberal	26.7	131	28.1
Democrat	25.1	121	26.0
Social Democrat	26.2	143	30.7
People's Cooperative	6.8	29	6.2
Communist	3.7	4	0.8
Minor Parties	5.7	25	5.4
Independents	5.8	13	2.8
	100.0	466	100.0

DEVELOPMENTS IN AUSTRIA, ISRAEL, JAPAN, INDIA, TURKEY

The figures show the Social Democrats in the lead in terms of seats though not of votes; the fact that with 26.2 per cent of the votes they secured 30.7 per cent of the seats would seem to prove that they had nothing to gain either from P.R. or from the election law of 1946,[30] although the party, and its leader, Katayama, continued to favor P.R.

As no clear majority existed, protracted negotiations were again necessary, this time taking twenty-eight days. It took another good week before the new Prime Minister, Mr. Katayama, was able to complete his cabinet. The cabinet, having required thirty-seven days to see the light of day, lasted eight months. A definite policy was all but impossible; the deadlock between the ministers (seven Socialists, seven Democrats, two from the People's Cooperative party) could seldom be overcome in time to permit effective action. Stop-gap measures were all that remained.

Katayama resigned on March 10, 1948, handing over his office to his Foreign Minister, Ashida. The latter could do no more than his predecessor against inflation and labor unrest; his cabinet fell over a major corruption scandal. Yoshida was recalled and, on October 15, 1948, elected by the Diet with 185 votes as against more than 200 abstentions. Naturally, he insisted on a dissolution and new elections, which were held on January 23, 1949. The following table[31] summarizes the results:

PARTY	PER CENT OF VOTE	NUMBER ELECTED	PER CENT ELECTED
Democratic Liberal	43.8	264	56.7
Democratic	15.8	68	14.6
Social Democratic	13.5	49	10.5
Communist	9.6	35	7.5
People's Cooperatives	3.4	14	3.0
Labor-Farmer	2.0	7	1.5
Social Renovation	1.3	5	1.1
New Liberal	0.6	2	0.4
Japan Farmer	0.8	1	0.2
Minor Parties	2.6	9	1.9
Independents	6.6	12	2.6
Total	100.0	466	100.0

BETWEEN DEMOCRACY AND ANARCHY

The feature most commented upon in the American press was the election of thirty-five Communists; with their allies, they were to constitute a Communist group in the House of fifty members. It will be seen that, for the first time, the Communists succeeded in gaining almost as large a percentage of the seats as of the votes — 7.5 as against 9.6. It is more important, however, to consider the percentage of votes actually obtained by the victorious Communist candidates in their respective constituencies. The result[32] is little short of amazing. The Communist candidate with the highest percentage, Mr. Shiga Yoshio, had 25.28 per cent of the popular vote, and the one with the lowest, Mr. Karasaw Toshiko, 8.43 per cent. In other words, under a majority system, all of the winning Communists (occasional exceptions on the basis of personal popularity are always possible, but also insignificant) would have been listed among the "also rans." The percentages were, of course, equally small on the part of some of the winning candidates of the other parties. Whereas the latter could, in case of the consolidation to be expected under a majority system, have won added votes either from candidates of the same party (the Communists concentrated all their strength on one candidate in each constituency), or from related parties, the Communists could not have done the former, and very rarely the latter.

The outstanding event of the election was, of course, the victory of Yoshida and his Democratic Liberals. He benefited from a strong popular revulsion against ineffective coalitions. Few objected to his winning 56 per cent of the House seats with 43.8 per cent of the votes; his majority was to be enlarged by the later accession of some of the deputies elected by the Democratic party. The new Yoshida cabinet represented quite a change from what had happened since 1946. After the first session of the new Diet ended, *The New York Times* reported, on June 1: "Japan's most productive postwar Diet session ended at midnight. It passed the first balanced budget since 1930 and made the first long needed moves toward cutting the country's top-heavy bureaucracy." [33]

The balanced budget sounded, of course, the death knell to inflation. Three weeks later *The New York Times* reported a substantial decline in note circulation, a ten per cent fall in prices, and a substantial reduction in black market prices and black market activities.[34] Thus, the most pressing problems of the country were solved as soon as there was a government capable of tackling them.

DEVELOPMENTS IN AUSTRIA, ISRAEL, JAPAN, INDIA, TURKEY

Such a government exists at the moment, but, like De Gasperi's government in Rome, one must add "for the time being." The Japanese system of voting, to be sure, is not a P.R. system comparable to the one used in Italy, but the limited vote offers, even in its restricted form, ample opportunity for party division. Furthermore, as in Italy, the fact that there is a government is not enough; there should also be a democratic opposition, strong enough to take over the burden of government when the voters demand "a change," and moderate enough to do so without disturbing continuity. There is no such opposition; Katayama's Socialist party lost ground, and is beset by too many internal crises to offer effective leadership in the near future. Yet, it would be ideally suited to this purpose. Katayama himself, a Christian, is not burdened by materialist dogmatism. Under his leadership the Japanese Socialist party could well become the equivalent of the British Labour party in strength as well as in moderation. At present it has neither; the left-wing causes much trouble, and the party as a whole is far from the strength needed even for effective opposition, although it has lately shown signs of regaining ground.

It would seem, then, that the majority system, if possible in the form of the plurality system, is needed both to do what can be done to obtain continued government majorities, and to assure the necessary consolidation within the present opposition. Single-member constituencies, to be sure, have been used in Japan before, and they gave rise to objections. They were, however, used before manhood suffrage went into effect in 1925, and before the occupation brought real freedom of voting. Universal suffrage might, as it did in England after 1867, induce a consolidation of political life, if combined with the plurality system. That would solve the task of securing majorities in a more natural way than the various devices contemplated for the purpose of creating a two-party system by more direct means.[35] Such devices always imply measures which run counter to the democratic character of political parties, which requires the possibility of a challenge by independents as well as by new parties. Nobody can, of course, guarantee that the plurality system will create a two-party system, and there will always be pessimists,[36] but certain things did change for the better in Japan in recent years.

If much remains to be done in Japan, certain matters need to be clarified in the United States. An important segment of SCAP, apparently, considered it is their task to strengthen the Japanese Left, and favored P.R. for this purpose. At first, the entire Left, including the Communists, were allowed to benefit from this desire. More recently, the Japanese Socialist party is mentioned as the one to favor. It should be borne in mind that, if we advocate democracy, we cannot favor one party alone. There must be at least two (and, if possible, only two). Realization of this fact would lead us to support every move to strengthen not just one particular party, but everything which makes for an efficient party *system,* the institutional requirements of which have been discussed above.

Measures of a non-political nature cannot be discussed here, but one point, in particular, must be borne in mind. Japanese society has certain minimum requirements of health which must be met before the state can be healthy. This implies, as General MacArthur has repeatedly stated with great force, a chance for the eighty million Japanese to support themselves. The Japanese must be able to live before they can have a democracy capable of standing on its own feet; they cannot forever remain dependent on American support.

India and Turkey

A brief reference must be made to two recent cases in which the requirements of affirmative democracy have been realized in spite of great difficulties. This applies, first of all, to India. In that vast subcontinent many of the pre-political conditions of democracy are absent. Illiteracy is high, and the material condition of the majority of the people is still such that the final success of democracy cannot be taken for granted.

It is all the more remarkable that what could have been done in the field of political institutions, has been done. The new constitution is long, taking in a great deal of material which might have been reserved to ordinary legislation. Also, it has the appearance of complexity, attempting to borrow from the American as well as from the British constitution. Yet, there seems to be no doubt that the general outlines of the parliamentary system will be followed. There is no trace of "frightened democracy"; the president may dissolve parliament as well as appoint and dismiss the prime minister (and, on his advice, the other ministers); the cabinet's responsibility to parliament, in this case the "House of the People," follows the ordinary simple lines rather than attempting to mend by constitutional paper provisions what has been rent by adopting a system of voting leading to the rise of irresponsible parties.

Similarly, while the constitution does not regulate the system of voting, the debates in the Constituent Assembly made it clear that the plurality system will continue to be used. Dr. Ambedkar, who guided the constitutional discussions, gave a well reasoned defense of the majority principle. India is, of course, threatened by heterogeneity as much as any country, and will need the full integrating force of the majority system to assist in her consolidation. The nuclei for the heterogeneous opposition exist. At the extreme Right, there are the radical Hindu societies and, at the Left, the Communists. The latter have been dealt with, and had to be dealt with, by the government through stern policy measures. It will be vital that there should be a government strong enough to defend itself but, at the same time, sufficiently sure of itself to permit effective checks on its actions. The radical Hindu societies are, in the absence of pro-Communist pressure from without, more important than the Communists. Time must tell whether they can be controlled; certainly, to give them, through P.R., the power to disrupt the present majority, would not help the course either of moderation or of integration.

There remains the task of forming a responsible opposition. The Socialists are attempting it; as long as the plurality system exists, the attempt is likely to be directed into constructive channels, although the formation of a responsible opposition is the most delicate part of the Indian political pattern.

We must repeat, in conclusion, that India's social conditions would, by themselves, point to failure rather than success of the democratic experiment. So far, India's leaders have acted with remarkable wisdom, although no one would want to predict with confidence that where material conditions are so difficult, even the best leadership, and the most coherent constitutional pattern, could assure final success for the democratic way of life.

Turkey offered the proponents of democracy the most welcome surprise which they have had in generations. The ruling People's party allowed itself to be voted out of office after having ruled, more or less dictatorially, for a generation. Elections held under the plurality system decided against it, and it went out of office without hesitation or complaint. There was, of course, no doubt as to who was to form the alternative cabinet, and thus there was no bargaining. Also, among the two opposition parties, the moderate one far outdistanced its rival. The expressions of good will which both sides offered to each other after the election are little short of amazing. The skeptical French would say: *Pourvu que ça dure*—"provided that it will last." Whether it will do so, no one can tell, but, at any rate, a good start has been made.

The winning Democratic party had about fifty-two per cent of the popular vote, and the outgoing Popular party forty-five per cent.[37] The former took three-fourths of the seats. This result also the former government party accepted without complaint, but the question arises whether, in this case, complaint would not have been justified. As mentioned in the case of Greece, there is no reason why such extreme results should not be prevented by adoption of a form of the limited vote[38] which would, in the case like the one in Turkey, reserve about forty per cent of the seats to the opposition. Such an arrangement leaves the government with a safe majority, but short of a two-thirds majority which, in fact, should materialize only in votes concurred in by the major parties as, for example, the adoption of constitutional amendments. It need not be repeated that such an arrangement does not require any interference with the single-member constituency and its effects upon party democracy and party vitality. Those additional opposition candidates could be declared elected who, among the defeated ones, polled the highest percentage of votes in their respective constituencies. In view of the uncertain prospects of democratic stability in the countries of the Near East and Far East, as well as the Balkans and other areas, such a system would be as commendable as it would be, for that matter, in the so-called "one-party states" (and what might be called the "one-party cities," including, for this purpose, New York City) in the United States. The bulk of this study has been given to the emphasis on the requirements of government authority, but it would be wrong not to underline the needs of civic responsibility and personal liberty as well.

Summary and Conclusions

The Need for a Political Marshall Plan

The above discussion of the governments of Continental Europe could be summarized by saying that instead of true democracy, they constitute something which lies between democracy and anarchy. It is not democracy, because of the lack of real authority—and the word, democracy, is partly derived from the Greek word *kratein*, which means to rule. Nor is it democracy in the sense that the people themselves make the basic decision as to the nature of their government; a type of party—which, in reality, is more "faction" than party—substitutes itself for the people, and acts as often in its own interests as in the interests of those whom it claims to represent.

Nor, of course, do the governments of Continental Europe constitute a case of anarchy. At times they go as far in this direction as it is possible to go, but reaching the logical limit would mean a vacuum, which nature abhors as much in politics as in physics. As the borderline of anarchy is reached, the pendulum swings in the opposite direction, and dictatorship develops. Whichever group then constitutes what Professor Gurian, in the Russian case, called "the active element in a universal anarchy,"[1] takes over, and the bulk of the people are inclined to acquiesce, because they feel that "it was about time." This proves Plato's theory[2] according to which "the most aggravated form of tyranny and slavery (arises) out of the most extreme form of liberty." The countries of post-war Continental Europe have so far escaped the fate of tyranny, but the very fear of such an outcome causes that erosion of authority which keeps democracy from being true to itself.

James Burnham was right when, discussing the state of Europe in 1949, he emphasized that of the major democratic countries only Britain had a government which was "a genuine government, a sovereign." He said: "The opposition . . . was loyal; loyal to the nation and to the government, no matter how sharply critical of the party that was leading the government."[3] Mr. Burnham continued:

"But in France and Germany and Italy, the chief and determining countries of the Continent, all was still in doubt. The citizens were contemptuous of their government, cynical, disillusioned, and often corrupt.

"There was evident in these three nations a partial dissolution of the community. The inhabitants were functioning as semi-autonomous individuals, groups, and factions, not as members of single national communities.

"Under such circumstances, the governments were not genuine governments, not truly sovereign (in Germany, of course, with the occupation and the East-West division, there could not in any case have been a genuine government). They were interim, liaison committees in which the various divisive real interests intersected and by a process of endless manipulation, were compromised just enough to keep things going.

"The mark of sovereignty is the ability to decide. These governments were incapable of decision . . .

"The ministers of these governments were chosen by the central committees of various of the many parties into which the formal political life of the countries was divided. Most of the parties and their central committees, however, had lost all living contact with the respective peoples. With the help of systems of proportional voting, which prevented any direct check by local constituencies, the central committees were self-perpetuating, and were able to select all candidates and functionaries. The party leaders were old in years and older still in political age; the parties themselves were the ghosts of a past era." [4]

In these passages, Mr. Burnham has summarized the contents of this book better than the author could have done it himself. Let us, then, limit ourselves to restating, as briefly as possible, those features of the political pattern of Continental Europe which point the way to remedial action. We must repeat that the divisive forces rampant on the European political scene need not have the field to themselves; they obtained their strength only because essential factors of social control are lacking. The case of French communism will illustrate the point.

At the time of the Liberation, French communism was bound to be a large and popular movement. Still, the course of events shows that when, in the municipal and provincial elections of 1945, the majority system—even the majority system in the crippled French form—was applied, communism was kept at the fringes of the French political pattern. With the use of P.R. in the election of the two constituent assemblies and the National Assembly, communism moved right into the center of French institutions. France's "premier party" had the votes to throw out of gear, by its mere presence in parliament, the mechanism of democracy, since the interplay of a responsible government and a responsible opposition was destroyed. When the Communists went into open opposition, they could move their parliamentary shock-troops, selected for brawn rather than for brain, into action, discrediting, and hoping to paralyze, the work of the majority.

It is nonsense to say that economic conditions alone were responsible for the strength of French communism. P.R. gave facilities to these extremists which were, in several respects, as useful to them as were those which its Weimar equivalent presented to the German Nazis.[5] The propaganda value of a large parliamentary group was immense, and the parliamentary indemnity as useful as the parliamentary immunity. Besides, the strength of the Communists placed the Socialists in an awkward position. The latter had to cooperate with parties holding views in contradiction to their own, and the workers were ready to believe the Communist agitators who called such action "a betrayal of the working class." Yet, had the Socialists refused to support the governments of the Third Force, at least with their votes, no positive majority would have been possible. The Socialists then found themselves, thanks to the opportunity given to the Communists by P.R. to oppose them effectively in every ward and village, in a position where they had to choose between utter irresponsibility and utter unpopularity. The Communists stood to gain what the Socialists lost by choosing responsibility.

If we ask how continued application of the majority system would affect the Communists, we must, as French observers do, distinguish between the "hard core" and the "soft shell" of French communism. The former, consisting of people thoroughly indoctrinated with Communist ideas, will, for some time to come, support communism regardless of the consequences. The latter consists of people who vote for the Communists primarily in order to protest. Generally speaking, the protest vote is practical; it rarely goes to a party without a chance, and never for long. American minor party history provides ample proof for this. Deprive the French Communists of a chance to elect their candidates in most of the country, as was done in the provincial elections of 1949, and the "soft shell" begins to peel off immediately. Repeat the process a few times, if necessary, in decisive elections, such as those for the National Assembly, and the "soft shell" will vanish. These voters will return to the older parties, at first on the basis of opportunistic considerations alone, but they will, in due course, accept the "indoctrination" of the more moderate groups as they accepted Communist indoctrination. This type of voter does not, of course, take any kind of politics too seriously.

In this connection we must bear in mind that there are two types of protest vote. The first is a reaction to bad economic conditions, and the second a reaction to bad, meaning unnatural, political conditions. Many Frenchmen find it difficult not to be repelled by the political system under which they live. They would agree with Alexander Hamilton who said: "No government, any more than an individual, will long be respected without being truly respectable; nor be truly respectable, without possessing a certain portion of order and stability." [6] It has been mentioned already that the awkward position in which the French Socialists found themselves as a result of P.R. drove many of their voters into the Communist camp.

The same happened later in the Center, at the expense primarily of the Popular Republicans. On the other hand, whatever may have to be said in criticism of De Gaulle's "Rally of the French People," that movement does not owe its existence simply to a caprice of its founder. The General had retired from practical politics; had matters developed satisfactorily, he would hardly have emerged from his retirement. Nor would he, in that case, have been able to gather the millions who, as it was, answered his call at once. Practically all of the De Gaullist vote was a protest vote, and it was clearly a protest against poor politics rather than against a poor economic situation. At the same time, the strength of the Communist party is a major source of strength for the DeGaullists; therefore, whatever would whittle down Communist strength would whittle down DeGaullist strength also.

It would seem, then, that the instrumentalities of positive democracy, beginning with the majority system, could do much to reduce the extremism of the Right, as well as of the Left, now rampant on the French political scene. If positive democracy is complete, and this requires in a country such as France that there be also a right of parliamentary dissolution,[7] the point would be reached where the enemies of the Republic would not only be repelled — as they were throughout the Third Republic — but also reconciled.

Negative democracy becomes a matter of concern for all of us where it affects the prospects of peace. It does so by aiding, in all of Western Europe, Communist fifth columns — by providing reasons for their existence as well as by making their votes effective, and their propaganda, partly financed by the state, easy. Negative democracy achieves the same result by undermining the will to resist aggression. Morale is dangerously low in Western Europe. People cherish freedom, to be sure, but they also want order, and the security which depends on it. The type of government now existing does not satisfy the desire for order. Furthermore, these governments will never succeed in converting the potential strength of their country into actual strength. When the Marshall Plan was discussed in the United States, figures were presented to show that if European man-power and European industrial resources were combined, a force comparable to that of the United States or Russia would come into being. It was overlooked that political weakness would cause a good part of these resources to lie fallow.

Domestic weaknesses also have much to do with the continued friction among European countries. The country which, at the end of the Second World War, should have assumed the task of European unification is France. French *governments,* however, had to act for France, and they were stop-gaps confined to stop-gap measures. A policy which looks to the future cannot produce full success immediately; years of planning and patience combined with firmness (but not hysteria!) must elapse before its fruits mature. To a French cabinet a success to be expected in a year did not exist. By that time, according to all odds of the political bookmakers, it would be relegated to the political limbo. For its survival it needed measures which the National Assembly would approve, or at any rate not disapprove of, within the next month, or perhaps the next week. The only case of a major positive initiative in the field of foreign policy was Foreign Minister Robert Schuman's proposal to pool the French and German heavy industries. It was an excellent move, but should have been made in 1945 rather than in 1950.

In this case, negative democracy entered the picture also on the German side. Dr. Adenauer was as anxious to come to terms with

France as Foreign Minister Schuman was anxious to come to terms with Western Germany. One has only to read the German press in order to see to how much nagging Adenauer was subjected. The opposition of the irascible Dr. Schumacher could have been discounted, at least temporarily, had the Chancellor been sure of his own majority, which he was not. Reference has been made to the difficulties caused by such members of the German party as the deputies Hedler and Ewers; the loss of their two votes alone could be decisive to a government which, in the face of any fullfledged attack, never had votes to spare. And there were other restive deputies on the government side, within the Free Democratic party as well as within the German party, not to mention the dissatisfied members of the CDU and the CSU.

Dr. Adenauer was determined to push Germany's entrance into the Council of Europe and the acceptance of the Schuman plan, but time would have to tell how many political scars his battle with the Bundestag would leave. *The Manchester Guardian,* commenting on the victory of the anti-British Wafd (the nationalist party) in Egypt, congratulated itself upon the creation of clear responsibilities and added: "It is the weak who can never compromise." [8] The trouble with compromising the differences between France and Germany has been that when there were, on both sides, democratic governments which wanted to compromise they both lacked the necessary strength. Matters were allowed to drift until the golden opportunity had passed. At present, outward encouragement (or pressure) may, to some extent, be substituted for domestic strength, but it will not produce the same results.

European as well as American observers know that there are reasons for concern arising from the field of foreign as well as of domestic politics. A special correspondent of *Le Monde* wrote recently:

"None of the bourgeois democracies of Europe fell on the field of battle under the blows of superior power; they all had succumbed previously to a rot within. All the SS did was to pick up the pieces . . ."

Turning to the present, the same writer added:

"Let us assume that the different countries of Western Europe were abandond to themselves, politically, economically, and militarily. And let us ask which ones of them are those which could be assumed, on the one hand, to have the political force needed in order to regain an economic equilibrium, and, on the other hand, the internal will to defend themselves. It seems that there are three: Socialist England, Fascist Spain, and National-Communist Yugoslavia." [9]

One may object to the term, "bourgeois democracies," and want to add that Britain's strength is more likely to stem from her democracy than from her socialism, but the basic facts are stated correctly. If so, what is the remedy?

It calls for adding a political Marshall plan to the economic Marshall Plan of the ECA, the diplomatic Marshall plan of the North Atlantic Pact, and the military Marshall plan of the Mutual Assistance Pact. The sequence in which the various versions were adopted was correct. Economic assistance had to come first because it was needed to hold a front otherwise threatened by immediate collapse. The diplomatic plan was necessary because it would have made little sense merely to fatten the goose which an aggressor might want to kill. Everything, finally, would have been an empty gesture without an adequate supply of arms.

Now, however, the time has come to make sure that there are governments in the countries of Continental Europe which can carry out their obligations, governments which are neither paralyzed nor in danger of being overthrown from within by a Communist or Fascist dictatorship. Those who drafted the "North Atlantic Defense Alliance" may have had this need in mind when they worded the first sentence of the second article to read: "The parties will contribute towards the further development of peaceful and friendly international relations by strengthening their free institutions, by bringing about better understanding of the principles upon which these institutions are founded, and by promoting conditions of stability and well-being."

This stated intention should be carried out. The leadership might come from the United States, not only on account of her great economic and, potentially at least, military power, but also on account of her early leadership in constitutional thought. The framers of the Philadelphia Constitution had the right approach to constitutional problems. They did not agree with extremists, such as the Greek writer, Polybius, for whom the constitution adopted was, "in every practical undertaking by a state . . . the most powerful agent for success or failure." [10] They were, as Madison made plain in No. 10 of

APPENDIX

(The following editorial, entitled "A Warning to Germany," is reprinted from *The New York Times* of November 11, 1948.)

"The echoes of Armistice Day, which ended the First World War, will register but faintly in a Germany laboring to dig itself out of the wreckage of the Second. Yet if there is one country which should heed the lessons of this day, that country is Germany. This applies not only to the inevitable consequences of unbridled ambition and ruthlessness but also to the internal organization which made it possible for a madman to seize a nation and plunge the whole world into war deliberately and with malice aforethought.

"Following the first Armistice, Germany adopted what it considered to be the most advanced democratic government in the world, modeled after the continental parliamentary system as exemplified in France and boasting of the latest electoral gadgets of the perfectionists. Among these gadgets was proportional representation of the worst type, the party list system, which divorced the candidates from their constituents and not only made the party supreme but put its fortunes above those of the country. This served the ambitions of professional politicians, but it atomized the electorate into more than a score of parties, deadlocked Parliament, paralyzed the coalition governments, and so disgusted the people that it killed off democracy by its very complexity and enabled a dictator to ride to power.

"Despite this, and despite the new demonstration of its evils in France, the Germans have not only returned to this system after their last defeat but are preparing to incorporate it into their new Constitution, now being framed in Bonn. Proportional representation, especially of the British type favored in the United States, may be innocuous in local affairs or in countries not rent by grave decisions among the people. But even in the United States it has produced more inequalities than it has remedied, and might have proved paralyzing had it been applied on a national scale in the last election. It has so proved itself in European countries split by fundamental ideological differences and unaccustomed to compromise and the democratic give-and-take. No element is more aware of this than the

REFERENCES

REFERENCES

INTRODUCTION

[1] The negative as well as the positive aspects of Rousseau have recently been analyzed in A. D. Lindsay, *The Modern Democratic State*, (Oxford, 1947), pp. 237 ff.

[2] For a very careful discussion of the general subject of the Introduction, see L. Freund, "Freiheit und Gleichheit als Zentralprobleme der Demokratie," *Kölner Zeitschrift für Soziologie*, Vol. I., 1948-49, pp. 373 ff.

[3] The above remarks are not intended to exclude any kind of freedom from the state. Fundamental rights have the very purpose of securing such freedom. They have a very evident positive purpose: to secure the free personality without which the free state is not possible. Only, it must be the freedom of the citizen rather than the freedom of the individual.

[4] Yves R. Simon, *The Nature and Functions of Authority*, (Milwaukee, 1940).

[5] *The History of Herodotus*, translated by G. Rawlinson, Vol. II, pp. 393-4.

[6] G. Mosca, *The Ruling Class*, (New York, 1939).

[7] R. M. Michels, *Political Parties*, (Glencoe, Ill., 1949).

[8] V. Pareto, *The Mind and Society*, (New York, 1935).

[9] Translated from F. W. Hegel, *Vorlesungen über die Philosophie der Geschichte*, (Leipzig, 1924), p. 339. (Translations from foreign languages are the author's unless otherwise indicated.)

[10] Here quoted from B. S. K. Padover, *The Complete Jefferson*, (New York, 1943), pp. 282 ff.

[11] John Morley, *Life of Gladstone*, Bk. II, p. 582. Here quoted from Ernst Troeltsch, *Die Soziallehren der christlichen Kirchen und Gruppen*, (Tübingen, 1923), p. 673.

[12] Charles Merriam, *The New Democracy and The New Despotism*, (New York, 1939), p. 44.

[13] John Locke, *The True End of Government*, Ch. XI.

[14] *Coningsby*, Bk. 5, Ch. IV.

[15] The term, "orgy of concentrated power," was used in a letter to the author by Dr. Michael Freund.

CHAPTER I

[1] Montesquieu, *Spirit of the Laws*, Bk. 2, Ch. II.

[2] Jerome Kerwin, "The Presidential Elections," *The Review of Politics*, April, 1948, p. 148.

[3] *La Quatrième République*, (New York, 1946), p. 65.

[4] (New York, 1940), pp. 95 ff.

[5] "How Democracy Was Extinguished in Spain," *The Daily Telegraph*, October 13, 1946.

[6] See the excerpts from a House of Commons speech by Sir Austen in: George Horwill, *Proportional Representation, Its Dangers and Its Defects*, (London, 1925), p. 132.

[7] *The Election of Representatives, Parliamentary and Municipal*, 4th ed., (London, 1873), pp. xv and 26-7.

[8] For the statistical details concerning British elections after the First World War, see: F. A. Hermens, *Democracy or Anarchy? A Study of Proportional Representation*, (Notre Dame, 1941), pp. 110-14.

[9] Ed. *The World's Classics*, pp. 137-8.

[10] *Ibid.*, p. xxiv.

[11] *Ibid.*, pp. 137-8.

[12] *The Times*, March 10, 1950. Somewhat different figures, based on a different classification, are given in: *The Times House of Commons, 1950*, (London, 1950), p. 275.

[13] "The Results Analysed," March 4, 1950, pp. 462 ff.

[14] *Ibid.*

[15] Quoted from Philip Viscount Snowden, *An Autobiography*, (London, 1934), p. 601.

[16] "The King's Government," March 4, 1950, pp. 457-8.

[17] April 27, 1950.

[18] "No Decision," February 25, 1950.

[19] "Britain's Labour Party at the Crossroads," *New York Times Magazine*, April 16, 1950, p. 26.

[20] March 2, 1950.

[21] "British Parties Held Close on Foreign Policy Stands," November 23, 1949.

[22] "L'Autorité de L'Angletere dans les Affaires Internationales n'est pas diminué," March 24, 1950.

[23] *The Times*, March 7, 1950.

[24] "No Easy Way," March 4, 1950, p. 460.

[25] March 15, 1950.

[26] *The Economist*, March 4, 1950.

[27] July 25, 1949.

[28] February 27, 1950.

[29] "No Easy Way," *op. cit.*, p. 461.

[30] House of Commons, *Parliamentary Debates*, Official Report, March 7, 1950. Mr. Churchill's speech was given considerable publicity by proponents of P.R., and in various countries of Continental Europe this writer noticed, in the summer of 1950, that a serious move towards a reform of the British electoral system was anticipated. When I was in London during the fall, my investigations at the headquarters of the three major parties showed that there was not the slightest prospect for any kind of change. I was told that Mr. Churchill's remarks had not even been cleared with his own party—"There were as many open mouths on his side of the House as on the other." Nor were Mr. Churchill's own intentions evaluated as very serious. It was remarked: "He was flying a kite." "He was throwing a bone to the (Liberal) dog."

Mr. Churchill's disapproval of a condition in which a smaller party would

REFERENCES

hold the political balance in the House of Commons excludes any deviation from the plurality system as much as does his classical defense of the British political system in his brilliant speech on the rebuilding of the House of Commons (*Parliamentary Debates,* Vol. 393, No. 114, Thursday, 28th Oct., 1943, pp. 404 ff.) Proponents of P.R. are, however, entitled to refer to the speech which he made during the Third Reading of the second Labour government's bill providing for the alternative vote. (*Parliamentary Debates,* Official Report, Vol. 253 (1930-31), pp. 100 ff.) The speech shows the same ambiguity as the one of March, 1950. Mr. Churchill expresses concern for the "under representation" of the Liberal party, but shrinks back from the implications of any remedy. Thus, he says: "I have always disliked proportional representation on account of its complications (which, of course, are peculiar to the Hare system —FAH), and I have not infrequently spoken of it in contemptuous terms, but I accept this view of the Conservative delegates upon the Three Party Conference." These delegates expressed themselves in favor of P.R. in the great cities, a solution which Mr. Churchill goes on to endorse in some detail. Its adoption would mean, of course, giving the opponents of Labour (a party which derives its major strength from the large cities) the partisan advantages of P.R. without any of its partisan disadvantages, as, with the plurality system retained in the other constituencies, Conservatives and Liberals would retain their advantage over Labour in their own strongholds.

If P.R. for the large cities is not adopted, Mr. Churchill favors the second ballot. Concerning the alternative vote, he continues: "It is the stupidest, the least scientific and the most unreal that the Government have embodied in their Bill. The decision of 100 or more constituencies, perhaps 200, is to be determined by the most worthless votes given for the most worthless candidates. That is what the Home Secretary told us to-day was 'establishing democracy on a broader and surer basis.' Imagine making the representation of great constituencies dependent on the second preference of the hindmost candidates. The hindmost candidate would become a personage of considerable importance, and the old phrase, 'Devil take the hindmost,' will acquire a new significance. I do not believe it will be beyond the resources of astute wirepullers to secure the right kind of hindmost candiates to be broken up in their party interests. There may well be a multiplicity of weak and fictitious candidates in order to make sure that the differences between No. 1 and No. 2 shall be settled, not by the second votes of No. 3, but by the second votes of No. 4 or No. 5, who may presumably give a more favorable turn to the party concerned. This method is surely the child of folly, and will become the parent of fraud. Neither the voters nor the candidates will be dealing with realities. An element of blind chance and accident will enter far more largely into our electoral decisions than even before, and respect for Parliament and Parliamentary processes will decline lower than it is at present." (pp. 106-7)

Mr. Churchill overlooks that the alternative vote is an essential ingredient of the Hare system of P.R., where its inconveniences are multiplied by the fact that more preferences can be expressed, and that the number of candidates among whom they may be distributed will be greater than under the alternative vote.

[31] Benjamin Welles, "British Liberals Predict Comeback," January 15, 1950.
[32] March 6, 1950.
[33] *Das Parlamentarische Wahlrecht,* Vol. I., (Berlin, 1932), p. 226.

[34] "No Easy Way," *op. cit.*
[35] L. F. Crisp, *The Parliamentary Government of the Australian Commonwealth,* (New Haven, 1949), pp. 68 ff.

CHAPTER II

[1] *The State,* (Boston, 1902), pp. 221-2.
[2] Plato, *The Republic,* Book II, par. 365.
[3] "La signification historique des élections françaises de 1928," *L'Année Politique,* July, 1928. On the entire problem of government instability in France, see the excellent book by A. Soulier, *L'Instabilité Ministérielle sous la Troisième République, 1871-1938,* (Paris, 1939).
[4] *Op. cit.,* pp. 125-6.
[5] See, in particular, Léon Blum's article, "Plus de République," *Le Populaire,* October 22, 1934.
[6] *Op. cit.,* pp. 297-8.
[7] "André Maurois, L'Eloge de la Stabilité," *Le Soir,* November 7, 1934.
[8] M. Prélot, "Sur le Soixantenaire de Notre Constitution," *Politique,* July-August, 1935, p. 591.
[9] K. Loewenstein, *Political Reconstruction,* (New York, 1946), p. 123.
[10] P. Birdsall in his Introduction to Gordon Wright, *The Reshaping of French Democracy,* (New York, 1948).
[11] W. Gurian, *Der Integrale Nationalismus,* (Frankfurt, 1931).
[12] G. Lachapelle: see the volumes which he published after each election, in particular *Elections Législatives, 26 avril et 3 Mai, 1936,* (Paris, 1936).
[13] The interview with Colonel de la Rocque is quoted here from *Echo de Paris,* May 3, 1936.

CHAPTER III

[1] Bonghi, "Gli ultimi fatti parlamentari," *Nuova Antologia,* January 1, 1895. Quoted from A. L. Lowell, *Government and Parties in Continental Europe,* (Boston and New York, 1896), p. 203.
[2] John H. Humphreys, *Objections to P.R. Answered,* (London, 1939), p. 23.
[3] G. Bandini, *La Riforma Elettorale con la Rappresentanza Proporzionale,* (Rome, 1910), pp. 582-3.
[4] G. Salvemini, "Come Eleggere La Costituente?" *Il Ponte,* November, 1945, pp. 675-6.
[5] L. Sturzo, *Italy and Fascismo,* (New York, 1927), p. 98.
[6] Lectures on Post-War Italy, delivered at Harvard University (mimeographed; no year given), Lecture I, p. 1.
[7] G. Giolitti, *Memoirs of My Life,* (London, 1923), p. 444.
[8] A. Esmein and H. Nézard, *Eléments de Droit Constitutionel Français et Comparé,* (Paris, 1927), Vol. I, p. 373.
[9] A. Malatesta, *Il Parlamento Italiano, Da Cavour a Mussolini,* (Milan, 1932), p. 212.
[10] *Op. cit.,* Lecture II, pp. 7-8.
[11] G. Volpe, *History of the Fascist Movement,* (Rome), p. 104.

REFERENCES

12 H. Schneider, *Making the Fascist State*, (New York, 1928), p. 80.
13 L. Sturzo, *op. cit.*, p. 118.
14 G. Salvemini, *The Fascist Dictatorship in Italy*, (New York, 1927), p. 111.
15 *Ibid.*, p. 113.
16 A Rossi, *Naissance du Fascisme*, (Paris, 1938), p. 201.
17 *Op. cit.*, Lecture II, p. 10.
18 *Storia del Movimento Fascista,* published in one volume with Mussolini's article, "La dottrina del Fascismo," p. 98. In the English translation (*History of the Fascist Movement, op. cit.,* p. 111), the sentence reads differently, the *realis* being used for the *irrealis*.
19 G. Pini and F. Bresadola, *Storia del Fascismo,* (Rome, 1928), p. 348.
20 *The Fascist Dictatorship in Italy, op. cit.,* p. 112.
21 Quoted from a speech made by Lord Craigavon in the Northern Irish Parliament, October 27, 1927, Government of Northern Ireland, House of Commons, *Parliamentary Debates*, Vol. VIII, No. 36, p. 2275.
22 *Verfassung und Verfassungsrecht,* (Munich and Leipzig, 1928), pp. 44-5.
23 Camera dei Deputati, *Discussioni*, Legislatura XXV, p. 19737.
24 *Of Civil Government*, Bk. 2, Ch. VIII, p. 166.
25 Bk. 1, Ch. I, p. 35.

CHAPTER IV

1 J. H. Humphreys, *op. cit.*, p. 24.
2 See on this and related matters: D. A. Ruestow, "Some Observations on Proportional Representation," *The Journal of Politics*, Vol. 12, pp. 12 ff.
3 Theodor Heuss, *Friedrich Naumann*, (Stuttgart, 1935), pp. 608-10.
4 C. G. Hoag and G. H. Hallett, Jr., *Proportional Representation*, (New York, 1926), pp. 134-5.
5 *Ibid.*
6 (Munich, 1935), p. 388.
7 Here quoted from: Department of State, *National Socialism: Basic Principles, Their Application by The Nazi Party's Foreign Organization, and the Use of Germans Abroad for Nazi Aims*, (Washington, 1943), p. 63.
8 *Ibid.*
9 *Gesammelte Schriften zur Politik,* (Munich, 1921), p. 391.
10 "Eigene Gedanken Alfred Webers ueber die Demokratie," *Frankfurter Zeitung*, October 15, 1929, 1st morn. ed.
11 *Prelude to Silence*, (New York, 1944), pp. 126-32.
12 *Am Grabe der Parteiherrschaft*, (Berlin, 1932), p. 30.
13 The calculations are based on the figures given in the statistics of the elections of 1930, Vol. 382, of the *Statistik des Deutschen Reiches*.
14 *Der Führer*, (Boston, 1944), pp. 539-40.
15 For a keen criticism of the major tenets of the economic interpretation of history as applied to politics, see L. Schwarzchild, "Historischer Mystizismus," *Das Neue Tagebuch*, February 16, 1935.
16 V. I. Lenin, *State and Revolution,* (New York, 1932) p. 8.

are the reason why Professor Zurcher was able to write: "No theoretical criticism of proportional representation has been more positively substantiated in practice than the charge that it would balkanize the party structure." (A. Zurcher, *The Experiment with Democracy in Central Europe,* [New York, 1933], p. 85. On the general theory of P.R., and for an excellent selected bibliography, see C. J. Friedrich, *Constitutional Government and Democracy,* [Boston, 1950], pp. 275 ff. and 633 ff.)

CHAPTER VII

[1] Gordon Wright, *op. cit.,* pp. 36-8 and p. 90. Senator Debré was good enough to read this chapter and to give me a memorandum which elucidates various problems concerning the Comité Général d'Etudes and the early relationships between General DeGaulle and the political parties. Since the text had already been set up in the form of page proofs, this information could not be incorporated. It is, however, contained in the chapter on post-war France in the German edition of *Democracy or Anarchy?, op. cit.*

[2] Michael Debré, "Sense de la Grandeur Française," *Les Cahiers Politiuques,* C.G.E. April, 1944, pp. 7-8. See also the following article entitled "Le Problème constitutionnel français," *ibid.,* pp. 8 ff.

[3] This summary of Debré's arguments follows his last-named article, *ibid.,* pp. 8 ff.

[4] Gordon Wright, *op. cit.,* pp. 38-9.

[5] *Ibid.*

[6] R. M. Dawson, *The Government of Canada,* (Toronto, 1949), pp. 78-9.

[7] See also R. Smend, *Verfassung und Verfassungsrecht, op. cit.,* pp. 78-79.

[8] Gordon Wright, *op. cit.,* pp. 38-9.

[9] For the statistical details, see *L'Année Politique,* 1944-45, (Paris, 1946), pp. 200-04 and pp. 292-4.

[10] *Ibid.,* p. 293.

[11] A. Leduc, "Gallic Trends: Will France Swing towards Democratic Socialism?" *The New Leader,* October 20, 1945.

[12] Raoul Husson, *Elections et Referendums,* (Paris, 1946), and *Elections et Referendums,* (Paris, 1947). For the percentage of unutilized votes, see the second volume, p. xxxiii.

[13] Gordon Wright, *op. cit.,* p. 261. The foundation of the RPF brought about considerable changes in the composition of parliamentary groups. For the details, see "Cinq Nouveaux Groupes à l'Assemblee Nationale," *Le Monde,* January 15, 1949.

[14] "Blum Bids Big Three Parties Unite to Rebuild France," *The New York Herald Tribune,* October 28, 1945.

[15] Raoul Husson, *op. cit.,* (1947), p. xxxiii.

[16] *Op. cit.,* p. 318.

[17] "Meaning of French Vote on New Constitution," *The Manchester Guardian Weekly,* October 18, 1946.

[18] *La Mort de l'Etat Républicain, op. cit.,* p. 185.

[19] Alexander Kendrick, *The Chicago Sun,* November 26, 1946.

[20] "Où l'On Souffle Le Chaud et Le Froid," *Temps Présent,* July 5, 1946.

[20(a)] Jules Moch, the Socialist leader, wrote on the occasion of the 42nd Congress of his party: "We forget quickly. Let us recall the year 1947. The Com-

REFERENCES

munist party saw its effectives grow and increased its pressure on the state. . . . At the same time Gaullism, like a straw fire, seemed to encompass all of public opinion. A dissolution of parliament was demanded everywhere. New elections would have yielded a Chamber absolutely incapable of governing, consisting, a third each, of Communists, Republicans, and DeGaullists. No designated Prime Minister could have obtained the 310 votes needed, according to the constitution, in order to obtain the 'investiture'." ("La Défense de la République," *Le Populaire,* June 13, 1950.)

Any reference to the inevitability of a heterogeneous majority as a result of a parliamentary dissolution in 1947 or 1948 implies a comparison between DeGaullists and National Socialists. To avoid misunderstandings, let it be emphasized that no identification of the two is intended; they are compared here only insofar as the mechanics of the parliamentary situation are concerned. The RPF contains different elements. Some of them will, if they prevail, push the movement towards dictatorship; others are sincerely interested in a reform of the Republic. The point of view of the latter has been expressed well by Professor René Capitant in his booklet, *Pour Une Constitution Fédérale, op. cit.,* and "Rapport sur la Revision de la Constitution," Rassemblement du Peuple Français, Conseil National, Seconde Session, (Mimeographed), dated Paris, September 28, 1948. Capitant emphasizes among his demands the adoption of the majority system and of a workable right of parliamentary dissolution. So far as the latter is concerned, it is to be used only after one cabinet has been overthrown by a new legislature. This is a limitation which, for example, British and Canadian writers would not accept, which, however, illustrates the moderation of these proposals.

[21] *Politique,* March, 1947, p. 20. For the details see *L'Année Politique,* 1947, (Paris, 1948), pp. 91 ff.; for the text of the decree, *ibid.,* p. 326. See also Harold Callender, "Auriol Spurns Figurehead Role in France; See Presidency Vital in Bolstering Unity," *The New York Times,* February 15, 1947.

[22] "Defense of the Republic," *The Manchester Guardian Weekly,* June 3, 1948; *L'Année Politique,* 1948, (Paris, 1949), pp. 332-3.

[23] "A Propos du Regime des Partis," *L'Aube,* June 23, 1948.

[24] Pertinax, "Resignation of De Gaulle Is Puzzling," *The Chicago Sun,* January 25, 1946.

[25] *Op. cit.,* pp. 222-3.

[25(a)] Bidault's cabinet was finally overthrown on June 24, 1950, the Socialists turning against it. Bidault was the first Prime Minister to ask the question of confidence in conformity with the provisions of the constitution. If this had been done a second time with the same negative result, the conditions for a dissolution of the National Assembly would have been granted. This fact made it easier for President Auriol to put pressure on the parties in order to induce them to make possible the formation of a new government. Still, the difficulties were considerable. After several others had rejected the offer to head a new cabinet, former Prime Minister Queuille accepted; he was, on June 30, personally approved by the Assembly, but his cabinet was overthrown on July 4. By that time the crisis seemed insoluble. Finally the former De Gaullist René Pleven was prevailed upon to try; he obtained his "investiture" on July 11, and approval for his cabinet on July 13th. The crisis coincided with the invasion of Korea. French diplomacy was, for several weeks, reduced to routine functions; the initiative gained with the Schuman plan was lost. Pleven attempted

BETWEEN DEMOCRACY AND ANARCHY

[53] "Election Talk in France," editorial, *The New York Times,* February 13, 1950.

[54] *L'Année Politique,* 1948, pp. 324-5.

[55] See the report in *Le Figaro* of September 11, 1950, entitled "A St.-Brieuc, M. Pleven a dit."

[56] Issue of October 30, 1950, p. 38.

[57] José de Broucker reports the salient facts in the Catholic daily, *The Sun Herald* (published in Kansas City, issue of December 5, 1950), under the headline, "Destructive Red Tactics Highlight French Crisis." He mentions the motives, which impelled Communists and DeGaullists to vote against Moch, and continues:

"However the RPF and the Communists do not make a majority, and since the Socialists cannot be suspected of voting against one of their leaders we are forced to think that a large number of MRP deputies voted in favor of the Communist proposal.

"There are two explanations of this extraordinary conduct. One is pure and and simple machiavellism. The MRP would have everything to gain from a political crisis, which would mean a conflict without issue since the Socialists would solidarize with Moch and refuse any further participation in a coalition government. In consequence nothing would be left but to dissolve parliament and call new general elections. And the elections would be conducted by the old electoral law since the new one has not been voted yet. And many members of the MRP believe that their party would get a better deal out of the old law than it can hope to get from the project that is being debated now."

CHAPTER VIII

[1] M. Dipiero, *Storia Critica dei Partiti Italiani,* (Rome, 1946), p. 175.

[2] W. M. Southam, *An International Electoral Commission,* (Ottawa, 1943). In Mr. Southam's words: "This system (the Hare system of P.R.), though *optional* to our Allies from the occupied countries, should be *imposed* by the Peace Conference on all Axis-controlled countries as a basic method for channelling their political activities into a democratic form of government. This, in effect, would be putting the Axis-controlled countries into a democratic 'political straight-jacket' from which, after a reasonable trial, they would not wish to escape." (*Ibid.,* p. 8.) On p. 2, we read: "This protective electoral proposal has been sent to the members of Parliament of the United Kingdom, and the Dominions of Canada, Australia, New Zealand, South Africa, and Eire; also to the members of all governments-in-exile in London, England, in Cairo, Egypt, and in Algiers, North Africa; and to the members of Congress and of the Administration, U.S.A., and others. Whether you agree with it or not, it would be helpful if those who read it would favor the State Department, Washington, D. C., U. S. A., or the British Foreign Office, London, England, with their opinion on the principle involved." The same page lists three printings during the year of publication.

[3] The American major was Robert E. Garrigan, who has given a humorous account of the election in: "An Italian Election under the Hare System," P.R. Department, *National Municipal Review,* June, 1946, pp. 316 ff. Mr. Garrigan complains that the Military Government "never showed the slightest inclination to learn" about the advantages of the Hare system. The election which he held was of a merely advisory nature. It is interesting to record his remarks concerning his attempt to "sell" the Hare system to the Italians: "It

REFERENCES

was easy to get approval for the Hare system. I simply said it was the most modern and advanced form of election. It had been so long since any of them had been concerned with the subject that none could argue the point, so they left the technical directions to me." (*Ibid.*, p. 317.) The unfamiliarity with elections, and the willingness to let a few people decide on the systems of elections, were general in Italy during that time.

[4] *Bolletino di informazioni e documentazioni del Ministero per la Costituente*, Vol. I, No. 2, November 30, 1945, p. 16.

[5] Signor Romualdo Bianchi in Rome, in a memorandum prepared for the author, dated February 8, 1950.

[6] "Un manifesto per le elezioni e la richesta di un referendum," *Tempo*, October 17, 1945.

[7] G. Salvemini, "Como eleggere la Costituente?" *op. cit.*, pp. 671 ff.

[8] L. Einaudi, "Contro La Proporzionale," Discorso Pronunciato Alla Consulta Nazionale Nella Seduta Dell'll Febbraio, 1946, (Rome, 1946).

[9] Istituto Centrale Di Statistica E Ministero Dell'Interno, *Elezioni Per l'Assemblea Constituente E Referendum Istituzionale*, 2 Giugno, 1946, (Rome, 1948), p. lii. The introduction to this volume contains an analysis of the election law, to which reference is made for details. See also: M. Grindrod, *The New Italy*, (London, 1947), pp. 44-7, and E. Wiskemann, *Italy*, (London, 1947), pp. 146 ff.

[10] G. Glisenti, Report published by NCWC News Service, dated June 30, 1947.

[11] For the statistical details, see *Il Popolo*, October 15, 1947, and *Unità*, October 14, 1947. Both newspapers give the results of the 1946 elections in comparison with those of 1947.

[11(a)] The term "neo-fascist" was commonly applied to the Qualunquists in the American press. The author was told repeatedly in Rome, however, that it was too strong, and that only later groups, such as the Italian Social Movement (MRI) could qualify for this designation.

[12] The various possibilities are discussed in an article entitled "Roma Senza Sindaco," *Il Popolo*, December 29, 1946.

[13] Anne O'Hare McCormick, *The New York Times*, April 7, 1947.

[14] "Insegnamenti delle Elezioni Romani," *Risorgimento Liberale*, editorial, October 17, 1947.

[15] G. Bellavista, "Proporzionale e Partitocrazia," *Il Giornale d'Italia*, July 23, 1949.—Don Sturzo has been a proponent of P.R. since the Second World War as he had been after the First. See, among others, his articles, "Il Sistema Proporzionale," *Il Popolo*, September 1 and 4, 1945; "Travaglio di partiti," *ibid.*, December 29, 1949; "Proporzionale e Blochi," *ibid.*, January 5, 1947. In the latter article he argued that there would be political blocs under either system of voting but that they were more dangerous under the majority system. He fears, apparently, that the "People's Bloc" of Communists and left-wing Socialists might secure a majority under a majority system. Actually, the example of the French Communists in the provincial elections of 1949 suggests the probability of a catastrophic defeat for the Communists under a majority system, even if in Italy the position of the Communists is better than in France insofar as they enjoy left-wing Socialist support. The latter might, however, be rather doubtful under the majority system, for reasons to be discussed in connection with the elections of 1948.

[16] For the text see: Repubblica Italiana, Ministero del'Interno, *Le Leggi Elettorali*, (Rome, 1948).

[17] February 17, 1948.

[18] "Italy's Victory," *Life*, May 3, 1948.

[19] Ministero dell'Interno, Istituto Centrale Di Statistica, *Elezioni Della Camera Dei Deputati E Del Senato Della Repubblica*, Dati Riassuntivi, (Rome, 1948), pp. 20-1. For a discussion of details which cannot be treated here, see M. Einaudi, "The Italian Elections of 1948," *The Review of Politics*, July, 1948, and I. Thomas, "The Italian Elections," *The Contemporary Review*, May, 1948.

[20] Anne O'Hare McCormick, "Coalition Government in Italy Is Working," *The New York Times*, February 16, 1949.

[21] Keith Wheeler, "Two-Party System Emerges in Italy," *The Chicago Sun-Times*, April 25, 1948.

[22] I. Thomas, *op. cit.*

[23] See the editorial under this title in the Socialist daily, *Avanti*, October 15, 1947.

[24] For details see F. Porru, "I risultati definitivi delle Regionali Sarde," *Il Tempo*, May 11, 1949, and A. Cortesi, "Left Parties Gain in Sardinia Voting," *The New York Times*, May 11, 1949.

[25] "Italian Monarchists Schemes and Stratagems," *The Manchester Guardian Weekly*, September 22, 1949.

[26] Title of an article by E. Corbino, *Il Tempo*, May 11, 1949.

[27] *Il Tempo*, May 11, 1949.

[28] See the report of a declaration made by De Gasperi to the delegations of the parliamentary groups, *Il Giornale d'Italia*, January 20, 1950.

[29] "Richieste e offerte del partito Liberale," *Il Giornale d'Italia*, January 19, 1950.

[29(a)] The proposed system was discussed by Oronzo Reale in the Republican weekly, *La Voce Repubblicana*, issue of December 10, 1950, under the title "La democrazia e i sistemi elettorali," and by Paolo Rossi in Saragat's weekly, *Giustizia*, issue of December 10, 1950, under the title "Una buona legge e i suoi cattivi critici." Both authors emphasize that, as a matter of principle, they favor P.R., but add that this system of voting has endangered a safe administration (in the words of Signor Rossi) "in hundreds of large centers and of illustrious cities where antagonistic forces confront each other in almost equal proportions." This point had, in the preceding discussion, been made by most observers, including Prime Minister de Gasperi; frequent reference was made to cities where the application of P.R. had led to incongruous results.

Some of the pertinent details of the systems of voting under consideration were discussed in the majority and minority reports on the government proposal for the election of regional councils, Camera Dei Deputati, N 986-A, "Relazione della I Commissione Permanente . . . Relatore Lucifredi, per la maggioranza; Relatore di minoranza Vigorelli, Sul Disegno Di Legge Presentato Dal Ministro Dell' Interno (Scelba). . . . Norme per la elezione dei Consigli regionali, Presentata alla Presidenza il 12 maggio, 1950." See also the Chamber documents, Nos. 984, 985, and 986, which deal respectively with the original government proposals for municipal, provincial, and regional elections.

[30] Hermann Luedemann. "Ohne Wagnis geht es nicht," *Die Welt*, January 15, 1948. By the same author, see also: "Starke Demokratie durch richtiges Wahlrecht," *Schleswig-Holsteinische Volkszeitung*, January 25, 1947;

REFERENCES

"Am Beispiel Bremen, Ein Beitrag zur Diskussion des Wahlsystems, SPD.," *Sozialdemokratischer Pressedienst*, November 18, 1947.

[31] M. Einaudi, "The Italian Land: Men, Nature, and Government," *Social Research*, March, 1950,

[32] G. Ferri, "Le Conseguenze Anarchiche della Rappresentanza Proporzionale," *Annuario di Diritto Comparato e di Studi Legislativi*, Vol. XXIV, 1948, p. 24.

[33] "Crisis Threatens Italy," *The New Leader*, May 13, 1950.

CHAPTER IX

[1] Dana Adams Schmidt, "2-Party Bent Seen in German Voting," *The New York Times*, May 28, 1946.

[2] American Association for a Democratic Germany, Facts about Occupied Germany, issue on "German Elections," January, 1947, p. 2.

[3] Foster Hailey, "Liberals Lose Out in Two-Party Race," *The New York Times*, February 24, 1950.

[4] American Association for a Democratic Germany, *op. cit.*, p. 2.

[5] Helene Wessel, "Der politische Weg der Deutschen Zentrumspartei," *Bericht über den Parteitag der Deutschen Zentrumspartei* in Werl am. 16. und 17. November, 1946, pp. 28-9.

[6] F. J. C. Hearnshaw, (New York, 1942), p. 260.

[7] "Proposals by Marshall and Molotov," *The New York Times*, March 23, 1950.

[8] "On the Record," *The Florida Times-Union*, June 18, 1949.

[9] P. 74.

[10] Pp. 75-6.

[11] Letter from Congressman (now Senator) Francis Case to the author, dated January 24, 1948.

[12] The clipping sent to the author by an American soldier bears no date; however, the context makes it likely that it was published some time in December, 1945, since Dr. Harries takes exception to a letter by a Dr. Waldschmidt, published December 3, 1945.

[13] "U. S. Drafting Plan on German Regime," March 20, 1947.

[14] K. Loewenstein, *Political Reconstruction, op. cit.*, p. 298.

[15] "Gegen Das Verhältniswahlrecht: Ein Aufruf Heidelberger Persönlichkeiten," *Die Wandlung*, February 7, 1947.

[16] *Der Tagesspiegel*, issues of February 15, and December 25, 1946, and January 1, 12, 19, 1947.

[17] "Zur Verhaeltniswahl; Ergebnisse zur Umfrage der Zeitschrift 'Wandlung'," *Die Main-post*, February 7, 1947.

[18] The letter was dated June 26, 1948, and I cannot, at this time, name the author. I gathered much of the information on the developments dealt with above during the summer of 1948, when I was teaching at the Universities of Muenster and Bonn; other information has been made available by some of those who participated in the decisions in question, or made later on-the-spot investigations.

[19] See the *Annual Report* of the Proportional Representation Society for 1946, (London, 1947). For an interesting comment, see mimeographed item

signed M.J.S., "The New 'D' Day, Invasion of Germany by British Single Transferable Vote Expert," forwarded to the author by a Cincinnati recipient.

[20] Mierendorff's views are succinctly expressed in his contribution to J. Schauff, *Neues Wahlrecht,* (Berlin, 1929), pp. 14 ff.

[21] Julius Leber, "Wahlreform? Alles aussprechen, was ist!" *Lübecker Volksbote,* December 20, 1947.

[22] "Proportional-System oder Einzelwahlkreise?" *New York Staatszeitung und Herold,* March 29, 1947.

[23] My information concerning Hilferding's opposition to P.R. was provided by one of his former colleagues in the Reichstag.

[24] Hermann Luedemann, "Ohne Wagnis geht es nicht," *op. cit.,* and "Starke Demokratie durch richtiges Wahlrecht," *op. cit.*

[25] *Das Wählen und das Regieren,* pp. 7-9. This pamphlet, published by the Deutsche Wählergesellschaft in 1949, contains the text of six speeches made in the Paul's Church in Frankfurt against the impending decision of the Parliamentary Council to adopt P.R.

[26] *Hitler and Beyond,* (New York, 1945), p. 39.

[27] For Professor Heuss' criticism of P.R., see, in particular, pp. 608-10 of his book, *Friedrich Naumann, op. cit.* Heuss primarily reports the views of Naumann, but on at least one occasion expresses himself in a manner which can only be interpreted as giving his own criticism of P.R.

[28] *Germany from Defeat to Defeat,* (London, 1943), pp. 64-6.

[29] During the period when the decision concerning the use of P.R. was made in the American zone, the mails had not as yet been reopened. On the implications, see my letter to the editor of *The New York Times,* published on February 1, 1946, under the title, "Vote in Hesse Questioned."

[30] For the election results, see Military Government in Germany, *Statistics of Elections in Germany, 1946,* Special Report of the Military Governor, U. S. zone.

[31] See the report by the DANA (Deutsche Nachrichten Agentur), dated December 12, 1946, and published in various German newspapers.

[32] The different systems of voting in the three major Laender of the British zone are discussed in *Die Wahl zum niedersächsischen Landtag vom 20 April, 1947,* (Hanover, 1947), prepared by Dr. Herbert C. Blank; the second part, pp. 58 ff., is particularly interesting.

[33] *Die Landeswahlen in Schleswig-Holstein,* herausgegeben vom Landeswahlleiter, (Kiel, 1947), p. 73.

[34] "Coalition Regimes for British Zone," April 22, 1947.

[35] "Laender-Parlamentarismus," *Die Welt,* January 6, 1948.

[36] "Staatskommissariat fehlt rechtliche Grundlage," July 28, 1948.

[37] Paul Wilhelm Wengler, "Maier's Patentdemokratie," February 11, 1950.

[38] "Verfassungsausschuss der Ministerpräsidenten der Westlichen Besatzungszonen," *Bericht über den Verfassungskonvent Auf Herrenchiemsee* vom 10-25 August, 1948.

[39] *Ibid.,* p. 7.

[40] *Ibid.,* p. 35.

[41] For the text of Dr. Luther's talks see: *Dem Wähler das Wahlrecht,* Veröffentlichung des Studienkreises Traunstein. . . . nach einem Gutachten des Reichskanzlers a. D. Dr. Hans Luther, erstattet vor dem Ausschuss für Wahlrechtsfragen des Parlamentarischen Rats in Bonn, 1949.

REFERENCES

[42] For the text of the various statements, as well as the German election law, see: *Documents on the Creation of the German Federal Constitution*, prepared by the Office of Military Government for Germany (U. S.), 1949, pp. 140 ff.

[43] The table is taken from: Otto Kirchheimer and Arnold H. Price, "Analysis and Effects of the Elections in Western Germany," *The Department of State Bulletin*, October 17, 1949, pp. 563 ff.

[44] S. R. Bolten, "Military Government and the German Political Parties," in: *Military Government, The Annals of the American Academy of Political and Social Science*, (January, 1950), pp. 55 ff. and p. 64.

[45] Adapted from "Die Verteilung der Abgeordnetensitze," *Frankfurter Neue Presse*, August 16, 1949. For a comprehensive tabulation of the election results, including a comparison with the Landtag elections of 1946-7, see: *Germany, 1947-9: The Story in Documents*, The Department of State, (Washington, 1950), pp. 317-19.

[46] The publications which are of particular interest in this connection are: Bayerisches Statistisches Landesamt, *Endgültige Ergebnisse der Wahlen zum ersten Bundestag am 14. August, 1949; Stimmergebnis der Wahlkreisvorschläge*, (mimeographed), (Munich, 1949); and Statistisches Landesamt Nord-Rhein Westfalen, *Gegenüberstellung der Ergebnisse der Landtagswahl. . . . und der Bundestagswahl vom 14.8.1949 im Lande Nord-Rhein-Westfalen nach der Wahlkreiseinteilung der Bundeswahl*, (mimeographed), (Duesseldorf, 1949). For an interesting discussion of the election results as compared with the probable effects of either absolute or relative majority systems, see E. P. Walk, in the appendix to G. B. von Hartmann, *Fuer und Wider das Mehrheitswahlrecht*, 2nd ed., (Frankfurt, 1950).

[47] Kirchheimer and Price, *op. cit.*, p. 566.

[48] "Die Wahl zum Bundestag am 14. August, 1949," *Wirtschaft und Statistik*, 1. Jg. N. F., Heft 5, p. 132.

[49] "Wer kann regieren?" *Westdeutsche Rundschau*, August 16, 1949.

[50] Military Government of Germany, *Statistics of Elections, op. cit.*, p. 11, for the first column; for the second, Bayerisches Statistisches Landesamt, *op. cit.*

[51] Peter Maslowski, *Neue Freie Presse* (Coburg), August 18, 1949. The new elections to the Bavarian Diet of November, 1950, did destroy the majority of the CSU. The Munich correspondent of the Kansas City daily, *Sun-Herald*, issue of December 5, remarked: "Now comes the dismal task for the politicians of figuring out the coalitions. It is more excitement, if less fun, than a horse race."

This is not the place to discuss in detail the new Diet elections which took place in 1950. In North Rhine-Westphalia the election system favored the strongest party, the CDU, which was placed in a position to form a majority either with the small Center party, or with the Free Democratic party, or both, or to resume the coalition with the Social Democrats. In spite of this relatively favorable result the negotiations for the formation of a new cabinet dragged on for months, resulting in a great deal of recrimination between the parties. The plurality system would, once again, have avoided these difficulties by giving the CDU a clear over-all majority. (For details, see F. Piefke, "Nordrhein-westfaelische Ergebnisse," *Der Waehler*, August, 1950.)

In Schleswig Holstein the election law was changed in order to prevent the non-Socialist coalition from obtaining a majority; this result was achieved by providing that no party could obtain seats from the reserve list which failed to present candidates in every constituency. The press paid much attention to the new party of expellees—theBHE—without considering that the rise of such a group was, in post-Potsdam Germany, an inevitable consequence of P.R. Schleswig-Holstein has a very large expellee population, but even in this case, two-thirds of the seats of the new group had to be won by way of the reserve list, and in the five cases where the party obtained a plurality its percentage of the total vote lay between 29.5 and 39.9, which is hardly enough to establish a new party under a majority system.

In Hessen the pressure of the *Deutsche Waehlergesellschaft* caused the government coalition to assist in eliminating the constitutional provision requiring P.R., which was done by way of a plebiscite, in which 78.4 per cent of those voting favored the change. The Diet was free to retain P.R. in the election law, however, which it did. Still, renewed representations by leading members of the *Deutsche Waehlergesellschaft* led to marked improvements in the bill, and the elections resulted in an over-all majority of the Social Democrats. (On the plebiscite and the new election law, see Ch. C. Baer, "Hessen's Landtag beraet Wahlgesetz," *Der Waehler*, August, 1950, and E. Bindert and Ch. C. Baer, "Vom Volksbegehren num Wahlgesetz," *Der Waehler*, September, 1950.)

The elections in Wuerttemberg-Baden showed, as did those in Bavaria and Hesse, Social Democratic advances and Christian Democratic losses, but are not otherwise remarkable.

[52] Jack Raymond, "Adenauer Is Nominated for Post of Chancellor in West Germany," *The New York Times*, September 15, 1949.

[53] Jack Raymond, "Adenauer Elected by a Single Vote," September 16, 1949.

[54] Alain Clément, "Adenauer's s'apprête à exercer une véritable régence sur l'Allemagne Occidentale," *Le Monde*, September 1, 1949.

[55] "German Parties," September 1, 1949.

[56] "Kreuz und Quer durch die Welt," November 28, 1949.

[57] Jack Raymond, September 18, 1949.

[58] F. A. Hermens, "The Danger of Stereotypes in Viewing Germany," *The Public Opinion Quarterly*, Winter, 1945-46; "The Reporters View Germany," *Forum*, August, 1949. See also the very revealing remarks in Marshall Knappen, *And Call It Peace*, (Chicago, 1947), pp. 191-3.

[59] "Bonn Deputy Withdraws Over Nazi-Style Speech," *The New York Times*, December 15, 1949.

[60] "Against Nationalism," *News From Germany*, published by the Executive Committee of the Social-Democratic party of Germany, February, 1950, p. 2.

[61] Jack Raymond, "Disorder Disrupts Bundestag Session; Repeated Intolerance of Views of Minorities of Right and Left Reflected at Bonn," *The New York Times*, September 23, 1949.

[62] "Against the Enemies of Democracy," *News From Germany, op. cit.*, March-April, 1950, pp. 7-9.

[63] "Germany's Overwhelming Problem Is Economic," *The New York Times*, January 30, 1950.

[64] "Economic Unity Vital to Germany," *St. Paul Pioneer Press*, June 21, 1947.

REFERENCES

[65] "Das Wählen und das Regieren," *op. cit.*

[66] E. W. Meyer, *Die Grundlagen für den Frieden mit Deutschland*, (Wiesbaden, 1949), p. 34.

[67] See Appendix.

[68] "Die Deutschen wünschen Demokratie," May 7, 1949.

[69] S. R. Bolten, *Military Government and the German Political Parties, op. cit.*, p. 64.

CHAPTER X

[1] On the constitutional problem see E. Hula, "Constitutional Developments in Austria," in J. K. Pollock, *Change and Crisis in European Government*, (New York, 1947), pp. 62 ff.

[2] *Austria, A Summary of Facts and Figures*, (New York, 1949), p. 22.

[3] "Nazi's Vote Is Key to Austrian Poll," October 7, 1949.

[4] The figures are, for the elections of 1949 as for those of 1945, taken from *Austrian Information*, published by the Information Department of the Austrian Consulate General in New York, Vol. II, No. 17, October 21, 1949. For the percentage of the seats (as well as for other details), see *Die Nationalratswahlen vom. 9. Oktober 1949*, Bearbeitet im Österreichischen Statistischen Zentralamt, (Vienna, 1950), p. 21. For the number of seats which, in 1945, would have been won under full P.R., see *Die Nationalratswahlen vom 25. November 1945*, Bearbeitet vom Oesterreichischen Statistischen Zentralamt, (Wein, 1946), p. 15, table 24.

[5] John McCormac, "Nazi-Tinged Party Gainer in Austria," *The New York Times*, October 11, 1949.

[6] For some details see Dr. A. Missong, "Wir und der VDU," *Österreichische Monatshefte*, November, 1949, pp. 53 ff.

[7] "Die Angst vor de OeVP," *Wiener Tageszeitung*, October 16, 1950.

[8] "Austria Party Rift Wide," *The New York Times*, November 5, 1949.

[9] "Coalition Cabinet Formed in Austria," *The New York Times*, November 8, 1949.

[10] It remains just appearance, as during the 1949 elections the order in which the candidates were listed by the party committees was in only one case changed by voters' preferences. See: *Die Nationalratswahlen vom 9 Oktober, 1949, op. cit.*, p. 21.

[11] For the details see articles 21, 22, 26, 30, 31, 32 of the *Constituent Assembly Elections Ordinance;* a typewritten copy of the English translation was made available to me by the Israeli Ministry of Justice. See also Dunner, *op. cit.*, p. 127.

[12] *Promise and Fulfillment*, (New York, 1950), p. 258.

[13] Anne O'Hare McCormick, "Pressing Issues Overcloud Israeli Interest in Charter," *The New York Times*, January 19, 1949.

[14] "Israeli Parties Start Drive for January 25 Election," *The New York Times*, January 15, 1950.

[15] See above, n. 11.

[16] Provided by Dr. Abraham Weinshall in a letter to the author, dated April 16, 1950.

[17] Dunner, *op. cit.*, pp. 130-1.

[18] Hal Lehrman has been reporting on political developments in Israel in the recent volumes of *Commentary*.

[19] Koestler, *op. cit.*, pp. 258-9.

[20] Professor Dunner (*op. cit.*, p. 125) says that P.R. "makes for excessive fragmentation, for indifference in the relation between voter and deputy, and it creates an omnipotent party machine."

[21] The letter from Dr. Weinshall to the author, cited above, ends with these observations on P.R.:
"There is a growing opposition to this system of elections, the main defects of which are: (a) splitting of votes; (b) dependence of the elected candidates upon their party bosses and not upon the electorate; (c) stressing of particular interests of each group instead of stressing the general interests of the population as a whole and the main issues confronting the state; (d) absence of a strong majority controlling the elected body and responsible for its policy; (e) absence of a strong and united opposition; (f) a low level of the elected candidates (whose loyalty towards the party is more appreciated than the personal qualification); (g) no bye-elections enabling to test the trend of the public opinion; (h) coalition government not based on one harmonic program, but on division of seats and distribution of influence and benefits."

[22] H. Vinacke, *A History of the Far East in Modern Times*, (New York, 1950), and H. Quigley, *Japanese Government and Politics*, (New York, 1932).

[23] Quigley, *op. cit.*, pp. 218 ff.

[24] For the details, see *ibid.*, pp. 271 ff.; for the text, pp. 378 ff. See also N. Kitazawa, *The Government of Japan*, (Princeton, 1939), p. 75, and W. B. Munro, *The Government of Europe*, with a supplementary chapter on Japan, p. 312; an excellent analysis of practical experience under this law is provided by K. Colegrove, "The Japanese General Election of 1928," *American Political Science Review*, Vol. XXII.

[25] Burton Crane, "Japan's Reds Map Big Election Drive," *The New York Times*, December 27, 1948.

[26] Memorandum for The Supreme Commander on the *Election Report*, submitted by the Chief of the Government Section of the U. S. Army, February 3, 1949.

[27] Lindesay Parrot, "Opposition Delays Japan's Poll Bill," *The New York Times*, March 26, 1947.

[28] (New York, 1949), p. 57.

[29] Memorandum on the *Election Report*, *op. cit.*

[30] Mr. Bisson says that "Japanese newsmen" calculated that the loss cost the Social Democrats "at least 50 seats," but does not give the basis for this estimate. (*Op. cit.*, p. 59.)

[31] *Memorandum on the Election Report*, *op. cit.*

[32] Dr. Justin Williams of the Government Section of SCAP was good enough to place the complete election results—the number of votes received by each candidate—at my disposal, and Mr. Jay T. Suagee of the Department of the Army, sent me, in a letter dated May 27, 1949, a corrected breakdown of the percentages secured by the winning Communists on the basis of later changes in the election returns.

[33] Burton Crane, "Busy Session Ends for Japanese Diet," June 1, 1949.

[34] Burton Crane, "Japan Turns Tide in Battle on Inflation; Price Levels Fall, Black Market Drops Too," June 23, 1949.

REFERENCES

[35] For a list see Lindesay Parrot, "Japan Drafts Plan of 2-Party System," *The New York Times*, July 14, 1947.

[36] See the opinions expressed by Mr. Ozaki to American newspaper men, as reported in "Democracy Held a Myth in Japan," *The New York Times*, May 20, 1950. Mr. Ozaki believes that even now Japanese parties represent more personal cliques than parties on the American model—a contention which many will not accept, no matter how much remains to be done to make Japanese parties truly popular.

[37] For some details, see Farnsworth Fowle, "Turkey's Democrats Plan Reforms," *The New York Times*, May 21, 1950.

[38] The limited vote is a form of majority voting when it makes certain of the election of a majority; it is a form of minority voting, with some, at least, of the characteristics of P.R., when in a multiple-member constituency the voter is allowed to vote for less than the majority of those to be elected.

CHAPTER XI

[1] W. Gurian, *Bolshevism: Theory and Practice*, (New York, 1937), pp. 61-2.

[2] Plato, *Republic*, Bks. VIII and IX.

[3] J. Burnham, *The Coming Defeat of Communism*, (New York, 1950), p. 49.

[4] J. Burnham, *op. cit.*, p. 50. Prof. C. J. Friedrich rightly says that the governments with which we are here concerned represent "the false parliamentary type as exemplified by France or Weimar Germany." ("Representation and Constitutional Reform in Europe," *The Western Political Quarterly*, June, 1948, p. 126.)

[5] See above, pp. 67-9.

[6] *The Federalist*, No. 62.

[7] Raymond Poincaré, who had held the position of President as well as Prime Minister, was one of those who "believed that a return to the normal method of dissolution, as practiced in Great Britain, would in itself cure all the ills of French parliamentarism." (B. Mirkine-Guetzévitch, "Some Constitutional Problems Facing the French Constituent Assembly," *Social Research*, March, 1946, p. 31.) At the time when Poincaré expressed those views, P.R. was not, of course, being applied.

[8] "Egypt," *The Manchester Guardian Weekly*, editorial, January 12, 1950.

[9] Jean-Jacques Servan Schreiber, "L'Amérique en Allemagne," *Le Monde*, (Sélections Hebdomadaires, du 10 au 16 mars 1950.)

[10] "Now, in every practical undertaking by a state we must regard as the most powerful agent for success or failure the form of its constitution; for from this as from a fountain-head all conceptions and plans of action not only proceed, but attain their consummation. . . ." (Here quoted from F. W. Coker, *Readings in Political Philosophy*, [New York, 1938], p. 115.)

[11] See his column in *The Cleveland Plain Dealer*, October 3, 1940.

[12] Professor Beard later developed a similar view when stating that "party, or, rather its management," might "become *a creative force* by drawing together interests which would otherwise be factional and, perhaps, vindictive." (*The Republic*, [New York, 1943], p. 269.)

[13] *The Fort Wayne News Sentinel*, October 4, 1948.

INDEX

(Since the Table of Contents is sufficiently detailed, this Index is confined to names of persons.)

Acheson, D., 254
Adams, J., xiv
Adenauer, K., 206, 209, 210, 211, 212, 213, 214, 215, 251, 252
Alessio, G., 54, 59, 60, 181
Ambedkar, B. R., 245
Amrein, A., 271
Anchuetz, G., 188
Aosta, Duke of, 56
Aquinas, T., 60
Arnold, K., 196, 210
Ashida, H., 241
Asquith, H., 20
Attlee, C., 22, 32, 213
Auriol, V., 138, 141, 273
Axelesson, G., 122

Bach, L., 271
Badoglio, P., 56-57, 166
Baer, C., 282
Bagehot, W., 12, 14, 17, 35, 36, 164, 267
Balfour, Lord, 14, 22
Bandini, G., 264
Barrachin, M., 154-155, 275
Barthélemy, J., 269
Beard, C., 254, 285
Bellavista, G., 170, 277
Benes, E., 91, 93
Bevan, A., 22
Beveridge, W., 22
Bevin, E., xiii, 23
Bianchi, R., 277
Bidault, G., 137, 140, 143, 153, 157, 273, 275
Bindert, E., 282
Birdsall, P., 264
Bisson, T., 240, 284
Blank, H., 280
Blum, L., 34, 35, 36, 131, 133, 135, 140, 141, 142, 150, 151, 152, 156, 264, 274
Blythe, E., 113
Bolten, S., 218, 219, 281, 283

Bonghi, R., 264
Bonomi, I., 51, 53, 161, 166
Brandt, W., 215
Braun, O., 73
Braunias, K., 27, 114, 121, 266, 270, 271
Brecht, A., 71, 78
Brentano, H., 213
Bresadola, F., 57, 265
Briand, A., 41
Briefs, G., 189, 266
Bright, J., 7
Brooke, B., 110
Broucher, J., 276
Bruening, H., 10, 67, 71, 73, 78, 101, 142
Brusselmans, F., 267
Buehler, O., 195, 196, 211
Buell, R., 88
Burnham, J., 247, 248, 285

Cadart, J., 275
Callender, H., 273
Capitant, R., 35, 129, 273
Case, F., 186, 279
Chamberlain, A., 7, 8, 262
Chmelar, J., 266
Churchill, R., 21
Churchill, W., 20-21, 26, 27, 32, 121, 262, 263
Clay, L., 188, 218
Clemenceau, G., 38, 44
Clément, A., 282
Cognoit, G., 127
Coker, F. W., 285
Colegrove, K., 284
Colijn, H., 116
Combes, J., 44
Corbett, J., 267
Corbino, E., 278
Cortesi, A., 169, 171, 278
Cosgrave, W., 106, 107, 112, 113, 117
Costello, J., 107, 108, 109, 111
Coty, R., 154, 155, 275

Craigavon, Lord, 265
Crane, B., 284
Crisp, L., 264
Croce, B., 161
Curzon, Lord, 57

Dahrendorf, 191, 217
Daudet, L., 41
Dawson, G., 129, 272
Debré, M., 125, 126, 127, 129, 135, 151, 272
Defournel, H., 136
DeGasperi, A., 160, 166, 168, 169, 170, 171, 173, 174, 176, 177, 179, 180, 181, 243, 278
DeGaulle, C., 125, 128, 129, 138, 139, 140, 142, 143, 144, 145, 150, 153, 154, 158, 250, 258, 272, 275
DeGreer, D. J., 116
Degrelle, L., 100, 102
Delcos, F., 155
Dennen, L., 180
De Valera, E., 106, 107, 108, 109, 112, 117, 269
Dipiero, M., 276
Disraeli, B., xvi, 48
Dollfuss, E., 86
Doumergue, G., 35, 37, 158
Dulles, J., 254
Dumusois, M., 145
Dunner, J., 227, 283, 284
Duttweiler, G., 119, 120
Duverger, M., 143, 144, 275
Duvieusart, J., 268

Eden, A., 20, 23
Einaudi, L., 161, 163, 164, 173, 174, 272
Einaudi, M., 179, 278, 279
Ekman, C., 114
Eldersveld, S., 270
Engels, F., 79, 80
Erhard, L., 207, 210
Esmein, A., 264
Ewers, H., 215
Eyskens, G., 104, 105

Facta, L., 53, 54, 55, 56, 57, 61, 67, 180
Ferri, G., 180, 279

Fey, E., 85
Figl, L., 221, 225
Fitzgerald, D., 113
Fitzgerald, J., 189
Fowle, F., 285
Freund, L., 261
Friedrich, C. J., 272, 285

Gallup, G., 92
Gambetta, L., 77
Garrigan, R., 276
Gedda, L., 171
Geiler, K., 216
Gessler, O., 78
Giolitti, G., 48, 50, 51, 52, 53, 54, 61, 85, 95, 166, 236, 264
Gladstone, W. E., xiv, 7, 24, 111
Glisenti, G., 277
Goebbels, J., 69
Goethe, J. W., 135
Goguel, F., 151, 152, 275
Gottwald, K., 93
Gouin, F., 140
Graham, M., 266
Grant, U., 78
Grevy, J., 77
Grindrod, M., 277
Grzesinski, A., 191
Gurian, W., 39, 247, 264, 271, 285
Gurion, B., 227, 231, 232

Haeberlin, H., 120
Hailey, F., 279
Hallett, G. H., 66, 67, 265
Hamilton, A., 157, 250
Hare, T., 8, 12
Harvey, T., 161
Hartmann, G. B. von, 281
Hauser, E., 268
Hearnshaw, F. J. C., 184, 279
Hedler, W., 214, 215
Hedtoft, H., 269
Hegel, F .W., xiv, 261
Heiden, C., 77
Heldmann, E., 217
Henlein, K., 89, 92
Herodotus, xii, 261
Herriot, E., 34, 35
Heuss, T., 191, 205, 211, 265, 280
Hilferding, R., 191

INDEX

Hellpach, W., 188
Hindenburg, P. von, 77, 78, 82, 103
Hitler, A., 54, 65, 67, 68, 75, 76, 77, 78, 82, 86, 89, 92, 183
Hodza, M., 91
Hogan, J., 107
d'Hondt, V., 202
Hoag, C. G., 66, 67, 265
Hoover, H., 76
Horwell, G., 262
Huber, E. R., 69
Hugenberg, A., 70
Hugo, V., 160
Hula, E., 283
Humphreys, J., 46, 189, 264, 265, 269
Husson, R., 133, 272, 274, 275

Jackson, A., xiii
Jászi, O., 84
Jaurès, J., 150
Jefferson, T., xiv
Jennings, I., 5
Joehr, W. A., 271
Jonkheere, E., 267

Kaegi, W., 271
Katayama, T., 241, 243
Kekkonen, U., 121
Kendrick, A., 272
Kerner, R., 266
Kerwin, J., 2, 261
Keynes, J. M., 24
Keyes, G., 222
Kirchheimer, O., 281
Kitazawa, N., 284
Kloeke, V. O., 271
Koch-Weser, E., 9, 191
Koestler, A., 229, 234, 284
Kraus, H. A., 225
Kroll, G., 201, 217

Labriola, A., 161
Lachapelle, G., 39, 264
La Follette, R., 75
Lalle, M., 154, 275
Laski, H., 22
Laval, P., 39
Leber, J., 191, 280
Lehrman, H., 231, 284
Lemass, S., 269

Lenin, V. I., 80, 265
Leo, J., 188
Leopold III, 77, 101, 102, 103, 104, 105, 268
Lindsay, A. D., 261
Lippmann, W., 254
Locke, J., xv, 59, 60, 261
Loritz, A., 209
Louis XIV, 30
Lowe, R., 3
Lowell, A., 264
Loewenstein, K., 37, 91, 122, 264, 266, 271, 279
Ludendorff, E., 66, 67
Luedemann, H., 179, 191, 278, 280
Luther, H., 200, 217, 258, 280
Luther, M., xvi, 183

MacArthur, D., 240, 244
Macdonald, R., 17, 32, 81, 266
Machiavelli, M., 183
Machray, R., 87, 266
MacMahon, P. M., de, 32, 33, 77
Madison, J., 253, 254
Malatesta, A., 264
Maslowski, P., 281
Marin, L., 30
Maritain, J., 128
Marie, A., 143
Marshall, G., 254
Marx, K., 24, 79, 81
Marx, W., 82
Masaryk, J., 91, 171
Maurois, A., 37, 264
Maurras, C., 39, 41
McBride, S., 107, 109, 110
McCloy, J. J., 198
McCormack, J., 223, 224, 283
McCormick, A., 168, 173, 216, 229, 277, 278, 283
Meissner, K., 215
Melbourne, Lord, 267
Menzel, W., 197
Merriam, C., xv, 261
Metaxas, J., 95, 97
Meyer, E. W., 217, 283
Michels, R., xiii, 261
Mierendorff, C., 190, 191, 280
Millerand, A., 39, 77
Mirkine-Guetzévitch, B., 4, 285

Missong, A., 283
Moch, J., 149, 159, 272, 274, 276
Molotov, V., 185
Montesquieu, C., 1, 261
Morley, J., 261
Morrison, H., xiii, 22
Mosca, G., xiii, 261
Mosley, O., 22
Mowrer, E. A., 9, 101
Munro, W., 284
Murrow, E. R., 195
Murry, G., 23
Mussolini, B., 52, 53, 54, 55, 56, 57, 61, 76, 88, 181
Musy, G. M., 120

Napoleon I, 30
Napoleon III, 54, 126
Naumann, F., 64, 65, 191, 280
Nenni, P., 171, 174, 175
Nezard, H., 264
Nitti, F., 50, 161

Oppenheim, F., 267
Orlando, V. E., 51, 161
Ozaki, Y., 285

Paasikivi, J., 122
Pacciardi, R., 181
Padover, S. R., 261
Pareto, V., xiii, 261
Parri, F., 166
Parrot, L., 240, 284, 285
Pergler, C., 91, 266
Pericles, xiv
Pertinax, 140, 273
Philip, A., 274
Pierlot, H., 102
Pilsudski, J., 87, 88
Pini, G., 57, 265
Pius XII, 166
Plastiras, N., 97, 98, 267
Plato, 73, 247, 264, 285
Pleven, R., 159, 273, 274
Poincaré, R., 44, 285
Pollock, J. K., 270, 283
Porru, F., 176
Prélot, M., 37, 264
Price, A. H., 281

Queuille, H., 137, 143, 149, 169, 273

Quigley, H., 236, 284

Radkey, O., 271
Ramadier, P., 138, 141, 142, 144
Raymond, J., 211, 282
Reale, O., 278
Reimann, M., 275
Renner, K., 84, 85, 220, 221
Reynold, G., 271
Ridder, J., 216
Roclore, M., 154, 275
Rocque, de la, 42, 43, 264
Rocques, M., 155, 275
Roosevelt, F., 76
Rossi, A., 265
Rossi, P., 278
Roucek, J., 266
Roure, R., 144
Rousseau, J. J., xi, xv, 35
Royall, K., 186
Ruestow, D., 265, 270

Salandra, A., 51
Salvemini, G., 50, 51, 54, 57, 58, 162, 163, 264, 265, 277
Sandelius, W., 114, 270
Saragat, G., 176, 177
Scelba, M., 180, 181
Schaelchin, H., 271
Schauff, J., 280
Schleicher, K. von, 78
Schmidt, D., 279
Schneider, H., 265
Schreiber, J., 285
Schroeder, G., 201
Schulthess, E., 120
Schumacher, K., 184, 191, 201, 209
Schumann, M., 139, 252
Schuman, R., 139, 143, 273
Schuerch, E., 271
Schwarzchild, L., 265
Seeckt, O., 78
Sedgwick, A., 97
Seignobos, C., 34
Simon, Y., xii, 261
Smend, R., 58, 169, 272
Smith, K., 254
Snowden, P., 262
Spiecker, K., 191
Sonnino, S., 48, 50

290

INDEX

Sophoulis, T., 96
Soulier, A., 264, 275
Southam, W., 276
Stalin, J., 183
Sternberger, D., 188, 217
Stresemann, G., 72, 81
Sturzo, L., 48, 50, 55, 165, 264, 265, 277
Suagee, J. T., 284
Sulzberger, C., 23, 98, 187, 266
Svinhofvud, O., 122

Taillade, M., 155, 275
Tardieu, A., 35
Thaelmann, E., 82
Theotokis, J., 97
Thiers, A., 36
Thomas, I., 174, 278
Thomas, N., 76
Thompson, D., 185
Thugutt, V., 87
Toskiko, K., 242
Tsaldaris, A., 97

Van Buren, M., 74
Van Zeeland, P., 101, 102
Venizelos, S., 95, 96, 97, 267
Victor Emmanuel III, 61, 77, 103
Vinacke, H., 236, 284
Volpe, G., 57, 264

Voorhis, J., xv

Waldeck-Rousseau, P. M. R., 44
Walk, E. P., 281
Ward, B., 22
Warren, L., 275
Weber, A., 70, 188
Weber, M., xii, 70
Weill-Raynal, E., 274
Weinshall, A., 229, 283, 284
Wellington, Duke of, 20, 21
Welles, B., 263
Wengler, P., 280
Wessel, H., 279
Westarp, K., 71, 72
Wheeler, K., 174, 278
Willms, G., 188
Willi, W., 271
Williams, J., 284
Wilson, W., 16, 31
Wiskemann, E., 277
Woeste, J., 105
Woodhouse, C., 94, 95, 266
Woodlock, T., 13, 229
Wright, G., 127, 141, 272

Yoshida, S., 239, 240, 241, 242
Yoshio, S., 242

Zilliacus, K., 14, 15
Zurcher, A., 271, 272